Scottish Record Society
New Series 12

The Gild Court Book of Dunfermline
1433 - 1597

SCOTTISH RECORD SOCIETY

Since its foundation in 1897, the Scottish Record Society has published numerous volumes of calendars and indices of public records and private muniments relating to Scotland. A list of the Society's publications is available on request.

Membership of the Society is open to all persons and institutions interested in its work. Further particulars may be obtained from the Honorary Secretary.

President

Professor Emeritus Gordon Donaldson
Ph.D., D.Litt., F.B.A., F.R.S.E.
H.M. Historiographer in Scotland

Treasurer

The Reverend Duncan Shaw, Ph.D., Th.Dr.
4 Sydney Terrace, Edinburgh, EH7 6SL

Secretary

James Kirk, Ph.D., D.Litt.
Department of Scottish History
University of Glasgow, Glasgow, G12 8QQ

SCOTTISH RECORD SOCIETY
NEW SERIES 12

The Gild Court Book of Dunfermline 1433-1597

Edited by
ELIZABETH P.D. TORRIE, Ph.D.

EDINBURGH, 1986

Published in 1986 by the
Scottish Record Society
Edinburgh.

Copyright ©   Scottish Record Society
and
Elizabeth P. D. Torrie 1986

ISBN 0 902054 08 2

ISSN 0 143-9448

*Printed in Great Britain by
John Geddes (Printers) Irvine*

CONTENTS

	Page
Preface	v
Introduction	xi
Abbreviations	xxxiii
Editorial Conventions	xxxiv
The Text	1
Index	175

PREFACE

The editing of this volume would not have been possible without the support of a number of people. Most of all I thank Professor Ian Cowan for his help and advice and Dr. John Durkan for his careful checking of my transcription of the original. Mr. John Torrie and Dr. James Brown have given me invaluable assistance, for which I am especially grateful. My thanks go also to Professor Geoffrey Barrow, Professor Gordon Donaldson, Dr. James Kirk, Dr. Michael Lynch, Dr. Roger Mason, Dr. Ann Mathieson and Mrs. Mairi Robinson.

I am indebted to the Incorporation of the Guildry of Dunfermline for the loan of the manuscript 'Gild Court Book of Dunfermline, 1433–1597', and for permission to reproduce three of the folios in this volume.

Pat Torrie

Folio 1 of the Gild Court Book of Dunfermline.

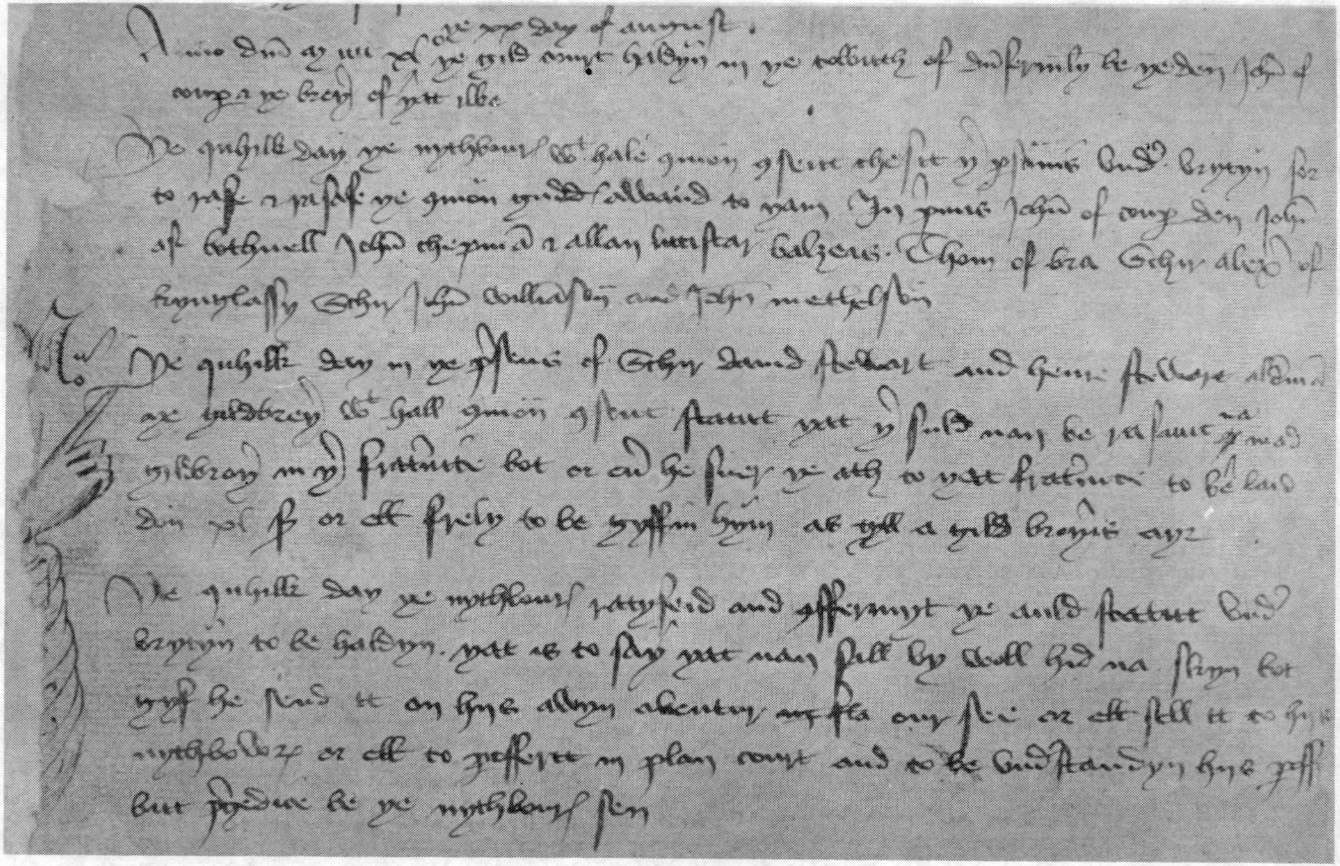

Portion of folio 4v of the Gild Court Book of Dunfermline.

Folio 59 of the Gild Court Book of Dunfermline.

INTRODUCTION

An early manuscript volume was discovered in autumn 1976 during an examination of the papers of the Incorporation of the Guildry of Dunfermline. This proved to be the Gild Court Book of Dunfermline, dating from 1433 to 1597. The volume was in a poor state of preservation. It consisted of one hundred and eight folios, some loose and worn, their original size probably being 11.7 x 8.4 inches. The paper was in parts thinning and torn. These with a further two folios, which appeared misplaced, were pressed into oak boards, one of which had split in two. Leather covers of a once very fine quality protected the boards. The watermarks on the paper are, however, clear. The main bulk of the paper has a dagger marking, of an unknown type,[1] and could have been imported from Germany, France or perhaps the Netherlands, where paper-making had commenced in 1428. A serpent design on folio 26 reveals its Rouen origin of a date normally considered by the evidence of the watermark to be between 1513 and 1522. Part of this folio, however, describes a gild court held in 1508. It is possible that this was copied into the blank bottom half of the folio at a later date, or perhaps the traditional suggestion that such paper was manufactured only from 1513 is a little conservative. The remaining paper is also French, of a type common along the Clermont-Ferrand, Lyon, Geneva line, with a gloved-hand watermark.

Fortunately, age has not destroyed any significant section of the folios. The text is, in the main, decipherable, and offers fine examples of fifteenth- and sixteenth-century handwriting, of a relatively plain form. Scribes who minuted the gild court meetings were often the same as those recording the burgh court proceedings in the 'Burgh Court Book of Dunfermline' from 1488 to 1584,[2] such as the common clerk, David Bra, in the late 1480s and 1490s, or notaries public such as John Cunningham whose hand may be seen on folio 72v of the Gild Court Book. Dean of Gild John Wilson wrote the gild minutes in 1519, and perhaps also in 1520 and 1521, and it is possible that this practice was followed by some of the other deans of gild.[3] The only decoration in the volume is on folio 88

INTRODUCTION

where notaries David Brown and James Kinghorn sign their names, and the drawing of hands to point out important enactments or statutes of the gild on folios 4v, 8v, 9v, 11v, 13v and 15v. This latter embellishment is also evidenced in the 'Burgh Court Book of Dunfermline'. Further examples are to be found in the fifteenth-century parchment Stirling gild records in the Central Region Archives at Stirling, and the Aberdeen gild records in Aberdeen City Archives.

Between 1978 and 1981 the Gild Court Book underwent restorative treatment at the Scottish Record Office. Conservation work consisted of the application of lime water to neutralise acid in the paper and thus prevent deterioration. Damaged parts were repaired with acid-free, hand-made paper, and each folio was covered on one side with very fine silk. This silk and a coating of gelatine size strengthens the paper and facilitates safe handling. The folios were then gathered together into fifteen sections and sewn with linen thread on to split vellum leather using the 'figure of eight' stitch clearly disclosed on the original binding. Modern covers were not put on the volume; and the old leather and oak binding was left untouched. During this process a reordering of the folios was made. This foliation, although not entirely consistent, is the one followed in the present edition, since it is more satisfactory than the pagination, in an unknown hand, as noted when the record was seen by the editor in 1976. As now sewn together the Gild Court Book includes folios 109 and 110, which are not transcribed in this edition since they form no part of the original volume, being seventeenth-century material. Other inconsistencies also stem from the reordering process. Folio 60 was originally folded in four, with writing on three quarters, the fourth being left blank. It is now bound into the volume, but would be better placed between folios 67v and 68 to maintain the correct sequence of date. Folio 108 has been reversed and in consequence 108v should be read before 108 recto. Folios 95 to 97 inclusive should either be placed at the end of the Gild Court Book, after the gild accounts, and foliated 106 to 108 inclusive, or at the beginning of the volume since this copying of the Gild Laws of Berwick is in an early hand, and was perhaps the first entry in the book. While suggesting these corrections, however, it should be stressed that the present foliation in no way inhibits a full comprehension of the text, whatever its original pagination.

The reappearance of this volume in 1976 was doubly significant. Firstly, the burgh records of Dunfermline were thought to be extant only from 1488. In 1917 Erskine

INTRODUCTION   xiii

Beveridge in his introduction to the transcription of the
'Burgh Court Book of Dunfermline', *The Burgh Records of
Dunfermline* (Edinburgh, 1917), recalled a tradition that
an earlier volume of burgh records had been lost in the
previous century.[4] The collected documents of G.H. Hutton,
the greater part dating from between 1788 and 1790 and
between 1809 and 1822, include a very few extracts which
may be from this earlier volume and a reading of them
suggests they formed part of a burgh court book, not a
gild court book.[5] Whether or not this was still in
existence in the first part of the nineteenth century,
burgh sources earlier than 1488 were not available to such
historians of Dunfermline as E. Henderson in 1879[6] or P.
Chalmers as early as 1844.[7] The twentieth-century editing
of the *Regality of Dunfermline Court Book, 1531-1538*
by J.M. Webster and A.A.M. Duncan (Dunfermline, 1953)
and the *Extracts from the Burgh Records of Dunfermline
in the Sixteenth and Seventeenth Centuries* (Dunfermline,1951)
by A. Shearer had of necessity to be undertaken without
the assistance of background information from the earlier
fifteenth century. Had these historians been in a position
to study the earlier gild records they might have placed
a different emphasis on some aspects of burgh life.

Secondly, within the broader context of Scottish gild
and burgh history this early book is important. The role
of the gild in medieval burgh life has been considered on
a number of occasions, but such studies have perhaps
been insufficiently based on primary sources. The gild
records of Scottish burghs have survived only sparsely.
There is reference to a meeting of the Edinburgh gild
court in 1403, which should more correctly be dated 1453,
in *Extracts from the Records of the Burgh of Edinburgh*,
and thereafter mention of isolated admissions to the gild,
but no gild court book as such survives which is earlier
than 1550.[8] Dundee and Glasgow have no medieval gild
records. However, a parchment roll in the Central Region
Archives Archives minutes the gild court of Stirling from
1460 to 1475 and the Perth 'Guildrie Book' dates from 1452.
There is a reference to the *curia gilde* of Aberdeen in
1437, and from 1441 the gild dealings are well documented
for this burgh. A few folios detail the proceedings of the
gild court of Ayr from 1428 to 1432.[9] These are the only
other fifteenth-century gild records for Scotland which
have so far come to light.

This Dunfermline gild court book commencing in 1433
is, therefore, of value, and not merely as welcome
additional source material to supplement the poorly
documented medieval gild history of Scotland. Its intrinsic

importance goes further. Dunfermline in the fifteenth and sixteenth centuries was not a royal burgh, nor a very large town, nor, it may reasonably be argued, was it of great standing among Scottish urban communities. But it is precisely because of these factors that this volume is of some merit. The burghs and gilds of Edinburgh, Aberdeen, Dundee, Stirling and Glasgow have all been studied.[10] These burghs were, however, in relatively privileged positions. Their wealth and, to a certain extent, their size set them apart from others; and perhaps too often in the past what has been shown to be true for the larger, wealthy burghs has been held, on little evidence, to be so for the smaller. The Dunfermline source material offers an insight into the daily routine of a small town which probably had much in common with the great majority of undocumented lesser burghs of Scotland.[11] A gild within any burgh was, however, far more than an inanimate municipal institution. It was a group of burgesses, not necessarily very wealthy or sophisticated, though certainly important within their own town. Doubtless the gild brother of many a Scottish burgh would have felt himself to have more in common with his rural neighbours than with the great merchant of the capital. It is precisely because of this lack of pretension –whether social, political or economic– that the gild member of Dunfermline as now revealed in fifteenth- and sixteenth-century documentation holds interest. With a greater knowledge of this small town and its inhabitants there may be an opportunity to come a little nearer to an understanding of that vast mass of medieval townspeople who have left so few records.

A manuscript record of 108 folios (six of which are blank) covering one hundred and sixty years can not be considered an abundant source. Its inadequacies may nevertheless be partially offset by a study of other contemporary records. The value of the 'Burgh Court Book of Dunfermline', for example, is considerably enhanced when considered with this 'Gild Court Book of Dunfermline'. Used in parallel the two give a relatively complete picture of the close involvement of the medieval Scottish burgh and its gild.

*

Gilds, as friendly societies, were common throughout western Europe from the eighth century.[12] Many assumed religious overtones, displayed in the Middle Ages by pageantry and material support of the church. In towns, however, these socio-religious groups often developed a further characteristic: that of the gild as an economic force, with a close interest in mercantile pursuits. In Scotland this latter facet became even more marked wherever emerging burghs, the possessors of mercantile privileges,[13] were granted a further right: that of a gild merchant.

The most reliable sources for early Scottish burghal history are the *Leges Burgorum*, reputedly of the reign of David I; statutes from the time of William the Lion; and the *Statuta Gilde*, the statutes of the gild of Berwick, the earlier part of which is attributed to 1249 and the later specifically dated 1281 and 1294. Reference is made to the gild merchant in *Leges Burgorum*, and in the reign of William the Lion official sanction was achieved:

> De libertate gilde mercatorie. Item statuit quod mercatores regni habeant gildam suam mercatoriam et ista gaudeant in pace cum libertate emendi et vendendi ubique infra limites libertatum burgorum ita quod quilibet sit contentus sua libertate et nullus occupet libertatem alterius ne forte in itinere Camerarii nostri condemnetur ut foristallator et puniatur.[14]

The rulings of the Berwick gild suggest an organisation already of some age, probably of pre-thirteenth-century origin. Perth and Roxburgh are known to have had gilds by the end of the twelfth century, since they are referred to in a charter of Roger, bishop of St. Andrews when the gild of that burgh was established.[15] These, along with Aberdeen (1222), Stirling (1226), Elgin (1234), Berwick (1249) and Dundee (1249 x 1286) were the first recorded in Scotland.[16]

How exactly these early associations functioned is now virtually impossible to recreate. The *Statuta Gilde* do, however, reveal a close identification of purpose, as a society for mutual self-help and conviviality between the gild of Berwick and the gilds of the Low Countries.[17] Yet in Scotland the emergence of gilds merchant was tightly, if not inextricably, linked to the emergence of burghs. The burgh was in many ways a community drawn together for trade, and recognised as such in twelfth- and thirteenth-century primary sources. But even when a specific right to a gild merchant was granted alongside a charter creating a burgh, this right to a gild was very much a corollary.[18] The gild, although of great influence, was not in origin the primary core of the burgh personnel, just as trade, although an essential facet, was not the sole *raison d'être* of the burgh. Traders in these early days, before true specialisation and the divorce of crafts and commerce, were more than probably craftsmen-traders and farmer-traders as much as merchant-traders. It is true to say, however, that wherever a gild merchant developed, that burgh had the means to gain the full potential from its mercantile privileges.

So close were the ties of burgh and gild that some historians have been tempted to view the gild merchant as the basis of early municipal government. [19] This extreme view is barely tenable. Early burgh laws and gild laws are framed in such a manner as to suggest that the gild merchant was controlled by the burgh and had no independent existence. The inclusion, for example, of clauses in *Statuta Gilde* dealing specifically with the municipal organisation of the burgh does not imply control of the burgh by the gild. [20] On the contrary, these Berwick regulations for the smooth-running of the gild suggest that the opposite was the case. Drawn up as they were by the mayor and worthy burgesses, they may provide evidence of a very serious attempt on the part of the burgh, having brought all gild members into one single gild, to control that gild. It is not surprising, however, that as the burgh organisation developed the gild members of the community gradually began to assume a greater role in administrative affairs. They were often the more substantial, and therefore influential, members of the townspeople, and, with their gild institution, the most vocal. Gild members, as able members of burgh society, rather than as gild members *per se*, adopted an increasingly dominant role in the municipal organisation. As a result the links between burgh and gild became still tighter.

Dunfermline's early history is a little obscure. It was a king's burgh by 1124 X 1127, but some form of settlement clearly existed before the reign of David I. This early burgh, however, appears to have lost favour after the reign of David I, and by the reign of William I a significant decline in Dunfermline as a royal centre is evident. [21] This would support the view that Dunfermline as a royal burgh 'probably decayed early'. [22] The reasons for this may never be completely certain, but it is quite probable that a suburb developing around the Benedictine abbey of Dunfermline gradually acquired dominance and there was a decline in the king's burgh. The *faubourg* became the *bourg*, and the Dunfermline of the early fourteenth century onwards was both topographically and legally a new town.

The transition from royal burgh to ecclesiastical

burgh of regality was complete by the reign of Robert I, when an undated charter gifted the great customs of wool, skins and leather, normally reserved for the crown, to the abbot and convent throughout their regality. [23] It is clear that along with the other burghs in the regality – Kirkcaldy, Musselburgh and Queensferry – Dunfermline was in a position to benefit more than indirectly from any trading privileges bestowed on the abbey from the early fourteenth century. The king also advised the magistrates and community of the town of Bruges of his intention to furnish the regality with a cocket in 1321, which would suggest a fair degree of trade between the regality and the Low Countries. [24] By 1363, however, two further royal favours quite specifically named the burgesses and merchants of the abbey as beneficiaries: there was confirmed to them the monopoly of buying and selling without payment of toll within the bounds not only of their burghs, but also of the entire regality; and the abbey and its burgesses and merchants were given a port at the grange of Gellet or West Rosyth. [25] The following year David II's charter in favour of the burgesses of Scotland, reiterating the mercantile liberties of burghs and their merchants, encouraged further the close tie of burgh and trade.

Probably soon after this, but certainly between the years 1365 and 1399, during the abbacy of John, possibly of Strathmiglo, a grant was made by the abbot of Dunfermline,

> burgensibus nostris de Dunfermelyn et eorum heredibus inperpetuum gyldam marcatricem...
> ...sicut burgenses domini nostri regis in burgis eiusdem domini nostri tenent et possident.[26]

It might be argued that this was merely confirming a right already held by the burgesses of Dunfermline, for reference is made to property held by the gild 'of old'. But whether an original grant, or merely confirmatory, by the latter part of the fourteenth century, with its gild merchant, the burgesses of Dunfermline were in a position to benefit fully from the trading rights inherent in the basic notion of a burgh.

The indications are that the burgh superior, the abbot of Dunfermline, accorded the burgesses a degree of self government which was rare in Scotland, England or Wales. [27] By the end of the fourteenth century Dunfermline had developed into a municipal unit with the theoretical right of independent action in legislative, judicial and financial matters, although it would be unwise to assume that in practice the burgh enjoyed absolute self-determination. All evidence would suggest that there was in Dunfermline an amicable *laissez-faire* relationship between abbot and burgh and gild. The town officers, the alderman and two bailies, do not appear to have been imposed from above.[28] They were 'of the burgh'. These men, supported by the community of burgesses through assizes and a council,[29] attended to all municipal business while apparently acceding willingly to the wishes of the superior, and at times actively seeking his support if the welfare of the burgh was thereby enhanced.

How the first generations of Dunfermline gild brethren conducted their daily lives, what role they played in the burghal organisation, or who formed their membership there is now no means of knowing. By the early 1430s, however, their fraternity numbered probably a little under fifty, which constituted a substantial minority of the 140 or so male burgesses in a town with a population of not much more that 1,000.[30] Gild business was, moreover, considered of sufficient import that a decision was made to record formally its dealings. For an initial outlay of two shillings for paper and a further 2s. 4d. for manufacture, the gild took possession of a book.[31] In 1433 the Gild Court Book of Dunfermline was commenced.

*

Designed as it was to minute the more official aspects of gild life, the pages of the Gild Court Book volume reveal an inevitable preoccupation with the gild's commercial activities. What set the majority of burghs apart from mere towns was their right to hold markets and fairs. These were not confined to burghs holding of the crown: Dunfermline had a weekly market and probably two fairs each year.[32] The regality of Dunfermline abbey was extensive, and within the area only the burghs of Dunfermline, Kirkcaldy, Queensferry and Musselburgh might trade. It is now clear from the Gild Court Book that the regality north of the Forth was divided between Dunfermline and Kirkcaldy.[33] Within this hinterland the gild claimed the sole right to deal in wool, hides, woolfells, furs and skins, and controlled the related skills and trades such as dyeing and tanning. The fraternity also attempted to keep for itself the sale of imports such as spices, wines, fine cloths and other specialised goods. This gild monopoly of dealing in the most lucrative commodities was jealously guarded and encroachment was severely punished. Members maintained their position by regulations against malpractice which were enforced by fines and banishment from the gild. Within the town the gild played an active part, with the burgh authorities, in controlling the supply, quality and price of foodstuffs, which might be sold by anyone at the official market, as long as toll was paid. It is, moreover, evident that Dunfermline, along with the other greater ecclesiastical burghs, had a share with the royal burghs in overseas trade, most notably along the north-west coast of Europe, into England, and in the Baltic. [34]

The Gild Court Book suggests that the gild aimed to keep a firm control of the local economy. Its commercial policy was wholly within the conventional patterns of trade followed by the east coast burghs of medieval Scotland. Vested interest sought to maintain the benefits of monopoly, and the traders' profits were arguably the primary concern. Such a system, however, did benefit the town. An adequate supply of necessities was ensured and at a reasonable market price for the burgh. Whatever the underlying motives, the public good was in general maintained. But where the true value of the gild most clearly emerges is when assessments are made of both gild and burgh finances. [35] They reveal a town that was not particularly wealthy, but one that remained solvent at least until the beginning of the sixteenth century, while fulfilling its financial commitments and upgrading its material surroundings. This was determined by one main factor: the gild, while dealing in far larger sums of money than were the burgh magistrates through the common purse, had a crucial financial role to play in the town. The town relied on the gild not only to loan funds and directly finance various burgh projects, but the fraternity also took upon itself many of the material improvements in Dunfermline. In 1448 and 1449, to cite only one example, £26. 3. 4d. was spent on repairs to the tolbooth. Of this, £21. 18. 6d. came directly from the gild brethren, and only £4. 4. 10d. from the common purse. [36] The gild accounts, now brought together at the end of the Gild Court Book, detail regrettably few years. Yet for the short time span they cover they demonstrate both the relative wealth of the gild and its role as financial and economic backbone of the burgh. They also underline the almost inextricable ties of gild and burgh.

These gild records as a whole, particularly when considered in association with the 'Burgh Court Book of Dunfermline', highlight the close involvement of the gild in what might be considered purely municipal matters, be they legislative, judicial or financial. In particular, the gild seems to have adopted a special interest in the material fabric of the town in which it invested heavily, and in decision-making over building lines and property maintenance. This intermingling of the functions of gild and burgh is not surprising in a burgh where approximately thirty percent of the male burgesses were gild brothers. Virtually the same men were prominent in gild and burgh, while within the town organisation there was no precise definition of areas of responsibility. This apparent confusion of role was at times assisted by the current clerk. Throughout much of the period when gild and burgh court are extant the same scribe minuted both gild court and burgh court business, and on occasion gild court affairs were erroneously minuted in the Burgh Court Book. The opposite may also have been the case. Formality was not, however, the keynote of the medieval burghal administration. As long as a particular municipal issue received attention, it did not seem of undue importance whether it was dealt with in a burgh or a gild court.

On the other hand, the gild maintained a close surveillance against encroachment into any of its own specific areas of responsibility or privilege. The alderman, as head of the burgh, often presided with the dean of gild at the gild courts held in the tolbooth, but the dean of gild, assisted by a sergeand, was the titular and practising head of the gild,[37] and it is clear that in spite of parliamentary efforts in 1469 to regulate the appointment of burghal officers, including deans of gilds, the Dunfermline gild officials were independent of the burgh elective system, and appointed from within and by the gild.[38] The gild had a very precise notion, moreover, that its rights were not to be eroded by even the abbot or the crown. Brethren were fined for complaints to the abbot against gild court decisions. By 1585 the gild was sufficiently self-assured that when approached by two traders seeking to do business in the town since they possessed a licence from the crown permitting them to trade in all burghs, the reply was unequivocal. Dunfermline was 'ane frie brucht of regalitie quharvpoun the kingis ma may [sic] nocht justlie intrude uny persoun vpoun thame for hurting of thair liberties'.[39]

Membership of the gild fraternity, however, implied far more than involvement in commercial activities and municipal affairs. Although probably never intended to record other than the more formal dealings of the gild, the Gild Court Book reveals clearly a vital aspect of the daily existence of the fraternity: it was a socio-religious group, retaining much in common with the early gilds of western Europe.

It was perhaps inevitable in a burgh dependent upon an abbey that close contact between church and laity should be maintained, and apparently happily maintained until well into the sixteenth century. Though church and town were never inter-dependent church life pervaded the secular and the abbey was sustained by the laity. A significant proportion of gild funds can be seen going directly to the support of the church, either through the regular supply of wax and candles, the occasional purchase of minor items such as candle-holders or door keys, or through the specific maintenance of altars and their chaplains. The gild took three altars under its patronage: the Holy Blood altar, St. Salvator's altar and, to a lesser extent, St. Ninian's altar.[40] There were a number of ways in which altars and chaplains could be sustained. The most common and profitable was to divert rentals due from gild property to a specific altar.[41] But the church might benefit by such gestures as, for example, Sir Andro Pacok being excused 20s. of his gild entry fee in exchange for a year's singing of mass at the Holy Blood altar.[42] The gild also played a dominant part in the collection throughout the burgh of light silver, a fund for the lighting of the parish church by candles. Probably all altars in the parish church, apart from those personally endowed, benefited from this, but in particular the gild altars, and that dedicated to the Rood and Our Lady, which was maintained specifically by the burgh.[43] Religious fervour was displayed in less materialistic ways. Holy days were times for fun, pageantry and processions.[44] On the latter occasions the gild members probably carried ahead of their group a gild cross, which they protected from the elements with a cowl. Equally, if not more important, on the death of a member of the fraternity all were obliged to attend the burial, and masses for the soul of the deceased were a mark of respect.

There is little evidence of any direct contacts with continental reforming thought before 1560. The Catholic cult seems to have continued according to traditional practice well into the sixteenth century. The first allusion to the Reformation crisis in the Gild Court Book is in November 1559, when the Lords of the Congregation were in retreat through Fife, pursued by French troops.[45] The pertinents of the Holy Blood altar had to be divided amongst gild members for safekeeping, since they lived in a ' troublous world', caught between warring factions.[46] How far the Protestant Reformation immediately altered the religious life of the gild cannot be known, although a minister held office by the time of the Reformation parliament in August 1560.[47] Yet the state of the parish church was such in 1563 that it is doubtful whether worship under the Protestant rite could have regularly been carried on in it. In that year the community of the burgh brought a complaint before the Privy Council to the effect that the abbot and sacristan of the abbey had so failed in their traditional role as maintainers of the roof, walls and windows of the parish church, and the consequent decay was such that there was 'greit danger and perrell ... to enter remane or bide within the said kirk'.[48] It is likely that gild altars were dismantled after 1560, although some altars in the abbey church and also a number of the monks survived until well into the 1580s.[49] There is, however, little suggestion in the Gild Court Book of changing spiritual habits amongst the fraternity other than a reference to the building of 'ane sufficient seat' in the parish church to accomodate the whole of the gildry in May 1561.[50] The indications are that for some time the two faiths co-existed. How easily can only be a matter of speculation.

Perhaps one of the most desirable benefits of gild life for this socio-religious group was that it was truly a fraternity, a brotherhood of men who joined together for mutual support. This inevitably implied obligations as well as privileges. Failure to act for the common good meant punishment by fine, or, ultimately, expulsion from the fraternity, and it is clear that maintenance of good order and true fellowship were an important aspect of gild court work. Charity was an essential part of gild life before and after the Reformation. Gild widows and orphans were supported, as well as the poor of the town. If a gild member fell upon hard times he would receive the moral and material support of his brothers in his mortal life and even at death their prayers for his soul would help him along the path to the next.[51]

The Gild Court Book and in particular the accounts, suggest that another aspect of their fraternity was also of prime importance to the members: conviviality. This might express itself in feasting but, more particularly, in drinking. It seems that gild life occasioned regular consumption of ale, beer and wine whether in private houses, one of the town's several taverns, or in the tolbooth, where the gild court was held. In 1443, for example, Dean of gild John of Coupir presented his annual account. Of a total of £1. 9s. 6d. expenses, burgh mail was 7d., paper and fee to a writer was 1s., expenses (unspecified) were 6s. 6d., and the remaining £1. 1s. 5d.

INTRODUCTION

was spent on drink. By the end of the fifteenth century gild conviviality was encouraged by an annual gild feast. In 1503 precise details of the necessities for such an occasion are detailed: wine 14s., a barrel of beer £1. 10s. 0d., ale 3s. The food requirements were merely 1s. 6d. for bread.[52]

Various facets of the everyday existence of gild brothers and other burgesses are revealed in the contemporary sources. For example, the burgh sasines transcribed in the Burgh Court Book, together with information from the Gild Court Book, give a clear picture of the urban setting, the site of market cross, tron, tolbooth, smithies, mills, tanning works, alehouses, town ports, and kilns; they show the size and lay-out of tofts, the burgages where repletion had begun, and those still unbuilt, and also of the construction of a few of these buildings. Most of all, however, these sasines highlight the fact that Dunfermline, in spite of its commercial centre and dominant ecclesiastical buildings, was a town with essentially a rural atmosphere with cultivated rigs and orchards, barns and stables within the burgh precincts. There is, moreover, precise evidence not only of the gild's interest in building development and road maintenance, but also of the areas of the town favoured by the brethren for investment in urban property.[53]

Much may be learned about the social background of the gild brothers at the end of the fifteenth century. For example, John Wilson, the dean of gild whose hand may be seen on folio 31v, and his wife, Marjorie Wallod, become more than mere names in official records when the inheritance of the widow Marjorie is catalogued to the last ladle in John Wilson's testament recorded in the Burgh Court Book.[54] A relatively clear picture of the interior of the houses of some of the brethren may be formed from information in the Burgh Court Book in particular. Details of beds, bedding, table, stools, chairs, clothing and cooking utensils suggest that for these more privileged members of burgh society life, while simple, was not one of mindless squalor.[55] Indeed, some houses possessed dry closets, and the property and roads in the north-west of the town benefited from an excellent drainage system which fed a culverted burn, which in its turn drove three mills.[56]

Within the folios of the Gild Court Book alone, however, there is much social comment. Plague was a continual threat and minuted in this volume is one of the earliest attempts, in 1444, by a Scottish urban society to effect protective measures against 'the pest'.[57] More constant was the danger to life and property from fire. The gild sought to alleviate its effects by reducing the entrance fee of aspiring brethren whose homes had been recently burned.[58] It is, however, clear that in spite of the risks to life some fifteenth-century gild families survived into their fourth, fifth and even further generations. And life was not all hardship. The Dunfermline townspeople enjoyed, amongst other amusements, a Robin Hood play well into the sixteenth century.[59] In short, this record offers evidence of the daily life of the gild brothers as well as their formal business; matters as diverse, for example, as the proportion of gild brethren who could sign their names, to the place of women in burgh society.[60]

The gild brothers were the most notable within this same burgh society, and one of the merits of this volume is that it shows precisely what sort of people formed the membership of a gild merchant. This has at times been the subject of confusion. There were basically four methods of entry: by inheritance, usually from father or grandfather, or through marriage to the daughter or widow of a gild brother, sometimes with the payment of a fee; as a result of good deeds to the gild or town; through the recommendation of an intermediary of influence, most notably the abbot, the Stewarts of Rosyth, or the crown; or by payment of a cash sum with a donation in cash or kind of spice and wine.[61] If one of these four qualifications could be fulfilled, the gild granted admission, as long as the applicant swore to obey gild rules and keep gild secrets, was a burgess of Dunfermline, and was male.

The concern to control the marriages of widows of gild brothers and the deterrents to encroachment into gild commercial privileges are clear indication that gild status was not only envied but closely guarded. It is, however, immediately apparent that a group forming approximately one third of the male burgess population was not an élitist society. Within its ranks men of very different social and professional standing were represented. A gild brother might be a member of the gentry or a laird, churchman, graduate, schoolmaster, overseas merchant, town clerk, tavern-keeper, cordiner, plumber, weaver, mason or skinner. The gild was not a preserve of merchants. Indeed, there are not many specific mentions of 'merchants' in the text. This does not mean that merchants were virtually non-existent within the fraternity; but rather that, as with other occupations, a man was not designated by employment, unless more than one member had the same name. A merchant in Scotland was not necessarily a wealthy specialist who traded overseas. He might be so, but, equally, such a man might have no greater pretensions than to sell his goods in his booth in the town. He, too, was a 'merchant'. There were few in Dunfermline who merited the title 'merchant' by the former description and, on this definition, the Dunfermline gild was not an exclusively 'merchant' gild at all. It may perhaps be significant that the clerks minuting the gild court proceedings never referred to the fraternity as the 'gild merchant'. In their eyes, the brotherhood was simply 'the gild'.

It has often been stated that the fifteenth and sixteenth centuries saw merchants and craftsmen of burghs in a constant struggle for power.[62] It might be wise to treat this notion with some caution. Tension and argument did develop when bodies became formalised. Dunfermline, however, was probably more typical of the majority of smaller burghs, with no incorporated crafts until the latter part of the sixteenth century.[63] Only as late as 1594 does there appear some evidence of ill-feeling between gild brethren and craftsmen, which is confirmed in the *Records of the Convention of the Royal Burghs of Scotland*.[64] Significantly, however, the prime point of contention for the gild was not the dealing in merchandise by craftsmen, but the dealing in merchandise by craftsmen who had not paid for the privilege. It was a financial, or even a social, issue, but not a matter of principle as regards merchant or craft status. It is true, however, that after craft incorporation eventually came into existence burgh politics developed an exclusiveness which had little place within the old framework of the gild merchant, which had survived for much of the sixteenth century.

The greatest merit of the volume is its portrayal of a small town, probably typical of the majority of Scottish burghs, which, while being aware of the political and religious changes of the fifteenth and sixteenth centuries, did not react as did the great centres. Life continued largely according to the old order. Here is recorded the routine existence of a gild fraternity, which in many ways displayed a traditional, even medieval conservatism, not yet greatly touched by the social stratifications and economic tensions that gradually pervaded larger and later burghs.[65]

Notes

1. C.M. Briquet, *Les Filigranes, Dictionnaire Historique des Marques du Papier dès leur Apparition vers 1282 jusqu'en 1600*, 4 vols., ed. A. Stevenson (The Paper Publications Society, Amsterdam, 1968), iv ('Watermark Illustrations').
2. SRO, B20/10/1.
3. MsGB, ff. 31v and 32.
4. *Dunf. Recs.*, p. vii.
5. NLS, Adv. Ms. 29-4-2 (vi). 'Huttons Collections', vol. vi. Linlithgow, Stirling, Kinross, Fife.
6. E. Henderson, *The Annals of Dunfermline and Vicinity from the Earliest period to the Present Time* (Glasgow 1879).
7. P. Chalmers, *Historical and Statistical Account of Dunfermline* (Edinburgh, 1844).
8. *Extracts from the Records of the Burgh of Edinburgh* (SBRS, 1869-92), 1.
9. Central Region Archives, PD6. 1/1, Gild Records 1460/75, Parchment Roll.
Perth Museum and Art Gallery, Archive 1/1, 'The Guildrie Book'.
Aberdeen City Archives, Aberdeen Gild Records, vol. v, ii, of series of Council Registers, 1441/1465.
SRO, PA5/2. 'The Ayr Manuscript', ff. 8v-10 and 85v. These folios have been published in *Archaelogical and Historical Collections relating to the Counties of Ayr and Wigton*, i (1878), and edited therein by T. Dickson, 'Proceedings of the Gild Court of Ayr, from the Ayr Manuscript', 223-230.
10. J. D. Marwick, *Edinburgh Guilds and Crafts. A sketch of the history of burgess-ship, guild brotherhood, and membership of crafts in the city* (Edinburgh, 1899). *Abdn. Recs.*
A.J. Warden, *Burgh Laws of Dundee, with the history statutes and proceedings of the Guild of Merchants and fraternities of craftsmen* (Edinburgh 1872).
D.B. Morris, *The Stirling Merchant Gild and the life of John Cowane* (Stirling, 1919).
D. Murray, *Early Burgh Organisation in Scotland as illustrated in the History of Glasgow and of some neighbouring Burghs*, 2 vols. (Glasgow, 1924), vol.i.
11. There was an overall tendency towards uniformity in burghal practice in Scotland. A deliberate effort was

made by burghs to maintain similarity by correspondence. *APS*, i, 722-724; *Abdn. Recs.*, i, 26-29. Complete identity in all detail was, however, not achieved. A manuscript source of April 1552 (Scottish Catholic Archives, Fort Augustus Ms. A.1. fo. 330r), for example, talks of the 'difference of messouris within the burrowis of this realme' and of 'the greit variance standing in divers and sundry burrowis ... of the chesing of the officiers sic as provest, bailies, thesorer, dene of gyld and counsall.' (I am indebted to Dr. Michael Lynch for indicating the existence of this latter source material.)

12. E. Coornaert, 'Les gildes médiévales', *Revue Histori-que*, cxix (1948).

13. The emergence of early towns and the creation of burghs are not detailed here. A.A.M. Duncan, *Scotland, the Making of the Kingdom* (Edinburgh, 1975), 463-488, and the earlier chapters of W.M. MacKenzie, *The Scottish Burghs* (Edinburgh, 1949) provide a full background.

14. *Leges Burgorum*, c. xciv.
    Assise Regis Willelmi, c. xxxix.

15. Charter 1189 x 1202, establishing a gild merchant in St. Andrews, copied onto fo. 35 recto of 'Registrum evidentiarum civitatis Sancti Andree'.
    University of St. Andrews Archives, B.65/1/1.

16. *APS*, i, 77; *Charters and other Documents Relating to the Royal Burgh of Stirling* (Scottish Burgh Records Society, 1884), No. 4; *The Records of Elgin* (New Spalding Club, 1903), 2 vols., i, 8; 'Statuta Gilde', c.1; charter of Robert I to burgesses of Dundee confirming their rights and liberties, Dundee District Archive and Record Centre, CC1, No. 16. There were probably gilds merchant established early in Inverkeithing, Dumbarton, Inverness and Edinburgh, but no primary source material to date has come to light to prove this. Ayr, Cupar, Montrose, Irvine and Forfar all had gilds before Dunfermline (*Charters of the Royal Burgh of Ayr* (Ayr and Wigton Archaeological Association, 1883,) No. 14; *APS*, i, 509; *Muniments of the Royal Burgh of Irvine*, 2 vols. (Edinburgh, 1890), i, No. 4; Montrose Burgh Archives, M/W1/1, 'Indenture 1376'.).

17. *Statuta Gilde* and the earlier *Leges Burgorum* were to a large extent borrowed. The latter in particular reflect in several chapters the 'customs' of New-

xxviii INTRODUCTION

castle and, to a lesser degree, Winchester, Northampton and Nottingham. The detailed assessment of borough customs by M. Bateson shows clearly the similarity of practices in Western Europe. M. Bateson, *Borough Customs*, 2 vols. (Selden Society, 1904), *passim*, as do A. Ballard and J. Tait, *British Borough Charters 1216-1307* (Cambridge, 1923), *passim*.

18. C. Gross, *The Gild Merchant, A Contribution to British Municipal History*, 2 vols. (Oxford, 1850), i, 85.

19. R. Miller, *Guide to the Procedure of the Dean of Guild Court of Edinburgh with a short history of the Guildry* (Edinburgh 1891), 8 and 9. J. Colston, *The Guildry of Edinburgh: Is it an Incorporation?* (Edinburgh, 1887), p.x, for example.

20. This is not the view of W.C. Dickinson in *Abdn. Recs.*, pp. cvii - cviii.

21. In the reign of David I, of ninety-seven royal acts of Scottish origin, eleven were issued at Dunfermline, compared with Edinburgh's fourteen, Stirling's twelve and Scone's eleven. (To the latter one might add also three issued at Perth.) By the reign of William I only twelve of the 437 surviving acts with Scottish place-dates emanate from Dunfermline, compared with Perth's forty-five, Stirling's forty-four and Edinburgh's thirty-four, and even these are dated early in the reign. *RRS*, i, 27-28; *RRS*, ii, 28.

22. G.S. Pryde, *The Burghs of Scotland* (Edinburgh, 1965), 43.

23. *RMS*, i, 24; *Dunf. Reg.*, No. 346.

24. *Dunf. Reg.*, No., 361.

25. *Dunf. Reg.*, No., 390 (Appendix I); *Dunf. Reg.*, No., 391 (Appendix II).

26. *Dunf. Reg.*, No., 595* (Appendix III).

27. Dunfermline's relationship with the abbey compares favourably with many other monastic towns in England and elsewhere. R.S. Gottfried, *Bury St. Edmunds and the Urban Crisis, 1290-1539* (Guildford, 1982), 167-172. N.M. Trenholme, *The English Monastic Boroughs* (Missouri, Columbia, 1927), *passim*. W.G. Hoskins and H.P.R. Finberg, *Devonshire Studies* (London, 1952), 189.

28. The chief officer was termed 'alderman' in the vernacular, until mid-sixteenth century when 'provost'

was favoured; in Latin it has always been 'prepositus'.

29. The reponsibility of manning assizes was shared by many burgesses. How the council was composed is not clear. Beveridge in the introduction to the transcribed 'Burgh Court Book' argued that a council emerged and superseded the assize and that the first reference to a council in Dunfermline was in 1515. This error was repeated by MacKenzie (W.M. MacKenzie, *The Scottish Burghs* (Edinburgh, 1949), 111) and Webster and Duncan (*Dunf. Ct. Bk.*, 23). The Gild Book, however, refers to a 'council' of the town on three occasions, in 1449, 1466 and 1476 (MsGB, ff. 7v. 10 and 107) and the 'Burgh Court Book' itself speaks specifically of a council in 1498 (*Dunf. Recs.*, 90). It is clear, that, at least during the fifteenth and early sixteenth centuries, the assize and council existed alongside each other.

30. A burgess roll, undated, but from the names inscribed, probably from the early 1500s would suggest there were only about 140 to 150 burgesses. *Dunf. Recs.*, 364 and Appendix vii of E.P.D. Torrie, 'The Gild of Dunfermline in the Fifteenth Century' (Unpublished Ph.D. thesis, Edinburgh, 1984). For details of the calculations for population figures, *ibid.*, 118–121.

31. MsGB, f. 100v.

32. MsGB, f. 9v.
Dunf. Recs., 5 and 121.
I.F. Grant, *The Social and Economic Development of Scotland before 1603* (Edinburgh, 1930), 367, and S.G.E. Lythe, 'Economic Life' in *Scottish Society in the Fifteenth Century*, ed. J.M. Brown (Edinburgh, 1977), 81, for example, argue that only royal burghs had the right to markets and fairs. This is not correct.

33. J.M. Webster and A.A.M. Duncan state that it was unlikely that the Dunfermline regality was apportioned between the regality burghs. (*Dunf. Ct. Bk.*, 25.) *Dunf. Reg.*, No. 424 and MsGB, 100, however, indicate some apportionment. It is clear that Dunfermline and Kirkcaldy were not in agreement over their respective hinterlands. Goatmilk from 1448 (MsGB, 100) and Kinglassie (MsGB, 5) came within Dunfermline's trading precinct. By 1583,

however, Kirkcaldy was claiming both to be within its hinterland.(N. Macbean (ed.), *The Kirkcaldy Burgh Records* (Kirkcaldy, 1908), 82.)

34. The belief that non-royal burghs were excluded from overseas trade still attracts some support, for example, J. Wormald, *Court, Kirk and Community. Scotland 1470-1625* (London, 1981), 49, and S.G.E. Lythe, 'Economic Life' in *Scottish Society in the Fifteenth Century*, ed. J.M. Brown (Edinburgh, 1977), 81. Flanders was a favoured market for Dunfermline merchants in the early sixteenth century; and by the last decade of the century commercial contacts with the Baltic regions were such that Dunfermline men were encouraged to settle in Prussia and Polish towns. Simon Hair, for example, who entered the Dunfermline gild in 1589 (MsGB, 83) may have been resident in Prussia by 1593 (Tack of Stany Acres, lying to the south of Dunfermline, granted by John Black, citizen of Swiecin in Prussia and burgess of Dunfermline, in favour of Simon Hair and his wife. Certified under the seal of the town of Lancirien (?) before the clerk of the town. Dated July 23, 1593. Muniments of the Earl of Elgin and Kincardine.)

35. Torrie, 'The Gild of Dunfermline in the Fifteenth Century', 209-221 and 262-285.

36. MsGB, f. 105.

37. The gild finances were, at least at times, under the control of a 'bursar' and accounts were supervised by 'auditors of the compt'.

38. *APS*, ii, 95. MsGB, ff.32,36v,50v,70, for example

39. MsGB, ff. 5 and 9.
    MsGB, 82.

40. The Holy Blood altars in the parish churches of Edinburgh, Perth, Dundee and St. Andrews came under the special patronage of the local gilds merchant. During the fifteenth and early sixteenth centuries many Holy Blood altars were founded in east coast ports and in other trading centres. (D. McRoberts, 'The Fetternear Banner', *Innes Review*,vii (1956), 77.)

41. MsGB, ff. 18v, 19v, 20.

42. MsGB, f. 28v.

43. *Dunf. Recs.*, 65.
44. I.B. Cowan, 'Church and Society' in *Scottish Society in the Fifteenth Century*, ed. J.M. Brown (London, 1977), 118.
45. *John Knox's History of the Reformation in Scotland*, ed., W.C. Dickinson, 2 vols., (London, 1949), i, 276.
46. MsGB, f. 59.
47. *John Knox's History of the Reformation in Scotland*, ed., W.C. Dickinson, i, 334.
48. *RPC*, i, 246-247.
49. M. Dilworth, 'Monks and Ministers after 1560' in *Records of the Scottish Church History Society*, xviii (1974), 216-220.
    RSS, viii, No. 2703.
50. MsGB, f. 64.
51. This aspect of gild life, and the gild of Dunfermline in the fifteenth century in general, is discussed in more detail in the relevant chapter by the editor in the forthcoming publication, *The Scottish Medieval Town*, edd. M. Lynch, M. Spearman and G. Stell.
52. MsGB, f. 104.
    MsGB, f. 24v.
53. Torrie, 'The Gild of Dunfermline in the Fifteenth Century', 100-155, 309-311.
54. *Dunf. Recs.*, 209.
55. A more detailed discussion is in Torrie, 'The Gild of Dunfermline in the Fifteenth Century', 286-332.
56. *Dunf. Recs.*, 307 and Torrie, 'The Gild of Dunfermline in the Fifteenth Century', 130-132, and 293-297.
57. MsGB, f. 103.
    Such proposals were early, and before those of Peebles where, it has been argued, the first Scottish local quarantine measures were taken. See, D. Henderson, *The Healers: a History of Medicine in Scotland* (Edinburgh, 1982), 13, and T.C. Smout, 'Coping with plague in sixteenth and seventeenth-century Scotland', *Scotia*, ii, No. i, 23.
58. MsGB, ff. 102v, 5v.
59. MsGB, f. 49.
    Medieval plays and ballads about Robin Hood in

England and Scotland had some similarities. R.B. Dobson and J. Taylor, *Rymes of Robin Hood* (London, 1976) and A,J, Mill, *Medieval Plays in Scotland* (Edinburgh, 1927), 24.

60. *Supra*, note 55.

61. This donation of spice and wine was also the practice of Perth ('Guildrie Book', 2) and Edinburgh (J.D. Marwick, *Edinburgh Guilds and Crafts*, 42). In Stirling, however, this part of the entrance fee was wine and wax (Stirling Gild Records, October 1461, for example).

62. I. F. Grant, *The Social and Economic Development of Scotland before 1603* (London, 1930), 135-136, for example.

63. D. Thomson, *The Dunfermline Hammermen. A History of the Incorporation of Hammermen in Dunfermline* (Paisley, 1909).
D. Thomson, *The Weavers Craft being a history of the Weavers Incorporation of Dunfermline* (Paisley, 1903).

64. MsGB, f. 88. *RCRB*, i, 448.

65. The evolvement of the gild as an urban institution and the change in the values and purposes of its members is evidenced in a seventeenth- and eighteenth-century manuscript volume, a gild court book of Dunfermline, immediately post-dating this volume, in the possession of the Incorporation of the Guildry of Dunfermline.

ABBREVIATIONS

Abdn. Recs.	Early Records of the Burgh of Aberdeen, 1317, 1398–1407, ed. W.C. Dickinson (Scottish History Society, 1957).
APS	The Acts of the Parliaments of Scotland, edd. T. Thomson and C. Innes (Edinburgh, 1814–75).
Dunf.Ct.Bk.	Regality of Dunfermline Court Book, 1531–1538, edd. J.M. Webster and A.A.M. Duncan (Dunfermline, 1953).
Dunf.Recs.	The Burgh Records of Dunfermline, ed. E. Beveridge (Edinburgh, 1917).
Dunf.Reg.	Registrum de Dunfermelyn, (Bannatyne Club, 1842).
MsGB	Gild Court Book of Dunfermline, 1433–1597.
NLS	National Library of Scotland, Edinburgh.
RCRB	Records of the Convention of the Royal Burghs of Scotland, ed. J.D. Marwick (Edinburgh, 1866–90).
RMS	Registrum Magni Sigilli Regum Scotorum, edd. J.M. Thomson and others (Edinburgh, 1882–1914).
RPC	The Register of the Privy Council of Scotland, edd. J.M. Burton and others (Edinburgh, 1877–98).
RRS	Regesta Regum Scottorum, i–ii, ed. G.W.S. Barrow (vol. ii with collaboration of W.W. Scott) (Edinburgh, 1960, 1971).
RSS	Registrum Secreti Sigilli Regum Scotorum, edd. M. Livingstone and others (Edinburgh, 1908).
SBRS	Scottish Burgh Records Society.
SRO	Scottish Record Office, Edinburgh.

EDITORIAL CONVENTIONS

In editing, the text has been altered from the original as little as possible. Original spellings of personal names, including variants and abbreviations, and place-names have been retained. Capitalisation and punctuation have been modernised where it facilitates a reading of the text. The scribes' 'y' for 'thorn' and 'z' for 'yogh' have been rendered 'th' and 'y' respectively; and 'z' as a fraction has been transcribed '$\frac{1}{2}$'. The double f -'ff'- has been retained. Very minor deletions of clerical errors have not been transcribed. Any editorial comments are italicised, and have been placed within square brackets. Deletions, margin notes and later additions, where discernible, are specified as such. Illegible text is indicated by one of the four notations: [.... ?], [*folio worn*], [*folio torn*], or [*text obscured*] where conservation work has concealed the original folio.

[*Fo. 1*]

The gild court haldyn in the tolbuth of Dunfermlyn the vii day of the moneth of November the yeir of Our Lord j^m cccc xxxiij yere. John of Coupir was made gyldbrothir for xl^s to be payit witht in a yer that is to say Candilmas Vitsunday and Mechelmes, plegis Davy Hake[t *? folio torn*] and Thom Granger. Item Alan Littistar tretit witht the gildbrethir for vi^s for his craft for a y[er *? folio torn*] hym self bourch. Item Thom Littistar tretit for his craft for iiii^s for a yer, Dawy Story pl[egis *? folio torn*].

The gyld court haldyn in the toulbouth of Dunfermlyn the xx day of February the yer of Our Lord j^m cccc xxxiij yer the quhilk day was decretit be the gyld brethir of the accion debatabil betwyx Wil Cristison and Huchon Masoun anentis a some of lyme be the consent of bath the partis that the said Wil Cristison and Huchon suld pass to Culros on the Monownday nyxt eftir and that Huchon on his coft sal tak twa nechbouris witht hym of this toun witht the childer that deliveryit the lyme and thar befor the Abbot of Culros to swer that Huchon and his childer deliverit that lyme that he rasavit fra Wil Cristison of his childer to the Abbot of Culros and never rasavit paiment tharfor and gif the abbot rafos to her the ath he sal suer the ath befor sufisand witnes and quhilk of partis that falyeis this to tyn the accion.

The gyld curt haldyn in the tolbuth the Seterday the iij day of Julii anno Domini j^m cccc xxxiii it was prwyt be a prwf that Jonet of Guthre had done syc trespass a gaynis Wylyam of Benyn and his wyf Jonet, for the qwilk scho was nocht worthy to remayn in the toun, bot of grace in fawor of hyr husbande as than and gyf it be efftir cuntyt on hyr syc a lyk trespas othir scho or ony othir doand withtowt ony gayncallying for to be banyst for evirmar and the said Jonet thar to remayn qwyl scho payt x^s and amerciat to the party that had convictyt thaim in syc degre as scho has of befor tym.

Item that ilk day Patoun Turnbul in amersiment for his unressnaly ppel[and *? folio worn*] of quarter a mark. [*deleted*: Item eodem die the den in amersiment of quarter a mark for he drw a schwrd to John Chepman].

The yer abone wryttyn the xxviij day of Julii Thom Cristysone in amersiament of vi^s viii^d for the myssaing of Dawy Story plegis for hym Jhon Wrych and Lawrens Boy[s? *folio torn*].

The said day Davy Story in amersiament of vi^s viii^d for hos myssaing the said Dawy sic, plegis for the said Dawy Patoun Dow and Wilyam of Walwode.

The gyld court haldyn the xx day of August anno etc xxxiiij that [ilk day? *folio worn*] Patoun Turnbul and Jon of Bothuyl ar awctualy made frendis for [all? *folio worn*] actyownys by gane and thair gudwiffis ilkan of thaim ar in amersiament of vi^s and vii^d and qwilk of thaim that be fundyn in a violent defaut til uthir he sal pay j^{cs} vii forqevyn to the gyld purs in tym to cum.

[*Fo. 1v*]

The court haldyn in the tolbuth of Dunfermlyn the xiij day of the moneth of October the yer [of? *text obscured*] Our Lorde j^m cccc xxxiiij yer that ilk day John Wilson cordowner tretit witht the nychtbowris f[or? *text obscured*] fredome to by hiddis vtuith the fredome for j yer and to pa thairfor vj^s viij^d.

The gild court haldyn in the tolbuth of Dunfermlyn the vj day of the moneth of November the yer of Our Lorde j^m cccc xxxiiij yer. That ilk day John Mechelson compleyeit apon Dawy Story and all things betuyx tham resplatit betuyx tham quh[il? *text obscured*] the next court. Item anentis John Mechelsoun and John of Coupir to pruf that the said Jo[hn? *text obscured*] Mechelson bouch skynis for vj^d. Item Dawy Story compleyeit apon John Wilson and that complant delayit quhil the next court. Item John Wilson in an vnlaw for the strowblyn of the aldirman and the den and his nychbouris the vnlaw x^s.

The gild court haldyn in tolbuth of Dunfermlyn the xxi day of November the yer of Our Lord j^m cccc xxxiiij yer. That ilk day Dawy Story in an vnlaw for the distrowbly[n? *text obscured*] of John Mechelsonis wyf [*deleted*: Dawy Story]. Item that ilk day John Mechelson wyf in vnlaw for the distroub[lin? *text obscured*] of Dawy Story. Item that na gild brothir occuby na fredom within the burch bot gif he hes a land and a tercet.

The gild court haldyn in the tolbuth of Dunfermlyn befor Thomas Cristysun dene of the gild the xxij day of Januar anno Domini j^m cccc xxxiiij that ilk day the brethir grantyt Law Fox that is to oys the gild fredome for a yer at his fadrys request. Item Jon of Coupir in the brethiris wil of amerciamentis for ane accyon betwix Jon Mechelsun and hym. Item Jon Wilsun and Jon of Coupir ilkan in amerciamentis for foule spech. Item [deleted: Rob] Jon of Coupir in amerciamentis for his dystrublyn of Jon Wricht the aldirman in wurd.

The gyld curt haldyn in the tolbuth of Dunfermlyn the v day of March the yer abone wrytyn the qwilk day the nichtburis grantyt fawor for a yer [addition: to Alan Ly[t star? text obscured]] that is to say qwyl Mechalmess for vj^s to be payd to the gyld purss.

[Fo. 2]

The gild court haldyn in the tolbuth of Dunfermlyn the vj day of May the yer of Our Lord j^m cccc xxxv yer. That ilk day Thom of Bray in amerciment for wrang saying betuyx hym and John Yung. Item that ilke day John Yung in amerciment for wrang spech betuyx him and Thom of Bra.

The gild court haldyn in the tolbuth of Dunfermlyn the xiiij day of May the yer of Our Lord j^m cccc xxxv yer. That ilke day John Mechelsoun and John of Coupir in the brethir wil for bying of skynis vtouth the [deleted: fredome] ton. Item that ilke day the brethir ordanit that that day the gild brethir sittis thai sele haf to thair culation xij^d and thai that cumys to the culation beand fra the sittyng sel pay j^d to thair ail. Item that John Jakson excludit the gild fredom quhil it be new bouch at the brethir for certan causis.

The Mechalmess that Huchun Masoun was dene of the gild John Wilson tretyt for the gyld fredome of hidis bying and barkyn for a yer for v^s.

[In margin: nota] The gyld court haldyn in the tolbuth of Dunfermlyn the xiij day of the moneth of October the yer of Our Lord j^m cccc xxxvj yer, Dawy Haket den of the gyld.

The gyld court haldyn in the tolbuth of Dunfermlyn the thrid day of the moneth of November the yer of Our Lorde j^m cccc xxxvj yer be [deleted: Dawy Haket dene] Henri Steuart aldirman and Dawy Haket dene.
That ilke day the gyld brethir graintit fredom to John Wilson cordouner to occupy the fredomys of the gyld lauchfully for hys tym for the som of xl^s to be paide at Pask and Midsummyr, dettour hym self and bourch Thom of Bra and Nychol Johnson.
The quhilk day Will of Annand wes mad gyld brothir at

the instans of the kying Den William of Hawyk and Lowrans Boys his eldfadir for the som of [xs *? folio worn*] to be pait at Fasterynewyn v^s at Witsunday next eftir v^s [bourch hym? *folio worn*] self. The quhilk day Alan Littistar wes mad gyld brothir for the som of xlv^s [to be paid *? folio worn*] at Pask and Lammes nex eftir, dettour hym self [bourch David of Bra John of Coupir *? folio worn*].

[*Fo. 2v*]

The quhilk day Lourens Fox wes made gild brothir for the som of xl^s. Thairof gyffyn him xx^s fre becaus of succeeding till his fadyr and to pay xx^s at Pask and Witsunday nixt eftyr, dettour hym self, John Mechelson and Will of Benyng plegis.

The quhilk day Robin Haket wes mad gild brothir for the som of xl^s of the quhilk some the gyld brethir gef hym fre x^s and to pay the xxx^s at Witsunday Lames and Mechelmes dettour hym self, bourch John Bothuele and John Mechel[son? *folio worn*].

Anno quo supra the xvij day of the moneth of November Wyl Jacson was maide gyld brothir for the sowm of fyfty schyllyngis in wyn syluir and al thyngis to be paide at Pace and Wytsonday next foluand. Plegis Wyl of Walwod and Jhon Yowng flessar and dettowr hym self.

Anno quo supra the gyld curt haldyn in the tolbuth be Davyd Hacat dene of the said fredome the xij day of the moneth of December Thom Cristyson presentit a letter testa[ment *? text obscured*] as the secund curt of Patoun Turnbul of the sown of xx^s, the said Pat[oun? *text obscured*] beand somond to the said accion absent jugit in ij^s, and to be somond to the next curt as the curt peremtowrlie.

Anno quo supra the gyld court haldyn in the tolbuth of Dunfermlyn the x day of March the quhilk day Nichol Bron was mad gyld brothir for the some of xl^s to be paid at thre termys, that is to say at Vitsunday next eftir j mark, at Martimes a mark and the nest Vitsunday thaireftir j mark, Schir Dawy Steuart borch the said Nichol dettour.

On Sanct Thomas day the appostyl befor Yule anno Domini j^{mo} ccc^o xxxvij^o Jon Wricht in amerciamentis of xl^s for the strikyn of Jon of Cowpir.
Item Jon of Cowpir in amerciamentis for his wrangwys spekyn aganys Jon Wricht. That ilk day Jon of Cowpir in amerciamentis of xl^s for his wrangwis strykyn of Thomas Crystyson.

Anno quo supra the gyld court haldyn in the tolbutht of

Dunfermlyn the xx day of the moneth Februar the quhilk day Alexander Boys wes mad gyldbrothir for our lord the abbottis request and Schir David Stewart na thyng payand bot the wyn. [*deleted*: Item that ilke day Nicholl Bron in amerciament for the defoulyn of our gildbrothir in a pak beren in the cuntray quhar he suld nocht and an vthir for forstallyn in the cuntray anenttis skynis byen the thrid for forstallyn in the marcat of skynis.]

[*Fo. 3*]

[*deleted*: Item the said Nichol the ferde fault is quhar the statut was ordanit that a nichbur suld pass hys peniworthis til hys nichburris that is woll hid and skyn the said Nicholl sauld hys peniworthis till fremit men and for the said iiij vnlauys the nichbouris ordanit to ras at thair will x^s.]

The gyld court haldyn in the tolbuth of Dunfermlyn be Dawy Haket den anno quo supra the xxvj day of Aprill the quhilk day the nychbouris of Mastirton trettit for the wranguys barken of hidd for xx^s, of the quhilk xx^s thai paid to the said den rich than x^s and the tothir x^s to pay at mydsummir day next eftir. Item fra John of Falsid $xviij^d$.

Item for hyddis sauld to Will of Bar xij^s, plegis John Goslyn to be paid withtin [? *folio torn*] dais.

Item the quhilk day Wil of Bar grant to the den and the brethir xij stekis lyand in bark with hym of vnfremanis the quhilk he errestit in hys hand rich than. Item John Robertson grantit to the den and the brethren iiij stekis lyand in bark of Dunloppis the quhilk the den erestit in hys hand.

[*deleted*: Item for a cartan. Item Will of Bar x^s for a cartan of hiddis baith fra the den and the brethir bourch John Goslyn.]

The gild court

[*Fo. 3v*]

Anno. etc. xxxviij

The viij day of November the yer abon wrytyn Wyl of Balmanoch was maid gildbrothir in the presens of Dawyd Hacat deyn and the gyld brethir for xl^s to be paid be Mychalmess next to cum, plegis Thom of Bra and Jhon of Cupyr.

The qihlk day the deyn and the brethir grantyt to Nychol Jhonsoun fawor of xx^s that he awch for John Wilson sowtar to be pait at iij termys, that is to say vj^s $viij^d$ at the term of Mertymass next to cum. vj^s $viij^d$ at Wytsonday next thairefftir and vj^s and viij^d at the next Martymes thar efftir, plegis his lande.

Anno quo supra the xxij day of November Jhon of Cupir in amerciament for his dystroblyn of Schir Wilyam Alansoun in worde.

Anno Domini j^m cccc xxxix yer the xij day of October the gild court haldyn in the tolbuth of Dunfermlyn be the den of the gyld of that ilke the brethir decretit and fand Will Jacson forstaller in to the byen of a cartan of skynnis fra the sallerer John Bothwell beand the marchand to the sallerer the quhilk skynnis eschet.

        Sum of entreis and proffitis in Dawy
        Haketts tym of twa yer xl lib viij^s vj^d.

[*Fo. 4*]

Anno Domini j^m cccc xxxviij^o the gild court haldyn in the tolbuth of Dunfermlyn be the den John of Coupir and the brethir the xix day of the moneth of Nouember.
The quhilk day Will of Gelland mad gyldbrethir for the soum of xl^s and the wyn siluir of the quhilk xl^s the brethir gef hym agan x^s for hys gud dedis doand till the makyn of a cawsay betuyx the Lym kill and our ton of Dunfermlyn. Borch Alan Littistar to be paid be Mechelmes nest eftir the date.
[*in margin:* nota] The quhilk day Johne Than sone and ayr till hys fadir Alexander Than was mad gyld brothir as ayr for the spice and the wyn.
[*in margin:* nota] The quhilk day Androu Hog was mad gyld brothir for the soum of xl^s to be paid be the nest Mechelmes nest eftir the date, borch John Than.
Anno Domini j^m cccc xxxix the gild court haldyn in the tolbuth of Dunfermlyn be the den Johne of Coupir and the brethir of that ilke the last day of Januer.
[*in margin:* nota] The quhilk day John Wrich at the den and the brethiris will for the defaut and myspersonyn of our balye Alan Littistar and to ras at thar will.
The quhilk day Alan Littistar than balye and hys wyf was put in frendschip with Johne Wrycht vndir a pan of x^s that gyf ony of tham defauttis till othir the pan to be rasit but remyssioun.
Anno Domini j^m cccc xxxix the gild court haldyn in the tolbuth of Dunfermlyn be the den Johne of Coupir and nychbouris the xiij day of Februar.
[*in margin*: nota] The quhilk day Thom Androson was mad gyld brothir and frely gyffyn for the abb[ots ? *folio torn*] request.
[*in margin*: nota] The quhilk day Den Rechard Bothuel

secrestan of Dunfermlyn vas mad gildbrothir for hys
fauouris till be don and for to be don in tym to cum.
[*in margin:* nota] The gild court haldyn in the tolbuth of
Dunfermlyn be the den Johne of Coupir and the bre[thir
folio torn] of ilke the xxiij day of Aprill the yer of Our
Lord j^m cccc xl yer.
The quhilk day John Blayk than almynnar was mad gildbrothir and fr[ely ? *folio torn*] gyffyn hym for fauour.
The quhilk day Will of Kyrcaldy tretit to hys fredom
and was mad gildbrothir throu ayrschip.

[*Fo. 4v*]
The quhilk day Will of Narn was mad gildbrothir and
gyffyn hym frely for fauour thai hade to hym.
The quhilk day Johne of Spens the herrauld was mad
gyldbrothir for the soum of xl^s of the quhilk soum the
gild brethir gef hym xx^s agan at the request of
Schir Stewart and to pay the tothir xx^s be the Martymes
nest eftyr, bourch Johne of Bothuel, dettour hym self.
Anno Domini j^m cccc xl^o the xx day of August the gild
court haldyn in the tolbuth of Dunfermlyn be the den
Johne of Coupir and the brethir of that ilke.
The quhilk day the nychbouris witht hale common consent
chesit thair persounis vndir vrytyn for to ras and rasaf
the common guddis awand to tham. Inprimis Johne of
Coupir den John of Bothuell John Chepman and Allan
Littistar balyeis Thom of Bra Schir Alexander of Kynglassy
Schir Johne Williamsoun and John Mechelsoun.
[*in margin: drawing of hand with pointing finger*] The quhilk day in the presens of Schir Dauid Stewart and Henre
Stewart aldirman the gildbrethir with hall common consent
statut that thair suld nan be rasauit na mad gildbrothir in thair fraternite but or euir he suer the ath to
that fraternite to be laid doun xl^s or ellis frely to be
gyffin hym as tyll a gild brothiris ayr.
The quhilk day the nychbouris ratyfeid and confffirmyt the
auld statut vndir vrytyn to be haldyn that is to say that
nan sall by woll hid na skyn bot gyf he send it on hys
awyn aventur our see or ellis sell it to hys nychbouris or ellis to profferit in plan court and to be vndir-
standyn hys proff[? *text obscured*] bot pregedice be the
nychbouris sen.

The gild court haldyn in the tolbuth of Dunfermlyn be the
den Alan Littistar and the brethir [*deleted:* anno Domini
j^m cccc xl] the xxij day of Januar anno Domini j^{mo} cccc^o xl^o.
The quhilk day Schir Alexander of Kynglassy and hys
seruandis and Will of Kynglassy was put in frendschip
witht Will the Ramsay and hys wyf and hys seruandis of

all the debatis movit betuyx tham to that day. And of the pan of v merkis laid betuyx tham of befor ilke an of tham fand dettour of the said pan. And that day rasit of ilke an of tham xl^d of the said pan and the lafe to be rasit at the brethirs will.

[*Fo. 5*]

The gild court haldyn in the tolbuth of Dunfermlyn be the den Alan Littistar and the brethir [of that ? *text obscured*] ilke the xj day of Februar anno Domini j^m cccc xl^o.

The quhilk day it vas ordanyt and consentyt be all the gyldbrethir that fraythinfurtht all actionis debatabill betuyx gildbrethir that are gret accionis of dettis or sic elik thyngis that be a sworn assiss of the said brethir vnsuspekit the accoun sall be determynit.

The quhilk day the nychbouris forgef Malice Lech xxx^s of hys fredom siluir for the hurtis that he tuk of the gild land and the x^s that he is [*deleted*: was] awand to be paid v^s at Vitsunday next eftir and v^s at Mechelmes, plegis John Chepman.

Memorandum that on Seterday the xviij day of Februar the yer of Our Lord j^m cccc xl in the gyld curt haldyn in the tolbuth of Dunfermlyn certane gudis war present and eschetyt takyn ovt of Kynglassy be the nychbouris of the said burgh fra Thom Cady. The qwilk gudis at the reuerens and reqvest of ovr lord the abbot and Schir Dawyd Steuart be the said nychboris was frely gyffyn to thaim. And our master Schir Dawyd had said sekerly that in tym to cum he sal mak na reqvest for hym na nan vthir in syklyk cace.

Anno etc. xlj^o the xxv day of November in the gild curt haldyn in the tolbuth in the presens of the aldirman and Wilyam of Kyrcaldy deyn of the gild it was fundyn be the nychburis that Alan Lytstar had brokyn thar stutut of sellyn of gild merchandis tyl vnfremen of this burgh quarfor the nychburis has decretyt that the said Alan sal be excludyt of al gild fredoum qvyl he opteynyt again at the aldirman the deyn and the brethir and pay xl^s to the brethir. Thir ar the namis of thaim that war thar. Inprimis the aldirman Henry Steuart the den the sacristan Jhon Chayn Jhon of Cupir Thom of Bra Jhon Wrych Schir Alexander Jhon Goslyn Jhon of Bothuel Thom Grangiar [*addition in margin*: [Da?] vy Hacat] Wyl of Narn Andro Hog Wilyam Logan Wilyam Gelland Schir Jhon Wilyamson Thom Cristysone Wilyam Jacsone Alexander Boys Nychol Broun Jhon Mechelsone Wilyam Balmanoch Malys Lech Wilyam Anande. Item Alan Martynsone.

Anno etc. xlj° the x day of March be for the aldirman the den and the brethir Will of Gelland was fundyn in amerciament for the distrublans of Jhon Goslyn in Thom Grangiaris hovs and the mendis ordanit betuex thaim and x markis ordanit to be put in Goslynis wil to be rasyt at the ordinans of the said brethir othir al or part qven thai thynk tym.

Item Jhon Goslyn fundyn in amerciamento [sic] for his complant makyn to the abbot apoun the said action qvil he had falyeit the law at the said brethir.

[Fo. 5v]

The gild court haldyn in the tolbuth of Dunfermlyn be the aldirman and the dene the xiiij day of Aprill the yer of Our Lord j^{mo} cccc^o and xlij.
The quhilk day Alexander Yrland sone and ayr to John Willsoun was mad gyldbruthir as ayr till hys fadyr the quhilk was a gildbruthir [deleted: for the] he payand the spice and the wyn.
[in margin: nota] The gild court haldin in the tolbuth of Dunfermlyn be the aldirman and the dene the xx day of September the yher of Our Lord j^m cccc xlij°.
That ilk day Dauid Wer was made gildbruthir at the instans of the abbot payand the spice and the wyne.

Michelmes.

The gild court haldyn in the tolbutht of Dunfermlyn be Henry Stewart aldirman and John of Coupir dene the ij day of Nouember the yere of Our Lord j^{mo} cccc xliij yer.
The quhilk day it was ordanit and statut witht hall common consent of the brethir that na sowtar sall bark ony hiddis and be his craft bot it that the horn and the er is elik lang as the law is.
The gild court haldin in the tolbuth of Dunfermlyn be John of Coupir den of the gylde the xxiij day of Nouember the yher of Oure Lord j^m cccc xliij.
That ilk day Wyll of Balmanoch grawntit the brekyn of the statute forsaid in the bying of v hydis the quhilk was jugit be the gyld brethir thar eschet, and than was rasit xij^d and dronkin the laffe at the nichtburis will.
Item that day Johne Wylsone soutar grawntit the brekyn of the said statute in bying of iiij hydis the qwhilk was jugit eschet, and than was rasit xij^d and dronkin the laffe ramanand at the nichtburis wyll.

The gild court haldyn in the tolbuth of Dunfermlyn be the aldirman Henre Stewart and John of Cvupir den of the gild the xxiij day of May the yer of Our Lord j^m cccc xliiij

yer.
The quhilk day John Sym ves resauit nychbour for caus he biggit and wes brynt he sall gyf till the culacioun vj^s viij^d and the wyn siluir dronkin. Item Will of Dunlop wes rasauit for the forsaid caus and he sall pay to the culacioun x^s witht the win siluir. Item Law of Furmornis wes rasauit nychbour for the forsaid caus [*deletion* : brint] that is to say brint and biggit and he sall gif to the culacioun x^s. Item John Baxtar wes mad nychbour for caus of biging and he sall pay to the culacioun x^s and the win siluir. Memorandum that John Symmys wyn syluir was drunkyn that ilk day. Item concordit witht Richard of Walwode for x^s and wyn syluir than payit. Item Law of Furmornys wyn syluir and all payit richt than.

[*Fo.* 6]

[*in margin* : nota] The gild court haldin in the tolbuth of Dunfermlyn be the aldirman and the den of gilde the thirde day of the moneth of October, the yhere of Oure Lord j^m cccc fourty and four.
[*in margin*: nota] That ilk day Robert Stewart was made gild brothir fre.

Anno etc. xliiij. In the presens of Johne of Bothuel den of the gilde and all the laffe of the fraternite vpon Saynt Thomas day befor Yhulle, Wylyhame of Kircaldy and Alane Litstar war pwt in frenschip and ilkane of thaim pwt in a mark to be rasyt at the wyllis of the sayd den and fraternite.

[*in margin*: nota] The gild court haldin in the tolbuth of Dunfermlyn be Johne of Bothuel den of gilde the xxvij day of Februar the yhere of Oure Lord j^m cccc xliiij.
That ilk day Moris Blaik was made gilde bruthir for xl^s and the wyn syluir of the qwilk som givyn to the almnar xx^s.

[*in margin* : nota] The gilde court haldyn in the tolbuth of Dunfermlyn be John of Bothuel den of the gilde the xiij day of Marche the yhere of Oure Lord j^m cccc xliiij.
That ilk day John of Coupir and Johne Chepman was pwt in to frenschip and ilkane of thaim in amerciamentis to be rasit at the wyll of the nichtbouris.

That ilk day Alan Littistar and Dauid Wer was put in frendschip and ilke an of thaim condampnit in an vnlaw to be rasit at the den and nychbouris will the said Alan of half a mark and the said Dauid of j mark.

[*in margin*: nota] The gilde court haldyn in the tolbuth of Dunfermlyn be Johne of Bothuel den of gylde the last day of the moneth of July the yhere of Oure Lord j^m cccc xlv.

COURT BOOK, 1433-1597 11

That ilk day it is acordyt betwen the gylde brethir and
Johne Wricht that bwt falyhe he suld pay be Candilmes
next thar eftir xlvij^s ij^d for the qwhilk soum to be payit
Thom of Bra and Thom Cristysone borch.

The gylde court haldin in the tolbuth of Dunfermlyn be
John of Bothuel den of the gilde the xxvij day of Nouember
the yhere of Oure Lord j^m cccc xlv. That ilk day it was
fwndyn be the gild brethir that Johne Sym, Wyll of
Balmanoch, Law of Furmornis and Wyll Logane ilkane has
brokyn the statute in hydis byi̇ng. Modefijt to John Sym
ij^s. Item Wyll of Balmanoch xij^d. Item Law of Furmornis
xviij^d. Item Wyll Logane xij^d.

[Fo. 6v]

[in margin : nota] The gylde court haldyn in the tolbuth
of Dunfermlyn be John of Bothuel den the xxj day of
December the yher of Our Lord j^m cccc xlv.
[in margin : nota] That ilk day Dotho Bakstar was made
gildbrothir for xl^s and the spice and the wyne of the
qwhilk soum thar was gevyn to the almnar x^s.
[in margin: nota] The gild court haldin in the tolbuth of
Dunfermlyn be John of Bothuel den the vii day of Maij the
yhere of Oure Lord j^m cccc xlvj.
[in margin: nota] That ilk day Elspeth of Ochterlowny pwt
hyr in the denys wyll anent the selling of Alexander of
Irlandis marchandis withoute leiffe, and fand the aldirman
Johne of Coupir borch to content thaim of the vnlaw at his
hame cuming. Item Moris Blaik seriand of the gild in
amerciamentis be causse he dyd nocht his office in the
pwnding of Wyll of Anand.

The yer of xlvj^o the x day of December the gild court
haldyn be the aldirman Johne of Cupyr and Jhon of Bothuel
dene of gyld. It vas determynyt be thaim and the brethir
betwex Wyl Jacson and Johne in furm and manir as foluis.
Inprimis it is ordanyt that fra the said day furth, the
said Wil Jacson suld neuir in word na in langage muff the
matiris gan befor to the Lord of Ogilvy vndir payn of
depriying of his fredoum for euir mar etc. Item[deleted:John]
Wyl Jacson fundyn dettour to John Jacson of xxxiij^s iiij^d.
Item Wil jacson dettour to Jhon Jacson of iiij^s anens the
Lord Tarwat. John Jacson in amerciament for his wrangwys
claym anens Sande Iraulyn. Item Jhon Jacson in amerciament for his wrangwys claym anens the takyn [?] of his
malyn. Item John Jacson in amerciament for the [deleted:che-
ppin] of his clath.
    Sum avand to John Jacson be Wyl Jacson the
    said day in al thyngis is xxxij^s ix^d.

12   DUNFERMLINE GILD

Thar vnlawis modyfyit to v pintis of maluasy John j quart and Wyl iij pyntis that ilk day drunkyn thar said amerciamentis.

[*in margin*: nota] The gyld court haldin in the tolbuth of Dunfermlyn be Johne of Bothuel den on Saynt Thomas day befor Yhulle the yher of Our Lord j^m cccc xlvj.

That ilk day Johne Wricht and his wyff was pwt in frenschip with Andro Hog and the said Andro and Johne Wrichtis wyff ilkan jugyt in amerciament for thar ill langage ilkan till othir. And to modefijt at the denys wyll and the brethir. Item Andro Hog in amerciamentis for his strublyn of John Wricht be word.

[*in margin*: nota] The quhilk day Andro Hog fand law borovis anens Johne Chepman thatt the said Johne suld be vnskayit of hym and his party as law wyll, plegis for the said Andro Hog Thom of Bra and Alan Lytstar.

[*in margin*: nota] The said John Chepman fand borowis for hym Wilyam of Kyrcaldy and Wyl Jacsone anens the said Andro.

Anno etc. xlvj.

[*in margin*: nota] The xiiij day of Januar Den Wilyam Boys sacristan of Dunfermlyn was maid gildbrothir throw resson of his fadir for his wyn siluir.

[*Fo.* 7]

Anno etc. xlvj.

The iiij day of Febrwar Wyl Flemyn and Thom Flemyn war maid gildbrethir at the instanis and request of our lord the abbot frely for thar wyn siluir.

Anno etc. xlvij^o.

iiij^o die mensis Nouembris the gildbrethir accordyt witht Wylly Logan to tap marchandis for j yer and he sal pay at the next sittyng v^s.

[*in margin*: nota] Item the nychtburis accordyt with John of Burn in the samyn manir for iij^s iiij^d to pay at Pask.

Anno quo supra.

Penultima die mensis Decembris be the gildbrethir al debatis betvex Alan Lytstar and John Chepm[an? *text obscured*] marchandis and al accionis to the said day fully deliuerit and endyt. And the said Alane ordanit to pay to the said John that day xv^s and Johne Chepman fra al clamis excludyt fra that day furth.

The iij day of Februar it is fundyn be the aldirman and the dene and the brethir that Wyll of Kyrcaldy had defaltyt gretly in langage to Johne Jacson and syn to Wyl Jacson and to the brethir to be modyfiit be thaim to a galon of wyn.

[*in margin*: nota] Item the said Wil Jacson in amerciamento

for his langage to be modyfiit to a qwart of wyn.
Item John Jacson in amerciamento for the said acton to half a galone.
Plegis for Wyl of Kyrcaldy John Wrych and Johne Mechalson.
Plegis for Johne Jacson Wyl Logan and Moryss Blayk.
Plegis for Wyl Jacson Thom of Bra and Alan Lytstar.
[in margin: nota] Alan Martyson in amerciamento for his wrangws haldyn of iij^s fra John Jacsone.
[in margin: nota] Alan Lytstar in amerciamento for his wrangwys haldyn of iiij^s vj^d fra Alan Martyson.
That ilk day the gildbrethir concordyt witht Law Fox and Law of Segy for the qwarel mell that pertenyt to the gildbrethir that thai sal pay for it iiij^s at the Pask next to cum.

[in margin: nota] The xxiiij day of Februar anno etc. xlvij Andro Gudsuan was maid gildbrothir of heritage.

[in margin: nota] The [deleted: a] gilde court haldin in the tolbuth of Dunfermlyn be johne of Bothuell den the ix day of Marche the yhere of Oure Lord j^m cccc xlvij.
[in margin: nota] That ilk day Johne of Burne was made gilde brothir fre at the instance of the Bischop of Santandrois payand the spice and the wyne.
    Anno etc. xlviij.
[in margin: nota] The xxiij day of the moneth of Nouember the gildbrethir forgaff frely to Malyss Lech x^s to his houss byggyn the quilk some he awch to the said brethir for his fredome siluir.
Anno etc xlviij^o the xxv day of Januar Johne Wrych aldirman and Schir Johne Wylyamson dene.
[in margin: nota] The quilk day Wyll Logan was maid gilld brothir for xxx^s and x^s giffyn of the xl^s at the instans of the almanar Den Johne Blayk and of his brothir Schir Henry Logan. Soluit.
[in margin: nota] The quilk day John Robertson and John of Tulch war maid gilldbrethir throw reson of thar fadiris.

[Fo. 7v]

[in margin: nota] The gyld court haldin in the tolbuth of Dunfermlyn be Schir John Wylyhamsone dene the vij day of Maij the yhere of Oure Lord j^m cccc xlix.
[in margin: nota] That ilk day Thom of Coupir was made gylde brothir for xl^s of the qwhilk gevin till him agane v^s.
Item James Strang was made gylde brothir for xl^s of the qwhilk gevin him agane xiij^s iiij^d.

[in margin: nota] Memorandum that the yhere of Oure Lord j^m cccc xlix the last day of June Johne Chepman balye on a part and Thom of Bra balye and Johne his sone

on the tothir part pwt in to frenschip and Johne of Bra
jugit in amerciament of halff a mark of the qwhilk to be
rasyt xl^d and Johne Chepman jugit in amerciamentis of
xl^d of the qwhilk to be rasyt xij^d. Item Thom of Brais
wyff and Johne Chepmannis war put in frenschip and the
said Johne Chepmannis wyff jugit in amerciament of a mark
of the qwhilk to be rasyt ij^s. All thir forsaid thingis war
done in the presens of Wylyham [deleted: Stewart Schir Jo]
Johne Wricht aldirman Schir Johne Wylyhamsone den witht
the laff of the consalle of the ton.

[in margin: nota] Memorandum quod anno Domini j^{mo} cccc
xlix quarto die mensis Augusti.
That ilk day Johne of Cokburne was made gylde brothir for
Johne of Bothuell throw the promyss and compositoun that
was made qwhen the toun was brint and the said Johne
has gevin of his gude wyll a dennyr with the spice and
wyne.
[in margin: nota] Item that ilk day Rob Patounson was
made gylde brothir for xx^s the qwhilk was gevin to the
thekin of the tolbuth.
Item that ilk day Thom Fowlar was made gylde brothir for
xxvj^s viij^d the qwhilk he payit than, and alswa he was
made burges fre the samyn tym.

[in margin: nota] Memorandum that the viij of Nouember
the yer of Our Lord j^m cccc xlix befor Johne of Coupyr
aldirman and Johne of Bothuel dene of the gild and the
brethir John Jacsone in amerciamento of xij^d betvex hym
and Johne of Byris.

The said day Alan Lytstar in amerciament of vj^d betvex
hym and Thom of Coupyr.

[in margin: nota] Memorandum that on Sant Thomas evyn
John Chepman and Wyll Jacsone war fwndyn ilkan distrublars
of vthir for the qwhilkis in the presens of the aldirman
Johne of Coupir and Johne of Bothuell dene thai war modefijt ilkan in xl^s and of the qwhilk some to be rasyt of
ilkane of thaim halff a mark without remyssion. And qwhilk
of thaim faltis till vthir in tym to cum all the halle xl^s
to be rasyt at the wyll of the said aldirman and dene of
gylde and the brethir.

[in margin: nota] Memorandum that the gyld court haldin
in the tolbuth of Dunfermlyn be Johne Bothuell dene of the
gyld the thryd day of October the yhere of Oure Lord
j^m cccc and fyvety.
[in margin: nota] That ilk day Johne Wricht was resauit
to the fredome of the gyld throu resone of his fadir
payand the spice and the wyne.
[in margin: nota] Item Philip Stoylle was resauit to the

fredome of the gyld throu resone of his fadir payand the spice and the wyne.
Item Johne Anderston son and ayr till Andro Anderston was mad gildbrothir throw ressone of his fadir and hys win paid.

[Fo. 8]

Anno Domini j^{mo} cccc liij the viij day of Dissember the gild court haldin be the den of the [gild ? *text obscured*] Johne Chepman. Quo die William Stewart was mad gild brothir in fauouris of hys awn request and for the wyn.

[*in margin*: nota] The gild court haldin in the tolbuth of Dunfermlyn be Johne Chepman den the xvj day of Ffebruar the yhere of Our Lord j^m cccc liij.
That ilk day Johne Fleming was made gildbrothir fre, payand the spice and the wyne.
Item Wyllyhame Stewart was made gildbrothir fre, payand the spice and the wyne.
Item James Hacate was made gildbrothir throu resone of his fadir, payand the spice and the wyne.

[*in margin*: nota] The gilde court haldin in the tolbuth of Dunfermlyn be Johne Chepman den the xxiij day of Februar the yhere of Oure Lord j^m cccc liij.
That ilk day Thom of Coupir was fundyn in amerciament for his foule speche made to John Sym and denying of selling of irne till hym as he bocht it, for the qwhilk he sall pay j quart of w[yn ? *text obscured*] the last of the amerciament ramyttit be the gild brethir.
Item John Sym in amerciament for his foule speche made to Thom Cristysone for the qwhilk he sall pay j pynt of wyne.

[*in margin*: nota] The gyld curt haldyn be Thom of Bra the xij day of October the yer of Our L[ord ? *text obscured*] etc liiij^o.
The quilk day Henry Foular payt ij^s for occupying of gild fredome in bar[kyn ? *text obscured*]
The quilk day Andro Lytstar dettor to the gild brethir of v^s for the fredoum [of ? *text obscured*] lyttyn qwyl the fest of Yowle next thair efftir, plegis Wil Jacsone.
That ilk day Henry Foular dettor of xl^d for fredome for a yer of barkyn of h[id ? *text obscured*] and hors hidis and lappis and nocht to by na hidis withtin this fredome.

The gild court haldin in the tolbuth of Dunfermlyn be Thom of Bra dene the viij day of Ffebruar the yhere of Oure Lord j^m cccc liiij.
[*in margin*: nota] That ilk day Pate Fleming was made gildbrothir fre at the instance of the abbot payand the spice and the wyne.

16 DUNFERMLINE GILD

The gild court haldin in the tolbuth of Dunfermlyn be Johne Chepman den the thrid day of Januar the yer of Our Lord j^m cccc lv.
That ilke day Androu Logan was mad gildbrothir for the soum of xl^s of the quhilk the nychbouris geff him agan in favour v^s.

[Fo. 8v]
Memorandum quod anno etc. lvj^o xxij die mensis Maij.
The quhilk day Wilyam Jacsone and Thom of Coupir balyeis war put in frenschip anent the discordis and debatis betwix thaim and for the strublans of the toun for the quhilkis ilkan has payit xij^d. And giff it be fundyn in tym to cum that ony of thaim kepis nocht thar frenschip till vthir and quhalk [deleted: falt] of thaim beis fundyn faltit at the sicht of the brethir thai sall pay halff a mark without remissione.

[in margin: nota] Memorandum quod anno Domini j^{mo} cccc lviij, xiij die mensis Maij John of Cokburne aldirman Johne Fleming dene of the gilde. That ilk day Lowry Foular entrit to the fredome of the gilde for xl^s of the quhilk he is remittyt a mark at the instance of the abbot, and payand the spice and the wyne.

[deleted: Memorandum quod anno Domini j^{mo} cccc lix^o xxvij^o die mensis Octobris Alane Litstar dene of the gilde. That ilk day Dauid Bra entrit to the fredome of the gilde for xiij^s iiij^d. The remanent was remittit till him of his gude being and for fauoris that the brethir of the gilde had to his fadir and hym. Item payand the spice and the wyne.

[in margin: drawing of hand with pointing finger] That ilk day it was ackit and consentit with the hale fraternite of the gilde that quhat tyme ony of the gild brethir discessit, the sergiand of the gilde sall warne all the gild brethir on the nycht befor to pass with that corsse to the erde. And ilk gilde brothir sall gir a messe be done for the saulle that ilk day or than within viij dayis at the ferrest. And giff ony of the gilde brethir levis this vndone the dene sall rasse on him xij^d without remissione and giff it for the saulle.

Michalmes.
[in margin: nota] The gild court haldin in the tolbuth of Dunfermlyn be Alan Litstar dene the vj day of September the yere of Our Lord j^m cccc lx.
[in margin: nota] The quhilk day Schir Robert Graunt was made gild brothir throu reson of his fadir and payit than xxx^d to the wyne quhilk was delyuerit to Lowry Foular

sergeand.
[*in margin* : nota] That ilk day Andro Butlar was made gilde brothir for xl^s the quhilk the said Alane dene resauit richt than. And the wyne siluir pait to Lowry Foular sergeand.
[*in margin* : nota] Item Dauid Bra was made gilde brothir for a mark of siluir the quhilk the said Alane dene resauit. And the wyne siluir payit to Lowry Foular sergeand.

Michalmes.

[*in margin*: nota] The gild court haldin in the tolbuth of Dunfermlyn be Thom of Coupir dene on Saint Thomas evin befor Yule anno etc. lx.
[*in margin*: nota] The quhilk day Johne of Hill was made gild brothir throu resone of his fadir payand the spice and the wyne.
Item Daue of Orok was made gild brothir for xl^s and at the raquest of the abbot thar was gevin him agane xiij^s iiij^d.

[*Fo. 9*]

[*in margin*: nota] The gilde court haldin in the tolbuth of Dunfermlyn be the dene Dauid Weir the xxiij day of Januar the yere of Oure Lord j^m cccc lxj.
[*in margin* : nota] That ilk day Andro Gervas was made gilde brothir for xl^s the quhilk he payit richt than and delyuerit to the said dene and the spice and the wyne to pay.

The gilde court haldin in the tolbuth of Dunfermlyn be the dene Thomas of Coupir vpone Saint Thomas day befor Yulle the yeir of Our Lord j^m cccc lxij.
[*in margin* : nota] The quhilk day Wyll of Spetell was resauit to the fredome of the gilde for xl^s the quhilk he payit richt than and delyuerit to the said dene.
[*in margin* : nota] Item that ilk day Andro Gudswane put him in the aldirmanis wyll and the denis of the dissobeying of the dene and complenyeing to the abbot, for the quhilkis accioune the said Andro was chargit to entir agane at the nex sytting.
[*in margin*: nota] The gild court haldin in the tolbuth of Dunfermlyn be Wilyam of Kircaldy aldirman and Thomas of Coupir dene of the gilde the xxvj day of Marche, the yer of Our Lord j^m cccc lxiij.
[*in margin*: nota] The quhilk day it was comptit and reknit betuix Johne of Coupir and Andro Butler his brothir anent the soum of xxiiij lib xiij^s iiij^d for a cartane of quhet that the said Johne had in marchandis of the said Androw, of the quhilk thar was previt be the said Johne

xxiiij lib and ij^s payit and anent the xj^s iiij^d to be rafound to the said Andro giff it mycht be gudli gottin of the dettouris. Item that ilk day Andro Butler fundyn a distrublar of the court be his worde.

[*in margin*: nota] The gilde court haldyn in the tolbuth of Dunfermlyn be Willyam of Kircaldy aldirman and Thomas of Coupir dene the vij day of Maij, the yer of Our Lorde j^m cccc lxiij^o. The quhilk day Schir Andro Hog was made brothir throu resone of his fadir payand the spice and the wyne, of the quhilk he payit richt than xxx^d to the said dene. Item Johne of Boyis was made brothir throu resone of his fadir and payit richt than xxxij^d to the said dene.

[*Fo. 9v*]

[*in margin* : nota] The gilde court haldin in the tolbuth of Dunfermlyn be Wilyam of Kircaldy aldirman and Thomas of Coupir den of gilde the xxvij day of August the yer of Our Lord j^m cccc lxiij.

[*in margin*: nota] The quhilk day the fredome was grauntyt till Andro Litstar quhill Michalmes cum a yer for v^s the quhilk he layde done richt than. And giff it hapnit in the mentyme hym to by the halle fredome that v^s to be alowit to him in the hale soum.

[*in margin* : nota] Item that ilk day Thom Cady was resauit to the fredome for xl^s the quhilk he layde done richt than and to pay the spyce and the wyne.

[*in margin* : nota] Item Rob of Walwode was resauit to the said fredome of the gilde for xl^s the quhilk he layde done richt than, and to pay the spice and wyne.

[*in margin* : nota] Item Johne of Walwode was resauit to the said fredome of the gild for xl^s quhilk he layde done richt than, the quhilk sowmis abone writyn delyuerit to the said dene.

Item of Rob of Walwodis soum lent to him xx^s	to be payit at the next Lammes plegis
Item to John of Walwodis soum lent to him xx^s	John of Coupir and the said dene

lxiij.

[*in margin: drawing of hand with pointing finger.*] Memorandum quod anno Domini j^{mo} cccc^o quinto die mensis Februarij it is appoyntit and accordit and fullely determinit be the aldirman balyeis and communite of the burgh of Dunfermlyn and apprevit confirmit and ratifijt be a venerable fadir in Crist Richard be Goddis tholing abbot of Dunfermlyn for plesaur of God Allmichti and commone profyt of the said burgh that in tym cuming for euir thar marcate day to be on the Setterday, and that na marcate be haldin within the said burgh vpone Sonday na yet on na festualle day na bothis be oppynnit na yete na marchandis be made vndir payne, in the first falt xij^d, the secund falt ij^s, the thride falt iij^s and to be excludit for yer and day of all marchandis within the said burgh.

[*in margin*: nota] The gilde court haldin in the tolbuth of Dunfermlyn be Johne of Coupir aldirman and Alane Litstar dene the xxiiij day of Nouember the yer of God j^m cccc lxiiij.

[*in margin*: nota] The quhilk day Andro Litstar was resauit to the fredome for xl^s of the quhilk soum thar was remittit till him xx^s at the instance of the abbot. And of the said xx^s alowit till him v^s quhilk he had payit of the yer gane befor for fauor of his fredome. Swa remanit xv^s and tharof gevin in almes to Finlay Broustaris wyff ij^s, and swa remanis in the said denys handis xiij^s, the said Andro to pay the spice and the wyne.

Memorandum that the vj day of Maij at the bidding of Wilyam Jacsone dene Thomas of Coupir and Wilyam Spetell balyeis the sayde dene has payit to Michale causamaker the xiij^s abone writyn.

[*Fo. 10*]

[*in margin*: nota] The gild court haldin in the tolbuth be Johne of Coupir aldirman and Thomas Coupir dene the xiij day of September the yer of Our Lord j^m cccc lxvj.

[*in margin*: nota] The quhilk day it was fundyn be the aldirman den of gilde and the consale of the toune that John Andersone was wrangwisli strikyn be Andro Gervas and drew his knyff till him quharfor he was jugit in amerciamentis of xl^s as the law giffis.

[*in margin*: nota] The gild court haldin in the tolbuth of Dunfermlyn be Johne of Coupir aldirman and Thomas of Coupir dene, the ferde day of the moneth of October the yer of Our Lord j^m cccc lxvj.

The quhilk day Johne Fleming was resauit to the freedome throu resone of his fadir and he layde doune richt than xxxij^d for his spice and wyne and delyuerit it to Andro Litstar sergeand.

[*in margin*: nota] Item that ilk day it was decretit and determyt be the said aldirman and dene and thir personis vndirwritin brethir of the gild, that the accioune betuix Alane Litstar on the ta part and Johne of Anderstone on the tothir part anent iiij pipis of wade quhilkis the said Alane clamyt the said John of to be his bocht and

sauld, and in presens of thir said personis the said Johne
band him to byde and stand at thar delyuerans, the said
personis ischit the court, and the said aldirman and dene
with the laffe of the court decretit and determit and
fullely endit, that the said iiij pipis of wad was the
said John Anderstounis and that he micht frely dispone
tharvpoun at his awn will, quhilk was schawin to thaim
at thar entre agane in the court, and thir ar the namis
of thaim beand present in the tyme Wilyam of Kircaldy,
Wilyam of Spetell and Dauid Bra balyeis, Wilyam Jacsone,
John Sym, Thomas Cristisone, Laurence Foular, Pate
Fleming, Law Furmornis, Andro Litstar, Thom Cady, Rob
of Walwode, Andro Gervas, John Fleming, with vthir
sindry.

[*in margin*: nota] The gild court haldin in the tolbuth of
Dunfermlyn be Wilyam of Kircaldy aldirman and Johne
Wrycht dene, the last day of September the yere of Oure
Lord j^m cccc lxix.

[*in margin*: nota] The quhilk day Johne of Anderstoune
was resauit to the fredome of the gild for xl^s the quhilk
he layde downe rycht than, and that soum was lent to
him agane, to be payit the tane halff agane, at the
Candilmes next thareftir, the tothir halff be the next
Witsonday thareftir with the spice and the wyne.

The gild court haldyn in the tolbuth of Dunfermlyn be the
aldirman Wilyam of Kircaldy and Thomas of Coupir dene
the xxviij day of October, the yer of Our Lord j^m cccc
lxix.

[*in margin*: nota] The quhilk day Nichole of Kirkcaldy was
resauit to the fredome fre payand the spice and the wyne.

[*Fo. 10v*]

[*in margin* : nota] The gild court haldin in the tolbuth
of Dunfermlyn be Wilyam of Kircaldy aldirman and Thomas
of Coupir the xviij day of Nouember the yer of Our Lord
j^m cccc lxix.

[*in margin*: nota] That ilk day Wyll Blakwode was resauit
to the fredome of the gild for xl^s quhilk he layde doun
richt than and tharof lent to him agane xx^s to be payit
be the next Pask, payand the spice and the wyne.

[*in margin*: nota] Item that ilk day Johne Malcome was
resauit to the fredome of the gild for xl^s quhilk he layde
doun richt than, and of that soum lent to him agane
xx^s to be payit be the next Pask, payand the spice and
the wyne.

The gild court haldin in the tolbuth of Dunfermlyn be
Schir Johne of Cokburne aldirman and Wilyam of Spetell,

on Saint Thomas evin, the yer of Our Lord j^m cccc lxx.
The quhilk day Thomas of Coupir and Lowrens Foular war put in frenschip anent certane debatis betuix thaim for the quhilk [deleted : thai adiugit] thai ar ilkan adiugit in amerciamentis that is to say the said Thomas xij^d, item the said Laurens ij^s and the said Laurens dettour of iij^s to the said Thomas for clath quhilk he contra tak fra him.

[in margin: nota] The gild court haldyn in the tolbuth of Dunfermlyn be Wilyam of Spetell den the ix day of the moneth of Februar the yer of Our Lord j^m cccc lxx.
The quhilk day Robyn of Boncle was resauit to the fredome and layde doun xl^s and payand the spyce and the vyne, the quhilk soum was lent to him agane.

The gild court haldyn in the tolbuth of Dunfermlyn be Thomas of Coupir aldirman and Robyn of Boncle dene, the ix day of Nouember the yer of Our Lord j^m cccc lxxj.
[in margin: nota] The quhilk day Johne Litstar was resauit to the fredome throu resone of his fadir, payand the spice and the wyne.

The gild court haldin in the tolbuth of Dunfermlyn be Thomas of Coupir aldirman Robert of Boncle dene, the xxiij day of Maij, the yer of Lord [sic] j^m cccc lxxij.
[in margin : nota] The quhilk day Will of Spetell and Thomas Cady war ilkan adiugit in vj^s viij^d becauss of thar foulle lengage ilkan till vthir. [deleted: law borch for Tho Cady Jo Brison. Item the said William of Spetell amerciamentis iij xl^s for his drawing of a knyff.] And [deleted: striking of Thomas Cady] law borous for William of Spetell, John Andersone and Rob Walwod. Law borous for Thom Cady Andro Gudeswane and Law Furmornis.

[Fo. 11]

[in margin : nota] The gild court haldin in the tolbuth of Dunfermlyn be Nichole of Kircaldy aldirman and Wilyam of Spetell dene of the gild the last day of October the yer of Our Lord j^m cccc lxxij.
[in margin: nota] The quhilk day Johne Wrycht was resauit to the fredome of the gild throu resone of his fadir.

[in margin: nota] The gild court haldin in the tolbuth of Dunfermlyn be the aldirman Nichole of Kirkcaldy and Wilyam of Spetell dene, the vij day of Nouember the yer of Our Lord j^m cccc lxxij.
[in margin: nota] The quhilk day Alexander Alansone was resauit to the fredome of the gild, for the quhilk he layde doune xl^s. Of the quhilk soum lent him agane

xx^S plegis tharfor Will Blacate and payand the spice and the wyne. Soluit.

[*in margin*: nota] The gild court haldin in the tolbuth of Dunfermlyn be Nychole of Kircaldy aldirman and Wilyam of Spetell dene, the xvj day of Januar, the yer of Our Lord j^m cccc, lxxij,.
The quhilk day Mastir Henry of Kircaldy was resauit to the fredom throu resone of his fadir payand the spice and the wyne.
Item that ilk day Johne of Kirkcaldy was resaut to the fredome of the gild for xl^S quhilk he layde doun rycht than of the quhilk thar was lent to him agane xx^S quhilk- is he promittit to pay agane quheneuir he beis chargit, and payand the spice and the wyne quhilk was gevin to him and Laurens Foular to the drynk in Flanderis.

The gilde court haldin in the tolbuth of Dunfermlyn be Schir Johne of Cokburne aldirman and Dauid Weir dene of the gild the xxiij day of Julij the yer of Our Lord j^m cccc lxx[iiij ? *text obscured*]
[*in margin* : nota] The quhilk day Cristell Cristisone was resauit to the fredome throu resone of his fadir payand the spice and the wyne.
[*in margin*: nota] That ilk day Thom Cady put him in the aldirmanis will and the denys of the wrang wyss selling of a dak of hydis to outmen and preoffrit thaim nocht to thar nichtburis.

The gilde court haldin in the tolbuth of Dunfermlyn be Laurens Foular dene of the gild the xxv day of Februar the yer of Our Lord j^m cccc lxxiiij.
[*in margin*: nota] The quhilk day Dauid Litstar was resauit to the fredome throu resone of his fadir payand the spice and the wyne.

[*Fo. 11v*]

[*in margin* : nota] The gild court haldin in the tolbuth be Laurens Foular dene of the gilde the iiij day of Marche, the yer of Our Lord j^m cccc lxxiiij.
[*in margin*: nota] The quhilk day Johne Sym was resauit to the fredome throu resone of his fadir payand the spice and the wyne.

[*in margin* : nota] The gilde court haldin in the tolbuth of Dunfermlyn be Johne of Kircaldy aldirman Andro Litstar dene of the gild the xiiij day of October.
Anno etc lxxv.
[*in margin: drawing of hand with pointing finger*] The qu- hilk day the personis vndirwrityn put thaim in the aldir- manis wyll and the denys of thar ganging furth of the toune and left it desolate in the tym of the pestilence

in contrar thar act, made and confirmyt, thir ar thar namys, Johne of Walwode, Rob of Walwode, Johne Anderstone, Dauid Litstar.

The gild court haldin in the tolbuth be Johne of Kircaldy aldirman, Andro Litstar dene the xxj day of October the yer of Our Lord j^m cccc lxxv.
[in margin: nota] The quhilk day Mastir Johne Frog was rasauit to the fredome for xl ^{s} the quhilk he layde doun rycht than, and tharof gevin him agane xx^s, payand the spice and wyne.
[in margin: nota] The gild court haldyn be the aldirman Johne of Kircaldy and Andro Litstar dene the ferde day of Nouember, the yer of Our Lord j^m cccc lxxv yeris.
[in margin: nota] That ilk day Wilyam Stewart was resauit to the fredome fre, payand the spice and wyn.
[in margin: nota] Item that ilk day Will Jacsone yunger was resauit to the fredome for xl^s, the quhilk he layde doun richt than and delyuerit to Andro Litstar dene.
Item that ilk day it was componit with Johne Broune and Rob Blacate for x^s to haffe the fredome for a yer the quhilk thai layde doun rycht than and deliuerit to Andro Litstar dene.

[in margin : Entre] The gild court haldin in the tolbuth of Dunfermlyn be Wilyam Stewart aldirman and Dauid Bra dene the xviij day of Januar, the yer of Our Lord j^m cccc lxx and vj yeris.
The quhilk day Johne of Walwode was resauit to the fredome throu resone of his wyff payand the spice and the toune [sic].
[in margin : nota] Item that ilk day Johne of Kircaldy is in amerciament for falt of aperans and to the answar and complaynt maid on him be Wilyam Jacsone.

[Fo. 12]

[in margin : nota] The gild court haldin be the aldirman Wilyam Stewart, and Dauid Bra dene, the xxiij day of August, the yer of Our Lord j^m cccc lxx and sevin yeris.
[in margin: nota] The quhilk day Johne of Kircaldy and Wilyam Jacsone yunger war convickit ilkane in amerciament of halff a mark for thar foule speche in thar presens of the dene and the brethir of the gild in playne court. And thar eftir the said Wilyam was conuickit of the dowing of the said Johne eftir thai war put vndir silence, and thareftir thai war put in frenschip. And that ilkane sall keip frenschip till vthir vndir payne of xl^s.

The gyld court haldyn be the aldirman John of Kyrcaudy and Wilyam of Spittel dene the xv day of Nouember the yer

of God j^m cccc lxx and viij yeris.
The qwhilk day Johne of Walwod the sone of Rycharde of Walwode was maid gildbrothir throw resone of his fadir for the spice and wyne.
The qwhilk day Jhone Browne in amerciament of v^s becaus he occupiit gild fredom.
Item [*sic*] qwhilk day Rob Blakat in amerciament of xxx^d becaus that he occupijt gild fredome.
The qwhylk day Rob Blackat wes made gilde brothir for xl^s the qwhilk xl^s wes deliuerit to Llowrens Foular bursur. The said bursur lent again to the said Rob Blackat xx^s and be payt again at Palm Sonday [*addition* : all payit to the said bursour.]

[*in margin*: nota] The gylde court haldin in the tolbuth of Dunfermlyn be Johne of Kircaldy aldirman and Wilyam of Spetell dene, the penultyn day of Nouember, the yer of Our Lord j^m cccc lxxviij yeris.
[*in margin*: nota] The quhilk day Johne Broune wa [*sic*] resauit to the fredome for xl^s the quhilk he layde doun richt than and delyuerit it to Laurens Foular bursar. Of the quhilk soum lent agane till him xx^s [*addition*: now hale payit] to be payit agane be Candilmas, and the spice and the wyne.
[*in margin* : nota] That ilk day Thom Smert was resauit to the fredome of the gilde throu resone of his grauntsyr Alexander Smert. And payand the spice and the wyne.

[*in margin*: nota] The gild court haldyn be Johne of Kircaldy and Wilyam of Spetell dene the xxix day of Januar anno etc. lxxviij.
The quhilk day Johne Wrycht was conuickit in amerciament for his contumasy for the hale brethir.

[*Fo. 12v*]

The gilde court haldin in the tolbuth be Johne of Kircaldy aldirman, Will of Spetell dene, the xvij day of Januar, the yer of Our Lord j^m cccc lxxviij.
That ilk day Dauid Bothuele was resauit to the fredome fre, payand the spice and the wyne.

[*in margin* : nota] The gild court haldin in the tolbuth be Johne of Kircaldy aldirman and Willyam Spetell den the vj day of Februar the yer of Our Lord j^m cccc lxxviij.
That ilk day Den Andro Tulch was resauit to the fredome throu resone of his fadir payand the spice and the wyne.

[*in margin*: nota] The gild court haldin in the tolbuth be Johne of Kircaldy aldirman Wilyam of Spetell dene the xij day of Marche, the yer of Our Lord j^m cccc lxxviij.

[*in margin*: nota] The gild court haldin in the tolbuth of Dunfermlyn be John of Kircaldy aldirman and Mastir Henry Kircaldy dene the xij day of Junij the yer of Our Lord j^m cccc lxxix.

[*in margin* : nota] The quhilk day Wilyam Jacsone was convickit of the wrangwiss strubling and inconueniant speking of Johne of Bothuele, for the quhilk he was adiugit in half a mark for ane vnlaw, and to ask the party forgevinnes and forber in tym to cum vndir payn of xl^s.

The gild court haldin in the tolbuth be John of Kircaldy aldirman and Mastir Henry Kircaldy the xix day of Nouember, the yer of Our Lord j^m cccc sevinte and nyne yeris.

[*in margin* : nota] The quhilk day Will of Balwny was resauit to the fredome at the instance of the abbot, payand the spice and the wyne.

The gild court haldyn at the burgh off Dunfermlyn in the tolbuth be Schir Jhon off Cockburne aldirman and Andro Butler den off the gild the xix day off Nouember the yeir off Our Lord j^m cccc achty and an yhiris.

The quhilk day Schir James Gudsuane wes resafit to the fredome payand the spyce and the wyne.

[*Fo. 13*]

The gild court haldin in the tolbutht of Dunfermlyn be Schir Johne of Cokburne aldirman and And[ro ? *text obscured*] Butlar dene of the gilde the first day of the moneth of December the yeir of Our Lorde j^m cccc lxxxj.

The gyld court haldyn in the tolbutht of Dunfermlyn be Schir Jhone of Cokburne aldirman and Llowrens Fowlar dene of the gild apone Thomas ewyn the yeir of God j^m cccc lxxxj yeir.

The qwhilk day Johne Blakkat wes maid gilbrothir for xl^s. The qwhilk wes laid downe and lent again till him and to be payt xx^s or Pas and other xx^s be Michelmes and gyff that the nychtburris mistires siluyr in the mentym he sall be warnit and be pay[it ? *text obscured*] wythyn xv days. Thir borowis Andro Butler and Rob Blakkat [*deleted* : All payt] awand xv^s of the haill sowme.

The gild court haldyn in the tolbutht of Dunfermlyn be the aldirman Schir Johne of Cokburne knycht Llorens Fowlar dene of the gilde and certane of nychtburris the ix day of March the yer of God j^m cccc lxxxj.

The qwylk day Robyn Scharp wes enterit to the fraternite and to the fredome for xl^s. The qwhilk wes laid doune and lent agayn to the said Robyn and to be payt within viij days eftir that he be schargit Andro Butlar and Robyn Blackat borowis for the said sowme and hym self dettour.

The gyld cowrt haldyn in the tolbuth of Dunfermly [sic] be the aldirman and the dene of the gyld and a certane of the nycburris the xiij day of Aprill the yeir of God j^m cccc lxxxj.

The quhilk day [deleted: Robyn Blakkat] Johne Blakcat laid done xx^s for his fredome and that was spendit on Passk Monunday be the aldirman and the nychburis.

The gild court haldyn in the tolbutht of Dunfermlyn be the aldirman and the dene of the gilde on Mychelmes ewyn the yer of God j^m cccc lxxxx[ij? text obscured].
[deleted: The qwhilk day Alane of Walwod wes maid gild brothir for xl^s. The qwhilk wes laid done and lent til hym agayn xxxvij^s and iij^d to be payt again on viij days warnyng.]

[Fo. 13v]

The gild court haldyn in the tolbutht of Dunfermlyne be the aldirman Schir Johne of Cokburne knycht and Dauid Bothtwell dene of the gilde and a certan of the nychtburis.

The gild court haldyn in the tolbutht of Dunfermlyne be the aldirman Schir Johne of Cokburne the ferd day of October the yer of God j^m cccc lxxxiij. The qwhilk day Llowrens Foular dene of gild Johne Wallod and Andro Butlar balyeis Llowrens Fowlar dene of gild.

The gild court haldyn in the tolbutht of Dunfermlyn be the aldirman Schir Johne of Cokburne and a certan of nychtburis.
The qwhilk day Johne Strang ves enterit to the fraternite throw resone of his fadir for the spice and wyn.

The gild court haldyn in the tolbutht of Dunfermlyne be the aldirman Schir Johne of Cokburne and Johne of Wallod dene the ix day of the monetht of October the yer of God j^m cccc lxxxiiij.
The quhilk day Dauy Coupyr wes maid gyld be resone of his fadyr for the spice and the wyn.

It is statut and ordanit be the aldirman balyeis and the gild brethir that na marchand sal by woll hid na skynnis on the haly day on to the tym of xii howris and ij marchandis sall haff thar owk a bowt to by thar marchandis and nane othiris to prewent thaim at samyn hour.

Llaw borowis for Will Jacson Rob Scharp and Dawy Litstar.
Llaw borowis for Robyn Wallod Rob Blakkat and John Blackat.

The gild court haldin in the tolbuth of Dunfermlyn be the aldirman Schir Johne of Cokburne and John of Wallod dene of the gild and the fraternite gaderit the penultima day of October etc. The qwhilk Robyn of Walwod wes put in frenschip and Wilyam Jacson and ackyt that qwhat tym that ony of thaim falts thai sal pay the hail wnlaw eftir the statut.

[Fo. 14]

The gild court haldyn in the tolbutht of Dunfermlyn be the aldirman Schir John of Cokburne John of Wallod dene of gild and a certane of nychtburris the v day of December the yer of God etc. lxxxiiij.
The qwhilk day Dauid Litstar and Johne Strang, law borowis for Dauid Litstar Wil Jacson and Alan Wallod, law borowis for Johne Strang Andro Gerues and Johne Browne.

The gild court haldyn in the tolbutht of Dunfermlyn be the aldirman and Johne of Wallod dene of the gild.
The qwhilk day Johne Androson the sone of vmqwhill Johne Androson wes maid gild brothir be reson of his fadir for the spice and the wyne.

The gild court haldyn in the tolbuth of Dunfermlyn be the aldirman and the den of gild and a part of the gild the xij day of Februarij the yer of God j^m cccc lxxxiiij.
The qwhilk day Wil of Spittel wes maid gild brothir for the spice and the wyn be reson of his fadir.

The gild court haldyn in the tolbutht of Dunfermlyn be the dene of the gild Schir James Gudsuane the viij day of October the yeir of God j^m cccc lxxx[v ? *folio worn*]
The qwhilk day John Orok wes maid gild bruthir [thro? *folio worn*] reson of his fadir for the spice and the wyn.
The qwhilk day Schir Jamys Gudsuane dene of the gild bursur resauit fra Alane of Wallod vj^s x^d of the gildmail of the yeir of God j^m cccc lxxxij and of Lowrens Foularis cont.
The qwhilk day Johne Malwyn wes maid gild brothir for xl^s, and laid it downe and it wes lent hym agayn.
The qwhilk day Mastir Johne Cristison wes maid gild brothir of dewocion for the spice and the wyn.

The gild court haldyn in the tolbutht of Dunfermlyn be the Schir James Gudsuan dene the xij day of Nouember the yer of God j^m cccc lxxxxv.

The qwhilk day Mastir Dauy Bardner and Dauid Grant war maid gild brethir be reson of the prior and Schir Robert Grant for spice and the wyn.

[Fo. 14v]

The gild court haldin in the tolbutht of Dunfermlyn be the aldirman and dene xxj day of October the yer of God j^m cccc lxxxv.

Entries.

The qwhilk day Thome Rogger wes maid gild brothir for xl^s and he laid it done and it wes lent hym again and to pay xx^s be Pas and othir xx^s als sone as we mystyr qwhen he is chargit.

The gild court haldyn in the tolbutht of Dunfermlyn be the aldirman and the dene of the gild and the gild brethir on Sanct Thomas ewyn. Absentis Mastir Dawy Bardner Schir Andro Thomson Alexander Alanson John Brown Dauid Grant Thom Roger Patrik Flemyn John Orok John Hyll Wil Jacson J. Malcom.

The gild court haldyn in the tolbutht of Dunfermlyn be Schir John of Cokburne aldirman Schir James Gudswane dene of the gild and the gild brethir.

[in margin: acta] The qwhilk day it is statut and ackit be the aldirman balyeis and dene and the [communite? text obscured] of the towne that the best qwhet salbe sald for vij^s. Item the best malt for half a mark. Item the best meil for iiij^s viij^d and the qwheit malt and meil that is nocht wortht the siluir for said to be sauld better chaip. And giff the nychtburris murmell the ail thai sal schaw to the balyeis and the balyeis and a part of the nychtburris sal sers and se qwheddir the falt be in the broster or in the malt. And giff the falt be in the molt the broster sal deliur the ail to the malt makar or v^s for the bol. And gyff the falt be in the broster the balyeis sal gar the nychtburris sal pris it has it is o wail and that na ail salbe derrer na viij^d ondir payn of scheit and al ordanit[? text obscured] done qwhul the law days eftir Pasc.

[in margin: nota] The quhilk day it vas statut and ordanyt be the gildbredir and the hale communite that na offisar aldirman or balye or ony othir that beris offis salbe forspekar for ony man or voman bot thar avn actione.

[Fo. 15]

The gild court haldyn in the tolbutht of Dunfermlyn be

the aldirman and the dene of the gilde and the nychtburris the xiij day of Maij the yer of God j^m cccc lxxxvj.
The quhilk day Johne Anderson presentit a bil of complaint
that his arschip ves haldy [*sic*] fra hym be the aldirman
and John of Wallod as borois for the deliuerans and the
den has chargit thaim to gar it be red wythin xv dais.

The gild court haldyn in the tolbutht of Dunfermlyn be
the aldirman and dene of the gild the thrid day of June
the yer of God j^m cccc lxxxvj.

The qwhilk day Johne Baxstar wes maid gild brothir
for xl^s. The qwhilk he laid doune and lent hym again and
to pay it again qwhen he is chargit.

The gild court haldin in the tolbutht of Dunfermlyne be
the aldirman Schir John of Cokburne and Schir [*deleted*: Joh]
Jamys Gudswane den the xvij day of June the yer of God
j^m cccc lxxxvj.
The qwhilk day Alane Cant wes maid gild brothir for
xl^s. The qwhilk day he laid done and gyffyn hym again
at the instance of the abbot.
The qwhilk day Johne Sym comperit and complenyeit apon
Johne Malcom that he held fra hym xiiij^s. The said
Johne Malcom present askit xv dais to ansuer. The qwhilk
wes grantit and he to ansuer as peremptour.

The gild court haldyn in the tolbutht of Dunfermlyn be
the aldirman and dene of the gild the viij day of Julij
the yer of God j^m cccc lxxxvj. The qwhilk day the accion
debatable betwix Andro Gerues and Dauid Litstar contenuit
to this day viij dais, falyeand thairof the next gild
court, and rycht sua the accioun betwix Johne Sym and
Johne Malcom continuit to the samyn day.

The gild court haldyn in the tolbutht of Dunfermlyne be
the aldirman and dene of the gild and a part of the gild
brethir the v day of August the yeir of God j^m cccc
lxxxvj. The qwhilk day, Item Johne Malcome dettur to
John Sym of x^s.
The qwhilk day Mastir Johne Patonsone wes maid gild
brothir be reson of hes fadir.
The qwhilk day the accioune debatable in betwix Dauid
Litstar and Andro Gerues and anence the ij markis it
is decretit that the said Dauid Litstar quit of his clayme.
Item Wil of Balloune and Andro Gerues ar somand to
ansuer ilkane til othir this day xv dais anens ij markis
the qwhilkis ilkane clamis othiris of [? *folio worn.*]

[*Fo. 15v*]

The gild court haldyn in Dunfermlyn be the Schir James

Gudswan dene of the gild and a part of the gild brethir the ix day of the monetht of September the yer of God j^m cccc lxxxvj.
[*in margin: drawing of small hand with finger pointing*]
The qwhylk day Schir Dauy Stewart wes maid gild bruthir be reson of his grant schir for the spice and the wyne.
The qwhilk day Johne of Mentetht wes maid gild brothir for xl^s. The qwhilk wes laid downe and giffyn hym agayn fre for the spice and wyn.

The qwhilk day Wil Jacsone at the instance of the dene and the gild brothir gaff to Andro Litstar respit of iiij lib. vj^s xv days and than to be payt.

The gild court haldyn in the tolbutht of Dunfermlyn be the aldirman and the dene of the gild Schir James Gudswan the xvj day of September the yer of God j^m cccc lxxxvj.
The qwhilk day it is decretit be the aldirman and the dene and the nychtburis that the ij markis debatable betwix Wilyam of Ballune and Andro Gerues it is decretit that thai ar baitht quit of othiris claym of the ij markis.
The qwhilk day gilld court haldyn in the tolbutht of Dunfermlyn be Schir Jamys Gudswane and Schir Johne of Cokburne aldirman and the gild brethir the last day of September the yer of God j^m cccc lxxxvj. Absentis Andro Gerues [*deleted*: Andro Litstar].
The qwhilk day Johne Leich wes maid gilde brothir throw resone of his fadir for the spice and the wyn. The qwhilk day Johne Baxter com dettur for x^s the qwhilk Malis Lech wes awand to the gild brethir for his fredom. The said Johne Baxter has payt the x^s to Schir Jamys Gudswan dene.

[*Fo. 16*]

[*in margin*: nota] The gild court haldyn in the tolbutht of Dunfermlyn be the aldirman and the dene of the gild and the gildbrethir the xxiij day of December the yer of God j^m cccc lxxxvj.

The qwhilk day Dauid Bra and Patrik Flemyn wer put in frenchip and qwha that ofendis til othiris sal pay at the wil of the gildbrethir xl^s and ilkan a galon of ail at the wil of the dene.

Item Wil Jacson and Patrik Flemyn wer put in frenchip and qwhat tym that Patrik Flemyn offendis til hym or he til hym sal pay vnforgyffyn xl^s.

The curt halddyn in the thobowt of Dunfermlin the xix day of January, the yer of God j^m cccc lxxxvij yeris. The quhilk day Willyam of Cokburne wes rasswyt to the

brethir of gild and maid gild brothir and paid thankfully
thairfoir in gold and siluir.

The gild court haldyn in the tolbutht of Dunfermlyne be
the aldirman the dene of the gild and a part of the gild
brethir the xvij day of Februarij the yer of God j^m cccc
lxxxvj. The qwhilk day Andro Gerues wes accusit of
strublans of the aldirman and the dene and the hale court
in ful langagis spekyn to Dauy Litstar balye for the
qwhilk and he was chargit throw the vertu of his aitht
and tinsel of his fredome to ask the aldirman the dene
and nychtburis, and Dauid Litstar forgyfnes for the
amerciamentis of his langage and he denyit to ask the
said Dauid forgyffnes. And thaireftir for his dissobeying
he wes chargit to remayne in the tolbutht ondir the
payne and chargis foirsaide and contemnandly he passit
furtht of the tolbutht but licens of the aldirman and dene
considering the aldirman and dene gaf him the chargis.

[*Fo. 16v*]

The gild court haldyn in the tolbutht of Dunfermlyn be the
aldirman the dene of the gild and the gild brethir the v
day of May the yer of God j^m cccc lxxxvij.

The qwilk day Schir James Gudswan gaff cownt of the
[*deleted*: gild] licht siluir. The said Schir James ful
payt of al that he laid downe to this day and of the
outcome put in the lycht stok ij^s and iij^d item.

The gild court haldyn in the tolbutht of Dunfermlyn be
the aldirman and the dene of the gild the xiiij day of
Julij the yer of God j^m cccc lxxxvij. As fundyn and
decretit that the ij ryggis vmqwhil Thome of Spens
liand one est part of Malaris Croft aw xxx^d to licht of
the Rud and Lady.

The qwhilk day the actione debatable betwix Lowrens Foular
and Rob Scharp is continuit to the next Tuisday that the
said Robert Scharp sal remane in the tolbutht qwhill he
prewe his payment lauchtfully or ellis mak hym payment.

The qwhilk day Schir Thomas Benynge ande Jhone Gerwes
come in be fore the deyne of the gilde Schir James Gudswane and the balyeis witht a part of the gilde brothir
thai baith beande bwnde to the for said dewyne and the
laif of the personis was present at the saide tyme and
thai decretyt at the for said Jhone suld pay to the said
Schir Thomas vj^s be the next Lammes folowande. Ande
fra thane furtht at the next Martymmes ij^s and at the
next Witsonday ij^s and say furtht termly ij^s quhyll the
tyme xl^s be laide done one a day bwte frawde or gyll
and of syk j lik monetht is gays bute pley or impedyment

of ony personis man or woman of golde or siluir ..

[Fo. 17]

The gild court haldyn in the tolbutht of Dunfermlyn be the aldirman Schir Johne of Cokburne and Schir James Gudsuane dene of the gild and a part of the gilde the xxviij day of September the yer of God j^m cccc lxxxvij.
The qwhilk day Alan Wallod wes maid dene of the gild for a yeir.
Item deliuerit be the nychtburis to Johne of Hill vj stane and ½ of wax.

The gild court haldyn in the tolbutht of Dunfermlyn be the aldirman Dauid Cowpyr and Alane of Wallod dene the xxvj day of October the yer of God j^m cccc lxxxvij.

The qwhilk day Thom Stewynsone wes maid gildbruthir be resone of his wyff for the spice and the wyne.

The xxiiij day of Nouember the yer of God j^m cccc lxxxvij all the lycht siluir is deliuerit to the conseruatouris thairof and that is xlv^s and x^d for al termes by passit excep vj^s and viij^d in the handis of Dauid Coupir.
Items vj^s vj^d and [sic] the handis of Dauid Litstar.

The gild court haldyn in the tolbutht of Dunfermlyne apon Sanct Thomas ewyn be the aldirman Dauid Coupir and Alan Wallod dene of the gild and a part of the gild brethir.

The qwhilk day it is ordanit be the aldirman and dene and the gilbrethir that the wyn that wes drunkyn in Dauid Bothwellis be the gildbrethir that [deleted: thair sall be] gyffin [deleted: to Dauy Coupir xx^s of the gild siluyr for xx^s of the mail of the Kyngis Sid Hil].
The qwhilk the gild sal pay xxxvj^s and thair persone sall pay it John Baxter xx^s Johne Malwyn x^s Thom Rogger vj^s to the comon purs at the comand of the aldirman.

[Fo. 17v]

The gild court haldyn in the tolbutht of Dunfermlyn be Dauid Coupir aldirman and a part of the gild brethir the penultima [deleted : xxii] day of Marche the yer of God j^m cccc lxxxviij.
The qwhilk day it is ordanit that John Baxter and Robert Lam sal gadir the licht siluyr for a yer and vphald the licht als gud has thai fynd it, thair borowis Wilyam Stewart Dauid Litstar and John Wallod.

The gild court haldyn in the tolbutht of Dunfermlyn be

COURT BOOK, 1433–1597

Dauid Coupir aldirman and Alan of Wallo dene and the gild brethir wytht a part of the dekynis of the towne the xxix day of September the yeir of God j^m cccc lxxxviij. Prepositus Dauid Coupir Wil Spitel decanus.

[*in margin*: gild brother] The qwhilk day Dene Thomas Monimeile sacristane wes maide gilde brothir fre for his gud demeritis and the spice and the wyn.

Wilyam of Spittel dene of the gild.

The gild court haldyn in the tolbutht of Dunfermlyn be the aldirman Dauid Coupir and the den of the gild Wilyam S and a part of the brethir.

[*deleted in whole or part*: Item Johne of Wallod of the Wynd gild seriande to Schir James Gudswane has payt to Wilyam of Spittel dene of the gyld vj^s x^d.
Item the said Wilyam dene of the gild has resauit vj^s x^d fra Johne Malcome in the yer of Alan of Wallod the qwhilk is payt to John of Wallode iij^s and Rob Blaccat vj^s x^d and J Malcom iij^s.]

The gild court haldyn in the tolbutht of Dunfermlyn be Dauid Coupir aldirman and Wilyam of Spittel dene of the gild and certan of the brethir the xv day of Jun the yer of God j^m cccc lxxxix yeris.
The qwhilk day

[*Fo. 18*]

The gild cowrt haldyn in the tolbutht of Dunfermlyn be Wilyam Stewart aldirman Johne of Wallod dene and the gild brethir the xxiiij day of October the yer of God j^m cccc lxxxix.

The qwhilk day Archibald Stewart wes maid gild brothir for his gud meratis and for Schir Dauy Stewartis request for the spice and wyn.

The qwhilk day Alexander Wilsone wes maid gild brothir be reson of his fadir and the spice and the wyn.

The gild court haldyn in the tolbutht of Dunfermlyn be Wilyam Stewart aldirman and Johne of Wallod dene of the gild and a part of the gild brethir the xxv day of Aprile the yer of God j^m cccc and nynte.

The gild court haldyn in the tolbutht of Dunfermlyn be the aldirman Dauid Coupir and Wilyam Spittell dene of the gild the xxvij day of Nouember the yer of God j^m cccc lxxxx.

The qwhilk day Wilyam Grant wes maid gild brothir be resone of his fadir and the spice and the wyn.

Stirlyne.

Thir ar the excresis of the ayris vj lib xiij^s iiij^d.

Llythtgwhow	–	iiij lib.
Inuirkethtyn	–	iij lib xiij^s iiij^d.
Kyngorne	–	iiij mark.
Cowpir	–	v lib vj^s iiij^d.
Pert	–	vj lib xiij^s iiij^d.

[Fo. 18v]

The gild cowrt haldyn in the tolbutht of Dunfermlyn be the aldirman and a part of gild brethir the xv day of Aprile the yer of God j^m cccc lxxxxj.

The qwhilk day Johne of Huton and Johne of Huton elder and yownger and Vil [in margin: Lam] has componit for the fredome for a yer ilkan half a mark and Ryche Patonson.

The gild court haldyn in the tolbutht of Dunfermlyn be Dauid Coupir aldirman Wilyam of Spittell dene of the gild and a part of the gild brethir the ix day of Julij the yer of God j^m cccc lxxxxj.

The qwhilk day the sacristane comperit befor the aldirman and dene and the gild brethir and thair in presens of thaim the said sacristane consentit for his tym that the nychtburis suld haff sic lik of offerans [deleted: of the offterans [sic] of the Haliblud altar and Sanct Margrettis altar has thai had of his predecessour of be for and subscriwit wytht the sacristanis awyn hand to the reparatione of the altaris. Ego Henricus Broune ad idem.

Rentale Sanct [sic] Saluatoris. Inprimis viij^d of Katrin Coupiris land in the Colyaraw on the west sid of that ilk betwix the land of Andro Litstar on the sutht [deleted: west] sid and the land of Moris Thomsone on the north sid.
Item of a hous bak sid of the said land iiij^s and vj^d to the hup hald of a derige for Will Logan.

Item xij^d of Cristel Cristisonis land to the reparatione of the altar and Wilyam of Spittell and Johne Baxter to be tututouris to the altar and to vphald the hers and keip the bred on the patron day and giff cownt thairof at the yeris end and gar the derige be done for Wilyam Logan.
Item of Rob of Murrais land xij^d to the samyn altar.

The qwhilk day Schir James Gudswan comperit and maid cownt of his annuell of his hous of thre yeris the said

Schir James awand thairof ix crownis and Mastir Dauy Bardnaris cownt rede in this sowme.

Michelmes.

The gilde court haldyn in the tolbutht of Dunfermlyn be Johne Mentetht aldirman Wilyam Jacsone dene and the gild brethir the xxix day of October the yer of God j^m cccc lxxxxj.

[*Fo. 19*]

The qwhilk day Andro Cristisone was maid gild brothir be resone of his grant schir [*deleted*: fadir] for the spice and wyne.

The gild court haldyn in the tolbutht of Dunfermlyn be John of Mentetht aldirman and Wilyam Jacsone dene and the gild brethir and a part of the communite the v day of Nouember the yer of j^m cccc lxxxxi.

The qwhilk day it is fundyn expedient be the nychtburris that thar sall be na dry tapstaris of aill wythtin the burchtg and giff thar be ony that ma be tantit tharwytht the aill sall be echeit the brostir sal tyn the aill and the tapstar amerciat of viij^s and the sers heir of to be obeiit and gif tha sers nocht to pay viij^s.

Item that na on fre man na woman sall occupy burges fredome ondir the payn of viij^s on forgiffyn etc.

Item it is statut that the [*deleted*: brost] malt makeris that sellis nocht sufficiand malt sall haff na othir payment for his malt bot the ail that is in place tharof and it be fundyn on sufficiand be sworne personis.

The gild cowrt haldyn in the tolbutht of Dunfermlyn be Johne of Mentetht aldirman Wilyam Jacson dene of the gild and the gild brethir the xiij day of Januer the yer of God j^m cccc lxxxxj.

[*in margin*: memorandum] The qwhilk day it is fundyn richt expedient that thir personis sal ophald the licht of the altaris inprimis Wilyam Stewart Dauid Coupir Alan Walwod and John Wricht to Sanct Rynyeins altar. Item to the Halibludis altar Dauid Litstar Thomas Rogger Rob Blackat John Blackat. Item Sanct Saluitouris altar Schir Johne Cokburne Wil Spittell John Baxter Alan Cant. Item Sanct Johnis altar John Mentetht Schir Jamys Gudswan Schir Andro Person.

The qwhilk day Dauid Bra has tane apon hym to bryng his ewidentis and hys rychtis this day viij dais the qwhilk is the xxj day of Januer and shaw till his nychtburis qwhat rycht he has to the twa acris in the north croft on the west sid of the samyn the tothir twa acris the tan at sid of the Lad Wynd the tothir at the town hillok the qwhilk he for x^s of the commonis falyeand thairof he sall refer till his nychtburis.

[Fo. 19v]

[in margin : memorandum] The qwhilk day John Persone wes maid gild brothir fre for his gild siluir he is bundyn to mak the muldis to the ill and to be mastir of the werk to the ill.

The gyld curt haldyne in the tolbuth of Dunfermlyne be the aldirman Jone of Menteht and Vilyem Jacsone dene of the gild and the gild brethir the xxi day of Januer and yer of God j^m cccc lxxxxj yeris.

The gild court haldyn in the tolbutht of Dunfermlyne be Johne Mentetht aldirman and the den of gild the last day of March the yer of God j^m cccc lxxxx and ij yeris.
The qwhilk day Schir James Gudswane has maid his cownt and restis in his hand v lib x^s and has promittit to find ij souerteis one Palm Sunewyn for the sowme for to be laid dowyne qwhen he is chargit.

[deleted: compotus William Cokburn and Alan Wallod] de anno preterito.
The qwhilk day gaff thar cont the commonis awand xl^d to thaim.
[deleted: The qwhilk] The gild cowrt haldyn in the tolbutht of Dunfermlyn be the aldirman John Mentetht of Mentetht and the dene of the gild and a part of the gild brethir the xxviij day of Julij the yer of God j^m cccc lxxxxij all cl [.... ?]

The qwhilk day in the gild cowrt the nychtburris etc.

[in margin: memorandum gild brethir] The qwhilk day dene Dauy Weir wes maid gildbrothir throw resone of his fadir for the spice and the wyn.

The gild cowrt haldyn in the tolbutht of Dunfermlyn be the aldirman John of Mentetht Alan of Walwod dene of the gild the xij day of Januer the yer of God j^m cccc lxxxxij.

Rentale Sancti Saluatoris.

Inprimis of Schir Jamys Gudswan land   –   v^s.
Item of Kate Cowpiris land   –   iij^s.
Item of Cristell Cristisonis land   –   xij^s.
Item of Rob Murra land   –   xij^s.

[Fo. 20]

The qwhylk day Schir Jamys Gudswane has deliuerit to the reparatioun of the Halibud altar of the annuel of his hous xxvij^s and vij^d.

The qwhilk day Dene Dauy Syme has fundyn John of Walwod suuerte that the annuell pertenyng to the seruice of Sanct Margaritis altar salbe furtht cumand and for Schir Robert Atkyn Thomas Rogger as executouris to Schir Thomas Benyn as law wil be for the aldirman and balyeis.

The qwhilk da the cownt of the gild maill maid be Wilyam Jacsone deliuerit be hym to John Malwyn vj^s x^d.

The gild covrt haldyn in the tolbutht of Dunfermlyn be the aldirman [deleted : John Mentetht] Dauid Cowpir and Wilyam Spittell den of the gild the v day of October the yer of God j^{mo} cccc^o lxxxxiij^o.

The gild court haldin in the tolbuth of Dunfermlyn be the aldirman Dauid Coupir and William Spital den of the gild the xix day of December the yer of God a thowsand four hundretht nynte and thre yeris on Sanct Thomas ewin.

The gyld court haldyn in the thwuth off Dunferymlyn be the aldirman Dauid Cwppyr and Wylyam off Spetyll den of the gyld the xxij day of Marce the yer off Our Lord j^m cccc nynte and iij yeris.

The gild court haldyne in the tolbutht off Dunfermlyne be the aldirman Dauid Coupir and Wilyam Jaksone dene of the gild the x day of October the yeir of God j^m cccc^c nynte and iiij yeris.

The gilde court haldyn in the tolbuth of Dunfermlyn be the aldirman Dauid Coupir and Wilyam Jaksoun den of the gilde the thrid day of Januer the yer of Gode j^m cccc nynte and iiij yeris.

[in margin: acta] The quhilk day Dauid Coupir aldirman and John Waluode j [s ?] borch and dettour to the gilde brethir for Schir James Gudswane for his annuell that he sall pay it within xx^{ti} dayis eftir that he be warnit of all the termes bygane.

[Fo. 20v]

Mechellmes.

The gyld cowrt haldyn in the tholbout off Downfyrmylyn be the aldirman Dawy Cwppyr and Jhon Wrych dayn off the gyld the xxxi day off Octobyr the yer of Our Lord

j^m cccc nytte and v yeris.
The quhilk day Johnne Willsone enterit to the gild fredome
for v cronis [addition: payt thairof of xxxi^s.]
The quhilk day Riche Pattonsone enterit to the gild
fredome for v cronis [addition: xxxj^s.]
The quhilk day Wilyame Lambert enterit to the gild
fredome for v cronis [addition: xxxj^s.]

The gyld court haldyne in the tolbutht of Dunfermlyne the
fyft day the Setterday of December the yeir of God j^m four
hundretht nynte and fife yeiris be the aldirman Dauid
Coupir and Johne Wrecht dene of gild and the gild
brethir.

The gyld court haldyne in the tolbutht of Dunfermlyne
the sewynt day of moneth of December the yeir of God
j^m iiij^c nynte and fyfe yeiris be the aldirman Dauid
Cowpir and John Wrycht dene of gild and the gild
brethir.

The quhilk day it is statute and ordanit be the aldirman Dauid Cowpir and Johnne Wrycht dene of gyld and
the gyld brethir that na bothte salbe opynnit na yit
na windo na nane merchandice maid opone the Sonday
wndir the payne of half a merk wnforgiffin.
[deleted: The qwhilk day it is appreift in the gild court
be the gild brethir that John Malwyne is fund a dissobeier
of the aldirman and dene of gild and of the gild seriand.]

The quhylk day Wyll Hart was maid gyld ffor the costis
sic lik as othir dowis [addition: pait xxxj ^{s}]. Wyll Hart
has pait xl^s and Jhon Wyllson sic lyk xl^s. Item Wyll
Lambart has pait hys forty ^{s}.
The expensys in Jhon Wrych hous be aldirman and the
deyn off the gyldis bredir xxxij^s.

The gild court haldin in the tolbutht of Dunfermlyn be
John of Vallud the dene of gilld and the aldirman and
gild brethir one Palm Sonday ewin the xviij day of
Marce the yer of God j^m cccc nynte and sex yeiris.
The qilk day Johne of Vallud dene of gild has tane the
gild cours in keping.

The quhilk day Richard Patonson pait his gild siluir.

[Fo. 21]

Memorandum the yeir of God a^m cccc nynte and sewyn
yerys the geld cowrt haldyn be the dayn off gyld Jhon
off Walwod and Dawy Cuppyr the last day of Septembar.
Wylyam Jakson is fund be the bredir off the gyl tyll hayf
trwbbelyt the hayll cowrt and dyueris of the bredir
with ewyll langag and in jurys in the mentym Schir

Jamy Gudswan and Jhon Baxtar efferys tham to stand at the corekson off the gyld brethir gyff thay haff maid ony fald to Wyllyam Jakson.

The gylld cowrt haldyn in the tholbowt be the aldirman Dawy Cwppyr Jhon off Walwod deyn off gyld and Resche Pattoson sargenttis.

The quhylk day Schir Jhon Allanson wos maid gyld for xl^s pait.

The quhilk day Schir Thomas Hvme of Langschav knycht was maid gild for xl^s pait and dovn laid and gifin thaim agan.

The quhilk day Wilyam Symson of Lathrisk enterit gild his xl^s dovn laid and gifin him agan.

The quhylk day Dawy Kyngowrn wos maid gyld brudir be reson off his wyff.

The quhylk day Jhon Fargeson wos maid gyld brudir for xl^s, to be pait quhen euir be chargys.

[Fo. 21v]

The quhilk day all the nychtbouris considerit the skyn that Wylyam Jakson had quhilk he coft fra Thom Calland vas coft fra the said Thom Calland and payit him thairfor nocht knavan na falt thairfor quhilk skyn as vas grantit be the said Thom Calland pertenyt to Vill Lambert thairfor the nychtbouris deliuerit that said skin suld be deliuerit agan to the said Thom Calland to be giffin to Vill Lambert as avnar of it, and the said Thom Calland to pay to the said Vilyam Jakson xviij^d for the said skin.

The gild court haldin in the tolbutht of Dunfermlyn the xxv day the Seterday of Julij the yer of God l^m cccc^c nynte and viij yeris be the aldirman Dauid Coupir John Vallod den of gild and the gild bredir.

The gild court haldin in the tolbutht of Dunfermlyn the xj day of August the yer of Our Lord m cccc^c nynte and viij yeris.

The quhilk day [deleted : the hale court] it is pronunsit in jugement be the aldirman and dene of gild be avis of the hale court that Johne Baxtar sall at his pleser occupye the gavill standand at the vest part of his hous the spacis and rovm of nyne jnch and sal raman in possessioun thairof. And gif ony partj has to persev ony thing pertenand to the said nyne inch in the said gavill deliuerit as is befor exprimyt that justis be ministerit as efferis but preiudice of ony partj. And in the mene tym that the said John bruk the sammyn landis pesably as lav vill. And als that the said John has all esiamentis fre apon the for frvnt of the said tenement extendant fra the said markis of nyne jnch fordvart to the chyngill and that it salbe leful to the offisaris of the tovn at the plesar of the said John Baxtar possessor of the land to ramuf als mekil of the star as standis wythin the said lyne of ix jnch befor expprimyt. And at our it is deliuerit and fundyn elikvis that the hale yard dik standis vthtin the said Johnis Baxtaris awn grond and vthtin the markis maid be the lynaris of befor.

The xxij day of the monetht of September the yer of Our Lord j^m cccc^c nynte and aucht yeris in the tolbutht of Dunfermlyn the gild court haldin Dauid Coupir aldirman and John Walvod dene of gild enterit Dene Robert Swynton a brudir of the gild.

[in margin: nota] The xxiji day of the monetht of Junij [deleted: Apri] the yer of Our Lord j^m cccc^c nynte and ix yeris in the tolbutht of Dunfermlyn the gild covrt haldin Wilyam Symson aldirman and Johne Baxtar dene of gild.
The quhilk day Henry Barbour and Johne Wallod enterit gild bredir deponit the atht and the money pait.
The quhilk day John Baxstar den of the gilde ressauit fra John of Waluode sergeande of the regalite of Dunfermlyn and Henry Barbour xl^s and of this deliuerit xxij^s to the portis makyn and to the aldirman for irn xx^{tjs} to the makyn of the bandis of the yettis.

[Fo. 22]

The gilde court haldin in the tolbutht of Dunfermlyn be the aldirman Wilyam Symsone and John Baxstar den of the gilde one Setterday the vj day of the monetht of September the yer of Gode ane thovsande four hundretht nynte and nyne yeris.

[in margin: gild brothir]. The quhilk day Johne of Balluny enterit to the fredome of gildry be resone of his fadir Wilyam of Ballune and deponit the aith thair-apon to observe and kep the statutis and ordinans of the aldirman and dene of gilde for thair tyme and the ackis made thairfor.

The gild court haldin in the tolbutht of Dunfermlyn the xix day of the monetht of October the yer of Our Lord j^m cccc^c nynte and ix yeris Vilyam Symson aldirman and Henry Barbor dene of gild.

The quhilk day John Walvod cordynar and Johne Walvod

skynnar and Johne Carnys cordinar enterit to the fredom of gildry deponit thar athtis the siluir tane and lent thaim agan. And the said Johne Vallod skynnar is oblist that he sal pul na voll skynnis na yit nane of his attorna vndir tynsal of his fredome.

The quhilk day it is deliuerit that Margret Lambert spous to Vil Lambert sal content and pay of the said Vilyammis gudis to Vilyam Jakson iiij lib of peter and a half xv vnce in the lib. trois vecht and that scho be compellit thairto vythtin term of lav.

The gild court haldin in the tolbutht of Dunfermlyn the secvnd day of the monetht of Nouember the yer of Our Lord j^m cccc^c nynte and ix yeris Vilyam Symson aldirman and Henry Barbour dene of gild.

The quhilk day Johne Jonson enterit gild be reson of Wilyam Dunlop his grantschir and gif ony othiris cummys to clame the fredom as nerrasf ar the said Johne sal pay for his fredome sik lik as othiris doyis.

[Fo. 22v]

The gild court haldin in the tolbutht of Dunfermlyn the xxiij day of the monetht of Nouember the yer of Our Lord j^m cccc^c nynte and ix yeris Vilyam Symson aldirman Henry Barbour dene of gild and the remanent of the laif of bredir.

The quhilk day Henry Barbor the said dene vas inquirit quharfor Schir James vas absent quhilk comperit nocht than and sufficiently prefit his varnyn, the aldirman dene and communite of the gild tharfor has continevit the matir to the den nixt covrt and has finaly condecendit and determyt vniuersaly to persev the Schir James for the annuell aucht of the Haly Blud land and the ofrandis pertenyng tharto sen the day that the said Schir James first intromittit tharwitht, and elikvis has finaly determyt to proceid aganys him in the landis that he has pertenyng to the Haly Blud and to provyd at thar povar according to justis for a sufficient chaplan til do dyvyn servis at the altar of the Haly Blud and mak him intromittor vytht all landis rentis annualis ofrandis and othiris possessionys and deuiteis pertening tharto, quhilk chaplan sal ansuer to the communite tharapon as accordis be the lav.

The quhilk day Johne Baxtar dene of the yer precedand maid covnt of all thingis tane be him vityin the tym of his offis all thingis covntit.

The quhilk day it is determyt be the aldirman dene and communite that the spous of Vilyam Lambert salbe compellit to deliuer to Vilyam Jakson incontinent eftir his hame cummyng the pepir [sic] quhilk scho vas adiugit in falyeand thairof hir gudis to be prisit to the vale of the said pepir [sic] as thar the pricis nov is.

The gild court haldin in the tolbuth of Dunfermlyn the xj day of January the yer of Our Lord j^m $cccc^c$ nynte and ix yeris Vilyam Symson aldirman Henry Barbour dene of gild and the remanent of the laif of the bredir of gild.

The quhilk day Johne Baxtar gaf in his covnt as eftir follovis. Inprimis he rasavit fra Johne Wallud and Henry Barbour xl^s. Item fra Ferge xix^s. Item fra Vilyam Hert for the cors siluir xj^s $iiij^d$. Item Rob Scharp $xiij^s$ $iiij^d$. Item for the intris of the terrare $xxxij^d$. Item resavit fra John Vallud his gudson [deleted: summa iiij lib vi^s $iiij^d$] $xiij^s$ ij^d.

        Summa totalis iiij lib. xix^s vj^d.

[Fo. 23]

        Expense eiusdem.

Inprimis deliuerit to Vilyam Symson the aldirman xx^s. Item to Johne Wilson xxx^s for vyne. Item to Allan Wallud xx^s. Item James Jakson $xvij^s$ vj^d. Item Pet Flemyn $iiij^s$. Item ij^s in breid to the pur folk. Item in colis ale and braid in the hovs vj^s $viij^d$.

        Summa expensarum iiij lib xix^s ij^d et sic restat competens $iiij^d$.

In Vigilia Palmarum anno Domini j^m quingintesimo the gild court haldin in the tolbutht of Dunfermlyn Wilyam Symsone aldirman and Henry Barbour den of gild and the remanent of the laif of the bredir of gild.

The quhilk day comperit Vilyam Andirson enterit gild brudir deponyt the atht the money pait and lent him al agane, and deliuerit be the sade Wilyam to Jhon of Waluod and Wilyame Spittall in the tym of the processione of the dede vj^s.

        Yull.

The hede court of the gildbrethir of the burche of Dunfermlyn be the aldirman Dauid Covpir and Jhone Wilsone dene of the gilde haldin one the xxvij day of the monetht of Januar the yer of Gode j^m and five hundretht yeris wytht the remanent of the laif of the brethir of gildry.

[in margin: acta] The quhilk day the aldirman Dauid Covpir and the dene of gilde witht the remanent of the laif of the gilde brethir has consentit and gevin leif to Cristyane Wrecht to mary quhome scho pleiss best and he to occupy the fredome of gilde for all the dayis of hir lif tyme.

[in margin: gild brothir]. The quhilk day Johne Wrecht enterit gilde brothir be resone of his fadir Johne Wrecht and deponit the gret aitht thairon to observe and kep the statutis of the gild brethir.

The gild court haldin in the tolbutht of Dunfermlyn the xxix day of January the yer of Our Lord j^m fif hundretht Dauid Covpir aldirman Johne Vilson dene of gild vytht the remanent of the laif of the bredir.

Compotum Henrici Barbur.

The quhilk day Henry Barbour gaf in his covnt of the denry of gild. In the first fra Johne Valuod cordynar xxx^d for his entra. Item fra Johne Carnys a mark and xxx^d for his entra. Item fra Johne Valuod skynnar x^s x^d and xxx^d for his entra. Item fra Johne Jonson xxx^d for his entra. Item Johne Valuod sergiand xxx^d for his entra. Item Henry Barbour xxx^d for his entra.

[addition: Restand awande to the dene now enterit ix markis and v^s vij^d restande awand of the gilde annuallis.]

Expense.
The sovm of the gild fest xlvj^s vi^d.

The quhilk day Vilya... Jakson and Robert Scharp ar bundyn to byd at the nychtbouris vnsuspek vyth[in? folio torn] iij dayis eftir that Vilyam Symson cummys hame thai beand varnyt to the gild court.

[Fo. 23v]

The covnt of the gild annualis rasavit.

The gild court haldin in the tolbutht of Dunfermlyn the vj day of Februar the er of Our Lord j^m fif hundretht Dauid Covpir aldirman Johne Vilson dene of gild and the remanent of the laif of the bredir of gild.

The quhilk day Vilyam Stevart of Rossicht complenet apon Johne Wallud sergiand saiand that he vas avand him xxxvj^s. And it is contynevit to this day xv dais.

The gild court haldin in the tolbutht of Dunfermlyn the xiij day of Februar the yer of Our Lord a thovsand fif hundreth Dauid Covpir aldirman Johne Vilson dene of gild and the remanent of the laif of the bredir of gild.

The gild fest made be the dene of gilde Jhon Wilsone and expendid thairupon to the gilde brethir lvj^s, and herof ressauit fra Wille Andirsone xx^s. Item fra Johne of Karnys xij^s. Item fra Jhon of Waluode skynnar xij^s. Item fra John of Waluode cordynar xij^s. Item v^s fra Jhon Fergussone in ane wnlaw. Item at the command of the aldirman to Henry Barbour gifin vij^s.

The gilde court haldin in the tolbutht of Dunfermlyn the xxvij day of Marche the yer of God j^m vi be Dauid Covpir aldirman and John Wilson dene of gilde wytht the remanent of the laif of the gilde brethir.

[*in margin*: compotum] The quhilk daye Henry Barbour dene of the gilde made his compt of the gilde cros and left restande in Wilyame Hertis handis xvj^s ij^d, and the cros to kep for this yer.

The gild court haldin in the tolbutht of Dunfermlyn the xj day of September the yer of Our Lord j^m v^c and ane yeris Dauid Covipir aldirman Johne Vilson dene of gild and the remanent of the laif of the bredir of gild.

The quhilk day Henry Hakkat of Petfuran enterit gild the sovm laid dovn and lent agane.

The expens of this yer belangin the gild fest made be Johne Vilsone dene of the gilde extending in all thingis to the sovme of x[viij ? *folio torn*] ij^d of this rasavit fra Ville Anderson iiij^s viij^d. Item fra jok Val[wod co? *folio torn*] rdynar iiij^s vj^d. Item fra Johne Waluod skynner iiij^s vj^d. Item fra Johne Carnys iiij^s vj^d.

[*Fo. 24*]

The gild covrt haldin in the tolbutht of Dunfermlyn the xxiij day of the monetht of September the yer of Our Lord j^m v^c and ij yeris Dauid Covpir aldirman Johne Wilson dene of gild wytht the laif of the bredir of the said gild.

The quhilk day Johne Ferguson was maid gild brudir for xl^s the spicis and the vyne, the gret atht sworn to occupy the statutis of the gild fredome and to occupy nane vnfre mennys gud to defraud the bredir, the siluir lent him agan at the vil of the bredir. Payit thairof for the mendyne of the gild cros vj^s viij^d. Item to the dene of gild vj^s viij^d.

The x day of October the yer of Our Lord j^m v^c and ij yeris the gild covrt haldin in the tolbuth of Dunfermlyn

Dauid Covpir aldirman Johne Vilson dene of gild vytht the laif of bredir of the said gild.
The quhilk day Adam Blacot enterit brodir for xl^S the siluir tane and lent agan, he bond to labour nane of his webstar craft excep his avn.

The tend day of Nouember the yer of God j^m v^c and ij yeris Johne Wilson dene of gild maid his covnt in the tolbutht of Dunfermlyn befor Dauid Covpir aldirman Wilyam Hert Vilyam Spitall balyeis Archbald Stevart Johne Mentetht Henry Barbour Johne Person and johne Waluod auditouris of the cont. And restand avand in the said Johnis handis sex pundis sevinten schillingis and sex pennes and all covntis declarit to the said day. And of the gild cors siluir restis avand in the said Johne Vilson denys hand xxiij^S viij^d.

Item gifyn for vax to be torchis xix^S. Item for the makyn of thaim xxvj^d. Item for the makyn of the treis xvij^d. Item gifyne in my lordis hal at Zule at the command of aldirman and nychtbouris xiiij^S.

The xxvj day of Nouember the yer of Our Lord j^m v^c and tua yeris the gild covrt haldin in the tolbutht of Dunfermlyn Dauid Covpir aldirman Johne Vilson dene of gild wytht laif of the bredir of the said gild.
The quhilk day Robert Brovne enterit brodir for xl^S the siluir tane and lent agane and pait that sammyn day xiiij^S.

The quhilk day Johne Flokart in the aldirmanis and dene of gildis vill.

The xj of Februar the yer of God j^m v^c and ij yeris Dauid Covpir aldirman Johne Vilson den of gild vytht the laif of the bredir the gild covrt haldin in the tolbutht of Dunfermlyne.

The quhilk day Richard Patonson comperit and schev [*deleted*: a borch] apon Vill Spitall batht the partis sall stand to consal of the bredir betuix that tym and viij dayis nixt follovand in hoip of concord or els tak the priualege of lav.

[*in margin*: memorandum] The quhilk day Wilyame Blacot enterit to the fredome of the gild brethir be resone of his fadir Wilyame Blacot and deponit the gret aitht herto.

[*Fo. 24v*]
The gild court haldin in the gild court in the tolbuth of Dunfermlyn the xx day of December the yer of Our Lord j^m v^c and thre yeris befor Dauid Covpir aldirman

and Johne Vilsone den of gild and the laif of the bredir.

The quhilk day Johne Waluod enterit gild be rycht of Johne Bra his granschir gif it be fvnd his ellis to pay at brediris vill the atht svorn to obserue the statutis and othiris contenit in the akis.

The quhilk day Dauid Movtrar enterit gild the siluir laid dovn and tane vp agan at the vil of the bredir the atht svorn to stand at the decreitis of the statutis.

The expens of the gild fest be Johne Vilsone dene of gild at Zule the yer of Our Lord j^m v^c and iij yeris. In primis in wyne xiiij^s. Item a barell of ber xxx^s. Item for breid xviij^d. Item a laid of colyis vj^d. Item in ale iij^s.

The gild covrt haldin in the tolbutht of Dunfermlyn xv day of September the yer of Our Lord j^m v^c and four yeris Dauid Covpir aldirman Johne Vilson dene of gild and the laif of the bredir.

The quhilk day Johne Fergusone has pait xlij^s viij^d of his gildschip.

The quhilk day Adam Blacot has pait xlij^s viij^d of his gildschip.

The quhilk day Robert Brovne has pait xlij^s viij^d of his gildschip.

The quhilk day Wilyam Anderson pait xlij^s viij^d of his gildschip.

The quhilk day Johne Carnis cordynar pait xlij^s viij^d of his gildschip.

The quhilk day Johne Vallud cordynar pait xlij^s viij^d of his gildschip.

The quhilk day Johne Vallud skynnar pait xlij^s viij^d of his gildschip.

[Fo. 25]

The gilde court haldin in the tolbutht of Dunfermlyn the vj day of the monetht of September the yer of Gode j^m v^c and v yeris be Dauid Covpir aldirman Henry Hackat dene of the gilde and the laif of the gilde brethir.

[*in margin*: nota] The quhilk day Schir Thomas Karnys chaplane enterit to the gilde fredome for all the dayis of his lyff.

The quhilk day Wilyam Cristisone enterit gilde brothir be resone of his fadir.

The gilde court haldin in the tolbutht of Dunfermlyn the last day of the monetht of October the yer of Gode j^m v^c and v yeris be Henry Bothuell and the laf of the gilde brethir.

The quhilk day the gilde brethir has continevit the vnlaw takin fra Adam Blacot to Sanct Thomas evin forrov Yull quhill the mair part of the congregatione of the said gilde brethir be gaddirit.

The gilde court haldin in the tolbutht of Dunfermlyn the xxj day of the monetht of December the yer of Gode j^m v^c and v yeris be Henry Bothuell aldirman and Johne Wilson dene of the gilde and the laif of the gilde brethir.

The quhilk day Johne Wilsone the den of gild gaf his compt of the gilde siluir and all thingis cuntit to this day and restand in the said Johnis handis viij^s ij^d.

The gylde court haldin in the tolbutht of the burcht of Dunfermlyn the xxvij day of the monetht of Marche the yer of Gode j^m v^c and vij yeris be the aldirman Dauid Covpir Henry Barbur dene of the gilde and the laif of the dene gilde brethir.

The quhilk day Dene Eduarde Skaithmur elimosinar of the abbay of Dunfermlyn Mastir Johne Turnbull vicar of Cleische and Schir Dauid Niniane parsone of Lude enterit to the fredome of the gilde brethir for all the dayis of thar lif tyme for suffragis to be done and tane.

[Fo. 25v]

The gilde court haldin in the tolbutht of Dunfermlyne the xxij day of Januar the yer of Gode j^m v^c and sevin yeris be Johne Willson dene of the gild and the laif of the gilde brethir.

[in margin: memorandum] The quhilk day the aldirman dene of the gilde witht consent of the remanent of the gilde brethir of the towne has consentit that Schir Dauid Ringane sall haue in fie and heretage the forlande abone and wndir belangande to the Haliblude liand one the northt syd of the Calsagate betuix the landis of Thomas Penny one the est part and the landis of Wilyam Mudy on the vest part. Ande he sall pay yerlie thairfore xiij^s iiij^d and to gif him sesying thairapone this day xv dayis and the act of the sesyng to be extendit in dew forme as efferis.

The gilde court haldin in the tolbutht of Dunfermlyn the xv day of Aprill the yer of Gode j^m v^c and viij yeris be the aldirman and dene of the gilde togiddir wytht the laif of the gilde brethir.

[in margin: compotus] Memorandum that one Settirday the

ferde day of the monetht of Nouember the yer of Gode
j^m v^c and viij yeris Johne Wilsone dene of the gilde
has gevin his compt of the gilde crose siluir and au
othir gilde siluiris and restand in his hand xxxviij^s iiij^d to
the cros.

The gilde court haldin in the tolbutht of Dunfermlyn be
the aldirman and the den of gilde togiddir wytht the
remanent of the gilde brethir the penult day of Februar
the yer of Gode j^m v^c and nyne yeris.

[*in margin*: for xl^S] The quhilk day Waltir Cristisone
enterit gild brothir and deponit the gret aitht thairto.
Item the samyn Waltir Cristy has pait xxv^S.

[*Fo. 26*]

[*deleted*: Item] The forstallaris of corne.

         Memorandum tuum Deum
         et unicum filium.

Robert Rovand in Drumcapye.
Georg Brovnne in Westir Luscour.
Allane Reid and Wille Reid in Cavil.
Johnne Roger in Petfirran.
johnne Bull in Gellat.

    The chepman that occupiis gild fredome.
         James be the
         g[race].

Wille Scurtuus Andro Scurtuus wyn.
Wille Scurtuus in Cragdukye.
Robert Anderson in Beitht.
Dauid Brovnne in Codane Beitht.
    Robertson Georg Robertson sovn in Beitht.
Swerd in Randill Craggis.
Yovng in Gellat.
Riche Atyine in Prumros.

The gylde cowrt haldyn in tovch buch of Dunfermlyne
be the aldirman and deyne of the gylde the xiij day of
Fabreuar the yere of Gode j^m v^c and vij yeyrris.

The quhylk day Andro Hacat was made gylde brothir for
xxxx^S and the spyis and the wyne payit thar of x^S and
the spyis and the wyne.

The quhylk day Wylyame Walcar was made gylde brothir
for xl^S and the spyis and the wyne payit thar of x^S and
the spyis and the wyne.

The quhylk day jamys Stewart was mayde gyld brothir
for xl^S and the spyis and the wyne payit heyr of x^S and
the spys and the wyne.

The quhylk day Jhon Fargusowne was mayde gylde brothir for xl^S and the spyis and the wyne payit heyr of x^S and spays and the wyne and sa thar is lent to euir man of thaime restande xxx^S qhyll the aldirman and deyne of gylde and the gylde brethir raquiyrs thaim thir witht. Summa restande non soluyt vj lib of thir personys abuynis wrytyn.

[Fo. 26v]

The quhylk day the actyowne debataly beteyx Jhon Wrycht and Rob Scharp is contunewyt qhyyl the nyxt Satirday the xx day of thir instant mwneth of Fabrewar and raffaryt to the sade Jhonys qewyf fayllande thar of the sade Rabe Scharp sall haf it to hys ath.

The qwhylk day

[Fo. 27]

The gilde court haldin in the tolbutht of the burcht of Dunfermlyne the sevynt day of the monetht of December the yer of God j^m v^C and ten yeris be the aldirman Henry Bothuell and Johne Willsone dene of the gilde togiddir wyth the remanent of the gilde brethir of the confraternite of the samyn.

[in margin: gilde xl^S] The quhilk day Lourence Fergujsone enterit gilde brothir for xl^S and lent him it agane quhill he be chargit and deponit the gret aitht to observe and kep the statutis of the samyn eftir his wndirstanding.
[addition: Item the said Lawrens has payt xxv^S.]

[in margin: compotus] The quhilk day Henry Barbur gaif his compt of gilde cros and gilde annuellis and the soume viij^S quhilk was deliuerit to John Wilsone dene of the gilde.

[in margin: compotus] The quhilk day John Wilson den of the gilde has gevin his compt of the gilde cros siluiris, annuellis and the entres of ij gilde brethir except the spis and the vyne. Et restat in manibus eius vj libri xj^S x^d. Item of the rest of the licht siluir iiij^S vj^d. Item gewin to Johne Wilson of this sovm in fynale payment of the hewcrist iij lib xix^S. Sic restat he awund fyftie sewin^S iiij^d.

[Fo. 27v]

Rentale Sancti Sanguinis.

In the first of ane hale tenement liand one the north syde

of the Calsagait betuix the land of Thom Penny and
Wilyam Cristison one the est part, the land of Johne
Baxstar and Will Mudy one the vest part.

Archbalde Edmonston payand yerlie xj^s for the bakland
and Jhok Blak payand for the forland yerlie v^s.

Item ane lande liande in the Nethirtoune and one the
southt syde of the samyn betuix the airris of wmquhil
Thom of Kynglassy one the est part and the airris of
wmquhill Thome of Burne one the vest part payande
yerlie vij^s.

Item ane aker of lande liand be vest Grantis Thorne
the airris of Andro Smyth one the est part and the land
of the elimosinar one the vest part payand yerlie to
Sanct Margretis bassyne in the abbay of Dunfermlyn
vj^s viij^d withtout ony vthir dvite aucht to ony vthir
landis.

[*in margin*: acta] The quhilk day the gildebrethir thocht
expedient that the aldirman Henry Bothuell and Schir Andro
Person chaplaine have the cur of the Haly Blude altar
ande to ressaue the offerandis of the same togiddir witht
the maillis and annuellis pertenyng to the sade altar ay
ande quhill thai be dischargit, and to gif thair compt
for the samyn.

[*Fo. 28*]

The gilde court haldin in the tolbutht of the burch of
Dunfermlyne one the xxiiij day of the monethi of December
the yer of Gode j^m v^c and x yeris be the aldirman and
the dene of gilde togiddir witht the remanent of the
gildebrethir.

[*in margin*: nota] The quhilk day James Prestone enterit
gilde brodir be resone of Dauid Coupir his gude
fadir.

[*in margin*: nota] The quhilk day Johne Burn enterit gilde
brothir be resone of John of Waluode of the Vynde his
grantschir.

The quhilk day Schir James Allanson wes made gild
brodir for his lif tyme for suffragis done and to be done.

The gild court haldin in the tolbutht of the burcht of
Dunfermlyn the first day of the monetht of Februar the
yeir of God ane thowsand fyfhundretht and ten yeris
be the aldirman Henry Bothuell Jhonne Wilsoune dene
of gild togiddir witht the ramanent of the gild brethir.

The quhilk day Schir Andro Pacok enterit gild brothir

for xx^s and deponit the aitht tharto.

The quhilk day Jhonne Wilsoun dene of gild gaf his compt of the expens of the yeir the gild fest quhilkis extendit to xxij^s ix^d and sa restis he awand xxxiiij^s vij^d. The samyn day the dene the elemosinar the Lard of Petfirran restis awand thair enteres siluir and all the laif of the enteres pait.

[Fo. 28v]

The gild court haldyn in the tolbutht of Dunfermlyng the xij day of the monetht of Aprill in the yeir of God j^{m}v^c and xj yheris be the aldirmane the dene of gild and the remanent of the gild brethir.

The quhilk day Lourens Ferguisoun et Robert Blacot aggreit and finaly concordit that Henry Greigis hidis be evinly diuidit and partit amang thaim jnduryn this yheir and forthir als lang as thay can aggre.

The quhilk day the aldirmane the dene of gild and the ramanant of the gild brethir decernit and ordanit ane tennement of land witht the yard and pertinens pertenying to the gildis lyand in the Nedirtoune of Dunfermlyng and one the southt part of the samyn betuix the landis pertenyng to Saint Michael altar one the est part and the landis of Jhon Purrok on the southt and west part to be set to Waltir Cristy gild brodir he payand tharfor yeirly the borow maill and xx^d to the gildis of yeirly annuall rent.

The court of the gilde brethir haldin in the tolbutht of Dunfermlyn be the aldirman Henry Hackat and Vilyam Spittall dene of the gilde togiddir wytht the remanent of the gilde brethir one the xxvij day of September the yer of Gode j^m v^c and xj yeris.

[in margin: nota] The quhilk day the gildebrethir has dischargit Schir Andro Pacok of the xx^{tjs} be the hale gild-brethir and exonerit him tharof imperpetuum for the Haly Blude mes singin for ane yer.

The quhilk day Lowrens Brownne was enterit gild be resonne of his fadir.

The gild court haldin in the tolbutht of Dunfermlyne the xx day of the monetht of December be Henry Hakkat aldirmane and Wilyem Spittail the dene of gild and the ramanent of the gild bredir the yeir of God abovnevritin.

The quhilk day Wilyem Spittail gaif his compt of Sanct Saluator altar and his charge vas xxiiij^s, and thairof

pait to the said altar in reparatioun and vphaldin of ane lamp vytht owly xiiij^s. And swa restis x^s the quhilk x^s pait be the said Villiem to the losing of Sanct Saluatour chellice befor the Den of Forthrik Johnne Hacket aldirman xxj yeir of
Memorandum that Setterdaye Sanct Thomas awyn the xx^{tj} day of December the yheir of God j^m v^c and xj yheris Johnne Vilson gaf his compt of the gild cors siluir and all othir gild siluir to this howr and all the forsaidis pait be him and the hal gildis exonerit and dischargit him tharof. Item the samyn day awand be Waltir Cristy [deleted: x] xv^s. Item Lowry Ferguisone [deleted: x]xv^s. Summa xxx^s.
Item the samyn daye Jhonne Vilson deliuerit to Wilyem Spittail of the rest of his compt iiij^s ix^d.
The rest of Lowrens Ferguison et Waltir Crysty et iiij^s ix^d in Wilyem Spittal hand giffin be the gildis to by thaim a bel to Wilyem Spittail Jhon Wilson Adam Blacot and John Ferguison.

[Fo. 29]

Memorandum the xx^{ti} day of December the yeir of God ane thowzand fifhundretht and tuelf yeiris one Sanct Thomas ewin James Prestone deyne of gyld and the laif of the gyld brethir present, the quhilk day Johnne of Cranis plumber was rasauit gyld bruthir witht consent all the brethir payand his dewhetis to the deyne of gild.

The quhilk day Alexander Arnoit enterit gild be resone of his wif Jonet Jaksone and payt thairfor the spys and the wyne.

The gild court haldin in the tolbutht of Dunfermling be the aldirmane and balyeis and the dene of gild and the ramanant of gild brothir the ferd day of Junij the yeir of God j^m and xiij yheris.

The quhilk day the compt maid be the gildis in presens of the aldirman and dene gild be Wilyem Spittaill dene of gild of the yeir last bipast of the annuellis pertenyng to the gildis and the gild cors, the quhilk extendit to vj^s ij^d, and it was gevin for part of payment of the bell.

The gild court haldin in the tolbuth of Dunfermling be the dene of gild Mastir Johnne Trumbul the aldirmane and balyeis and the ramanent of gild bredir the x day of Nouember the yeir of God j^m v^c and xiij yeris.

The quhilk daye Dauid Stevart lard of Rossitht was maid gild and sworne thar to.

The court of the gild haldin in the tolbuth of Dunfermling

be the deyne of the gild the aldirman and the laif of the gild brethir the thrid day of December the yeir of God j^m v^c and xiij yheris.

The quhilk day Schir Johnne Hill chaplane was enterit to the gild brothir be resonne of his fadir and sworne thar to.

The quhilk Thomas Fyne was maid gild for v crovnis and lent agayn to the said Tho and sworne thar to.

[*in margin*: Anno Domini j^m v^c xiij] The xxj daye of the moneth of March in presens of the aldirman the deyn of gild the balyeis and a part of the gildbrethir Johnne Wrycht and Johnne Wilson maid thair compt of the lych siluir gaddering be the space of yeir that wis the yeir of Gode j^m v^c [*deleted*: xij yheris] xj yheris, and thar charg was xiiii lib ix^s viij. Of that sovme spendit vpon the belhous and hinging of the bell the sovme be the said Johnne Wrycht and Johne Wilson the sovme xiiii lib xiij^s viij^d, and sua the forsaidis Johnne and John ar exonerit and dischargit of the forsaid sovme of lych siluir and hawand Johne Wilsone of his part of the bel siluir v^s iiij^d and to Wilyem Spittell x^s.

[Fo. 29v]

Xxvij die mensis Maij anno Domini j^m v^c xiiij^o per Magistrum Johanem Cristini [*sic*] decanum gilde etc. The quhilk day Willyam Spittall Johne Vilson Adam Blacot and John Fergussone war payit for ane bell and all vncostis tharof and grantis thaim veill and thankfully payit for the samyn of the soume of xxij libris and for vncostis xiiij libris xiij^s viij^d, and quitclaimit the gilde brethir tharof.

The court haldin the tolbuth of Dunfermling be Johne Wrycht deyne of gild and the remanent of the gild brethir the xix day of Januar the yeir of God j^m v^c xiiij yeris.

[*in margin* : compotus] The quhilk day Mastir Johne Trumbul maid his compt to the forsaid deyne of gild and the gild brethir of the lycht siluir fra the xvj day anno j^m v^c xiij of Nouember to Yhovul evyn the xxiiij day of December in the yeir of God j^m v^c xiiij yeris. His charg was xxj lib. xiij^s xj^d, and spendit tharof baith yeris for wax xvij lib vj^d and bell siluir and othir vncostis, and swa restis v lib ix^s v^d in the said Mastir Johnne hand.

xxj die mensis Januarij anno j^m v^c xiiij.

The quhilk day the haill gild brethir determit that Wille Danyel suld haf xiiij^s for the tyme bigane, and in tym to cum thai wald provid for the rynging of the bell thar self as thaj thocht maist expedient.

The xxvj daye of the monetht of Januar the yeir of God j^m v^c xiiij.

The quhilk daye Johnne Burne youngar pait xxj^s for ane annuel pertenyng to the Hale Blud altar in payment of termeis bigane.

[*deleted*: The quhilk daye Schir Andro Pacok maid his compt of the Haly Blud offerand of twa yeris and it came to vj lib ix^s j^d, and of the said sovme in the Lard of Petfirran haund and be the actis and his hand writ the sovme of v lib. xij^s and thar restis in Schir Andro Pacok hand xvij^s j^d half. And likvis restand in the Lard of Petfirran hand rasauit fra Williem Lambert xiiij^s.]

The quhilk daye the haill gildis set to Johnne Burne ane land in the Neddirtoune lyand betuix Thome Burne land on the west part and Thome Horne land on the est part for vij^s of annuel to be pait yeirly to the Haly Blud altar.

The quhilk daye Williem Lambert restis avand to the Haly Blud altar xxj^s viij^d. And the hail comunite has set him ane akkir of land of v yeris nixt and jmmediat falloand the dait of thair presens.

xxx die mensis Januarij anno Domini j^m v^c xiiij in presencia prepositj decani gilde.

The quhilk day Schir Allan Glen maid his compt of the Haly Blud offerand for twa yeris and sa lang as the fest of Yovl last bipast to this da and hes deliuerit iij lib xvijj^s xij^d vj^d of it and to thaim at sang the mes ix^s. Item for vax xxxij^d.

[*Fo. 30*]

The viij day of Merche the yeir of God j^m v^c and xv yerris the gyld curt haldyne the said day be deyne of gyld aldirman and the gilbrethir decretis that Wilyem Lambert sal steik wp the bowhell one the est part of the stair maid betuix hym and Schir Andro Pacok eftir the contrac maid be the linaris that na nouaciones suld be maid.

The quhilk day Adam Blacot and Wilyem Grant balyeis of Dunfermling deliuerit in the tolbuth the sovme of vj lib and vj^s quhilk was borrovit of the lycht siluir for the paying of taxt, and the gilde dischargit thame thairof.

The quhilk day Johnne Wrycht gaf his compt of the vax and all vncostis pertenyng to the kirk and thai dischargit him of all thingis to this day.

The x day of the monetht of Januar the yeir of God j^m v^c xvj yeris.
The quhilk daye Mastir Johne Trumbul gaif in presens of the den of gild and the gild bredir the sovme of v lib to be put in the box of the lycht siluir and thre lib and xj^s of the Haly Blud siluir and sa he has pait all sovmis that he aucht to the said comonite and was dischargit tharof, and has deliuerit the box and the keis.

The secund day of Maij the yeir of God j^m v^c and xvij yeiris Johne Wilsone bailye maid his compt of the recept of the lycht siluir be hym in the yeir of God j^m v^c and xvj yeiris in presens of the deyne Johne Wrycht and Wilyem Spittall witht vthiris diuers of the bying of the wax and the vp puttyng of the bell in the new stepall, extendand til xiij lib and odir siluir, and the said Johne has put in the box that restis vnspendit – iij lib iij^s xj^d ob.

[*in margin*: nota] xiij die mensis Nouembris anno Domini j^m v^c xvij^o.
The quhilk day Wilyam Valcar and John Scobe var vnlawit in the gild court be the aldirman John Hackat of Petfuran Adam Blacat den of the gild and the remanent of the gilde bredir and ilkan of thaim to pay halfa mark betuix this and Candilmes nixt to cum.
The quhilk day Johnne Pattonson enterit gild be reson of his fadir.
The ilk day Allane Covpir was maid gild and sworne thairto.

xv die Januar the yeir of God j^m v^c xviij yeris.
The quhilk day Adam Blacot dene of gild gaif his compt of the gild fest to the aldirman and the remanent of the gild bredir the quhilk drev – iij lib ij^s.

[*Fo. 30v*]

The first day of Februar the yeir of God j^m v^c xvij yeiris in presens of the aldirman deyne of gild.

The quhilk day Williem Lambert gaif his compt for ane akkir pertenyng to the Hale Blud altar of the ald compt xxj^s and viij^d, and at this last compt vthir xxxvj^s.

The gild court haldin in the tolbutht of Dunfermling be the aldirman den of gild and the the gild bredir the xiij day of Februar the yeir of God j^m v^c xvij yeris.

The quhilk day Andro Hockat vas maid gildbrodir for

xl^s the spis and wyn pait and x^s of the said xl^s pait the samyn day.

The quhilk day Williem Walcar vas rasauit gildbrodir for xl^s and sworne tharto the spis and the wyn pait and x^s of siluir.

The quhilk day James Stevart was rasauit gildbrodir for xl^s and sworne tharto the spis and wyn pait and x^s of siluir.

The quhilk day Johnne Ferguison was resauit gildbrodir for xl^s and sworne tharto the spis and wyn pait and x^s of siluir.

The court of the gild bredir haldin in the tolbutht of Dunfermling the sext day of the monetht of March the yeir of God j^m v^c xvij be the aldirmane John Hackat aldirmane Adam Blacot dene of gild and the remanent of the gildbrethir.

The quhilk day Schir Andro Pacok deliuerit the Hale Blude siluir that he was awand in presens of the aldirman dene of gilde and the gild brether foirsaid. And the said gilde exonerit quytclaimit and dischargit the said Schir Andro of the payment tharof now and forevir.

The quhilk day Schir Johnne Hil deliuerit the Hale Blud siluir that he was avand in presens of the aldirman den of gild and the gildbredir forsaid, and the said gild exonerit quitclaimit and dischargit the said Schir Johnne of the payment thairof nov and forevir.
The samyn day Johnne of Burne paid xxj^s for annuellis of the Hale Blud altar of termes bigane.
The quhilk day the haill gild bredir diuisat x^s to be gevyn to Schir Andro Robertson fra this tym quhill Witsounday for singing at the evynsang and hie mes quhill the said fest of Vitsounday and to be tane of the gild siluir.

[Fo. 31]

[deleted probably: The quhilk day I Jhon Hakat off Petfuran grantis me awand to the Hally Blud alter the sovme off v lib xij^s. Manew propria etc. And hais payit this some to the Hally Blud tabarnakill]

The secund day of October the hail gildis decretit thai wald nocht rasaif na man natif of Innerkething gild bredir.
The samyn day the aldirman den of gild and the laif of the gildbredir has ramittit and forgevin frelie to John Scobe his vnlays for all thingis bigane to this

day.

Curia gilde tenta apud Dunfermlyne xxiij die Octobris anno Domini j^m v^c decimo octauo in presencia Johanne Hakhed aldirmani Johanne Fergusone decani gilde.

The quhilk day aldirmane dene of gild ordanis that Johne Wrycht Johne Wilsone Adam Blacat sall gif thar compt the nixt Satirday of the deine of gildschip and Wilyem Blacat Hendre Greg to gif compt for Sanct Saluatouris altar the said day and the lycht gaddaris to bring in batht the ald siluir and the new and quhay failyeis tharin to be chargit to remaine in the tolbwitht be the saide aldirmane deine of gild and the laif of gilbrethir.

The gild curt haldin in the towubutht of Dunfermlyne be the aldirmane deine of gild and laif of the gild brethir the xxvij of Nouember the yeir of God j^m v^c and xviij yeiris.

The quhilk day Robert Gray was maid gilde brothir at the jnstance of ane maist reuerend fadir Andro arsbischorp of Sanctandrois for thre sume of xxxij^d and ane ynglis cop and the Robert suerne thar to in presens of the brethir. Raptim per decanum etc.

The qwhilk day the auldirman and den off gild wytht the ramenaynt off the gild bredyr ordand that Arscbald Stewart and Thomas Fyne suld be in gud peis and cherite and gyff ony off the saidis twa personis makis offence tyll othir owdyr in word or deid it beand knawyne qwhilk off tham beis fundyn in the falt he sall pay to Hally Blud alter halff stane off wakis be the gild bredyr and sal als aisc the aldirman fforgyffnes.

[*Fo. 31v*]

The xxviij day of the monetht of Januar the yeir of God j^m v^c xviij per Johannem Ferguson decanum gilde.
The quhilk day John Hovtone vas maid gild for xl^s and suorne tharto, xx^s tharof pait.
The aldirman dene of gild and the remanent of the gild bredir ordanit that the licht gaddiris and all thai that aw ony thing to the Haly Blud altar or ony kirk gud to bring it in this day xv dais.

xxiij die mensis Marcij anno Domini j^m v^c xviij.

The quhilk day Johne Ferguison den of gild gaif his compt of the gild fest to the aldirman and the ramanent of the gild bredir the expens maid be him is – iij lib xij^s viij^d.

xxvj die mensis Nouembris anno Domini j^m v^c xix^o.
The quhilk day the Deine of Forthrik gaif his compt of the efferand of the Halibluid siluir to the deine of gyld Johne Wilsone Wilyem Spittaill Johne Fergusone bailyeis, and laif of the brethir fra the xxvij day of October in the yeir of God j^m v^c and xviij yeiris to the foirsaid day of Nouember in the yeir of God j^m v^c xix yeiris. His resait cumis to xlvj^s iiij^d, and of that pait the chapillains and the clerkis, and to Symont Caruour x^s j^d. And sua restis xv^s viij^d for the quhilk deliuerit four pund of wax to Johne Ferguisone that ingadirit of the smaw offerandis.

Decanus manu propria.

The vij day of the monetht of Julij anno Domini j^m v^c xx yeris.
The quhilk day the haill gild bredir decretit and ordanit that Williem Cristison suld the ask the baillie Johnne Ferguison forgevinnas of the falt he maid to him and the said Williem Cristison suld nocht falt to nane officiar of the said tovne vndir the payne of xx^{tjs} in tyme to cum or ane stane of wax at the wil of the gild brothir quhillis Johne or Wilyem faltis til othir.

The gild cowrt haldyn in the towbowtht off the Dunfermlyne be the aldirman and the den off the gyld bredir the xj day off Nouembar the yeir off God j^m v^c and xx yeiris.

The qwhylk day Wellem Lambart gyff in his cownt off ane akir of land pertenyng to the Hally Blud altar and staw rest awand in the said Wellem hand off the termis be fforpast restis the sawm off xlviij^s iiij^d and twa bolls off malt off this instant yeir excepand halff a mark to be gyffyn to the tarar off Dunfermlyne.
[*addition*: Cristian Reid the spovs of Williem Lambert restis awannd to the Haly Blud altar the xv day of Nouember the yeir of God j^m v^c xxj yeris xxvij^s iiij^d.]

The quhilk day Villiem Lambert vif hes pait xxvij^s iiij^d of the rest of the Haly Blud akir of the sovme resauit fra Villiem Vallud that his fadir wes awand to Villiem Lambert and his vif and left hym to pay be his fadir in legasye xix^s viij^d.

[*Fo. 32*]

Anno Domini m^o v^o vicesimo primo.

The quhilk day the haldirmane bailyeis and the laif of the gild brethir chesat Adam Blakat deine of gild and suerne thairto.

The xxvj day of October the geld cowrt haldyn in the

towbowtht of Dunfermlyne be Jhone Hakat aldirmane and Ademe Blakot den of gyld and the ramenent of the gyld bredir.
The qwhylk day it is pprewyt that Robert Prowd coft hydis and occupyit the gild fredoume and weis leid to v^s of wnlaw and gyf he contewinws to pay x^s euirik tyme.
Lambartis wyf is contenewit of the akir of land and the payment thar of qwhyll this day xv dayis.
The qwhylk day Jhon Wrecht wes callit tyll anssur to Mastir Jhone Cristysune instance to anssur to the byll of scowmowndis giffyne ine be the said Mastir Jhon has the first cowrt and to ansur to the next cowr has law wyll has he that wes scowmownd be the officiar.
The qwhylk day James Werkmane wes enterit gyld brodir ffore xl^s and the spice and the wyne and the xl^s laid on the bwrd and lent to hym agane qwhyll he be schargit be the aldirman and den of gyld and sowrne thar to.

One Sanct Thomas ewyne the xxj yeir of God etc.

The quhilk day Wilyem Spittall bailye and Johne Hakat aldirmane gaf in thar comptis of the lycht siluir in the said yeir to the for said of Sanct Thomas ewine extendand til sex pund xij^s and $iiij^d$, the compt maid tharof be for the dene of gild and the brethir restis hawand to the foir saidis Johne and Wilyem $xiij^s$ j^d. And hawand be Johne Duncane Wilyem Blak and Robe Brand of annuellis and the cow siluir and $viij^s$.

The qwhilk day the marchandis grantis tham payit off the selwir off the Haley Blud tabbyrnekill the qwhylk extendis to xlij libris and restand in the kest off the Hally Blud seluir xxx^s vj^d and in Jhon of Carnis hand xj^s.

iij lib $xvij^s$ $vj^{d\,\frac{1}{2}}$.

[Fo. 32v]

x die Maii anno Domini j^m v^c xxij.

The quhilk day Villiem Spittaill hes maid his compt of the lycht siluir extendand to iij lib $xvij^s$ vj^d. And disponit of the said sovme iij lib xij^d to the operacione of the kirk and restand in the box $xxiiij^s$ $vjjj^{d\,\frac{1}{2}}$.

The. xx^o die mensis Decembris anno vt supra.
The quhilk day Johne Troter pait the forsaid sovme be for the aldirman and ane certane of the gild [deleted: siluir] bredir.

Curia ca
The gild court haldyn by the aldirman and Allan Covpir dene of the gild witht the la[if ? *folio torn*] of the bredir the xxiij day of December the yeir of God j^m v^c xxij yeiris.
The quhilk day Patrik Wemis lard of Pettincrif wes [*deleted*: maid] enterit gild brodir and the gild siluir and vthir dewiteis gevin quit excep the spice and the wyine.

xij die Decembris anno Domini j^m v^c xxiij.

The gyld court haldin in the tolbutht of Dunfermlyn the xij day of December the yeir of God j^m v^c xxiij yeiris be Johne Hackat aldirman Villiem Spittall dene of gyld and the remanent of the [*deleted*: dene] gyld bredir.
The quhilk day the dene of the gyld and the remanent of the gyld bredir determit and ordanit that Johne Ferguson youngar that he sal mak the half berrall of vly that he sald to Dauid Hackat sufficient stuf or ellis to pay xxvj^s to the said Dauid Hackat this day viij dayis.

ix^o die mensis Januarij anno Domini j^m v^c xxiij.

The gyld court haldin in the tolbutht of Dunfermling the ix day of Januar the yeir of God j^m v^c xxiij yeiris be Johne Halkat aldirman Villiem Spittael dene of the gild the laif of gyld bredir.
The quhilk day Allan Covpir hes tane to preif this day viij dais that he deliuerit vj berrelis of olye to Johne Patirsone.
The quhilk day Allan Covpir ackit hym self that the olye fresit or this day viij dais that the said Allan sal tak it again, and it be nocht frost.
The quhilk day it is comprimittit betuix honorable personis ay ar to say Villiem Spittal one the ta part Johne Wrycht on the tothir part to this affek as aftir fallovi[s ?*folio torn*] that is to say anens the oxone that wes tane as baitht the parteis alleigis and al vthir debatable matiris, and thaj ar sworne to abid at thir per personis vndir writin thaj ar to say the Lard of Petfirran and Robert Stevart for the part of Johne Wrycht, the Lard of Pettincrief and Maistir Andro Stevart for the part of Villiem Spittall. And the forsaid personis ar sworne to deliuer eftir thair convenience gif thaj can, and to deliuer betuix this day and viij days. And gif the forsaid personis can nocht aggre vpon the deliuerans thaj sal haif povir to cheis ane od man.

[Fo. 33]

The quhilk day Mastir Andro Stevart wes enterit gyld brodir and wes suorne tharto the gild siluir and vthir deuiteis gevin quit.

The quhilk day Gavin Lawsoune vas enterit gild brodir be resoune of Elezebeth Ferguison his spovs and suorne.
The quhilk day James Murray enterit gild brodir for 1^s and suorne tharto.

The gild court haldyne be the dene of the gyld Mastir Andro Stevart and the remanent of the laif of the gild bredir the xx day of Januar the yeir of God j^m v^c xxiij yeiris.
The quhilk day Villiem Spittall and Thomas Fyne hes maid thair compt of the lycht siluir extendand to the sovme of x pundis xiiij^s iij^d ob. And disponit of the said sovme in al thingis to the operacioune of the kirk x pund xj^s vij^d. Sa restis in tresserer handis xxxij^d ob of the hail sovme foirsaid that the said Villiem and Thomas hes laid dovne. Item apon the said day Villiem Grant brocht xx^d. And the said Mastir Andro enterit the said day that is the xx day of Januar to the lycht siluir.
The quhilk day Villiem Spittall maid his compt of the dene of gild siluir and he hes laid dovne iiij^s j^d for the gild cors. Item in the handis of Gavane Lavsone xxx^d for Thom Stevinsone land. Item xij^d for the land of John Wrycht at the cors. Item xx iij^d for Vat Cristy and thai ar all the hail gild annuellis of the quhilk cors siluir and annuellis the dene of the gild and the laif of the gild bredir dischargis the said Villiem to this day, excep the gild bredir siluir the quhilk restis in the buk onetane vp be hym the said Villiem.

The first day of the monetht of Marche the yeir of God j^m v^c xxvj yeris.
The gyld court haldyn be the den of the gyld Johnne Pattounsoune the aldirmane and the remanent of gild brodir the first day of the monetht of March the yeir of God j^m v^c xxvj yeris.

The quhilk day Robert Murray was enterit gyld brodir for 1^s and suorne tharto.
The quhilk day Jaime Ferguisoune enterit gyld brodir for 1^s and suorne tharto.
The quhilk day Lourens Scobie vas enterit gyld brodir for 1^s and suorne tharto.
The quhilk day Villiem Hil vas enterit gild brodir for 1^s and suorne tharto.

The quhilk day Thomas Dallgles vas enterit gild brodir for 1^S and suorne tharto.
The quhilk day Thomas Scobie vas enterit gild brodir and suorne tharto. Pait vt.
The quhilk day Adam Brand vas enterit gyld brodir and suorne tharto. Pait vt supra.
The quhilk day Robert Wilsoune vas enterit gild brodir and suorne tharto. Pait vt supra.
The quhilk day Williem Nechol was enterit gild brodir and suorne tharto. Pait vt supra.
The quhilk day Richart Logtoune was enterit gild brodir and suorne tharto. Pait vt supra.

The quhilk day Mastir Andro Stevart den of gild has maid his compt of the lycht siluir befor the aldirman and the remanent of the gyld bredir and deliuerit to the forsaid John [*? folio torn*] dene of gyld cors callit gyld cors iiij^S ij^d.

[*Fo. 33v*]

Anno Domini j^m v^c xxvj mensis Marcij die primo pait be the personis vndirvritin.

In primis Thomas Scobie xxx^S restand awand x^S the spice and wyn ane jnglis cop to the dene.
Item Richart Logtoune xxx^S. Restant vt supra.
Item Adam Brand xxxx^S. Vt supra pait xl^S.
Item Thomas Dawgles xxx^S. Restant vt supra.
Item Robert Wilsoun xxxx^S. Vt supra pait xl^S.
Item Laurens Scobie xxxx^S. Vt supra pait xl^S.
Item Jaime Ferguisoune xxx^S. Restant vt supra. [*addition*: gevin quit the laif be the gyld.]
Penultima die mensis Octobris anno Domini j^m v^c xxix per Laurencium Ferguison decanum gilde et confratres.
The quhilk day Williem Wallud enterit gild be resoun of his fadir and suorne tharto.

xxj die mensis Februarij anno xxix^o.
The quhilk day Patrik Wemis was maid dene of the gild and sworne tharto.

xxj die mensis Augusti anno Domini j^m v^c xxx^o.
The court haldyn be Patrik Wemis dene of the gild and the laif of the gild bredir.

The quhilk day Symon Caruour comperit in jugsment and offerit hyme to pay and content to the [*deleted*: alderman] dene of the gild and the laif of the tovnschip the haill sovme that he hes rasauit withtin ane monetht or ellis to tak xij markis for his almery, and in all thingis and he to compleit the samyn in al thingis.

The quhilk day Schir Johnne Hill comperit in jugsment and gaif our al the annuellis pertenyn to the Haly Blud altar and thaj to tak vp the samyn anuellis and the akyr at this Vitsounday bypast in anno j^{mo} v^c xxx^o and this annuellis [deleted: and akir] sal pay for the mes sining witht the gild cors siluir for the sining at the altar.

xvij die mensis Septembris anno Domini j^m v^c xxx^o.

The quhilk day it was appuntit and finaly concordit betuix Patrik Wems dene of the gild and the laif of the toune one the ta part and Symone Caruor one the tothir part anent the almery, quhilk thaj war content and the said Symon of xiij markis and a half for his warkmanschip of the said almery, and sway the said dene of the gild hes pait the said Symon the forsaid day of the lycht siluir xl^s and swa restis onpait to the said Symon de claro iij markis v^s and $iiij^d$.

[Fo. 34]

The quhilk day James Warkmen hes pait to the dene of the gild Patrik Wemis of his gild siluir x^s and the laif of the remanent gevin quit in wil of the gild bredir.

xxj die mensis Octobris anno Domini j^{mo} v^v xxx^o curia tenta per Patricium Wemis decanum gilde et confratres etc.

The quhilk day Johne Patonsone comperit in jugsment and persevit Villiem Blacot ffor the payment of the half gavill biggit betuix the said Villiem and [deleted: Villiem] Johnne landis the said [deleted: Johne tha] Villiem deniit that euir he promittit ane penny to the said Johne for the biggin of the said gavill and alsua the said Villiem deniit that euir he bad Villiem Spittell cum to the said Johne to mak ony condicione or to profir hym ony siluir, apon the quhilkis the forsaid Johne offerit to the said Villiem aitht and he suld gif hym quit, the quhilk the said William deponit the aitht apon the promiss, and attour the gild bredir wardit apon the samyn and fand.

The quhilk day the gildbrethir he wardit and fund that Thom Davgles hes failyeit to Johnne Huttone gif he hes tane mair penneworth fra his alleigit callit v[?] souerty nocht xx s. s. extendis to, and to call the said Villiem befor, to se the verite tharof.

The quhilk day Patrik Wemis dene of the gild and the laif of the gild brodir hes ordand Schir Villiem Grant to resaif the gild cors in keping and to ansuer for the siluir to the dene of the gild.

The quhilk day Henry Bad hes oblist hyme in jugsment to entir burgis apon Furisday nixt to cum, and thareftir to entir gild brodir quhen he is chargit tharto, and attour the said Henry is cumit in will for the occupeing of the fredome.

The quhilk day the actioune persevit be James Fergusoune apone Villiem Andirsone for the haldyn fra hyme of xiiij ^{s} gret, the nychtbouris hes fund be ane interlocutour of the court that the said Villiem is avand the said xiiij gret.

[Fo. 34v]

xx^{mo} die mensis Decembris anno Domini j^{mo} v^c xxxj^o curia tenta per Patricium Wemis decanum gilde et confratres etc.

The quhilk day Henry Bad was enterit gildbrodir for 1^s and x^s gevin quit.

The quhilk day the bredir was contentit that Schir Andro Quhit suld [deleted: haif the siluir] say the messis for the bredir that deis.

The quhilk day the gild bredir was contentit to tak wp the feist agan.

The quhilk day Schir Thomas Malcum was enterit gild brodir for al the dais of his lyftyme for the suffraige dovne and to be dovne.

xxvj^{to} die mensis Octobris anno Domini j^{mo} v^c xxxij^o curia tenta per Patricium Wemis decanum gilde and confratres etc.

The quhilk day Laurens Fergusone was maid dene of the gild and Patrik Wemis to help him and was suorne tharto.

The quhilk day Johne Arnot was maid gyld brodir be resone of his fadir Alexander Arnot and enterit thairto.

The quhilk day James Blyth was enterit gyld brodir fre for the spice and the wyne and that for the raquest of Dene James Crechtone sacristan and suorne thairto.

The quhilk day Johne Multray was gyld brodir for 1^s and x gevin quit and suorne thairto.

The quhilk day the dene of the gyld and the laif of the bredir hes grantit to gif to Schir Andro Quhit xl^s be yeir induryn thair willis for seruice maid and to be maid and that to be tayne of the gild siluir and the annuellis.

[Fo. 35]

xiiij^o die mensis Nouembris anno Domini j^{mo} v^c xxxij^o curia tenta per Laurencium Fergusone decanum gilde et confratres etc.

The quhilk day Patrik Wemis hes gevin in restand in Robert Gray hand for the Haly Blud akyr twa yeiris profit, and sua the said Patrik the dene of the gyld and the gyld bredir hes assignit the said ferme to tax vp and to pay the bredir that wantis for Sanct Margaret [deleted:altar] tabernikill ay and quhill thaj be pait, thar ar the names that sais thaj want in the fyrst to Allan Cwpir Laurens Fergusone Adam Blacot Villiem Andirsone.

The quhilk day the dene of the gyld commandit Allan Cowpir to remane in the tolbutht ay and quhill he pait xlvij^s v^d for the lycht siluir. He said he wald nocht remane bot pas his way and tyne his fredome and sway passit him away and wald quit his fredome.

The quhilk day Petir Hacheid was enterit gyldbrothir for 1^s and gevin quit at the raquest of the aldirman and suorne thairto.

xx^o die mensis Nouembris anno vt [supra ?] curia tenta per Laurencium Fergusone decanum gilde et confratres etc.

The quhilk day Henry Bad hes pait xx^s of his gyldsiluir and sua restis vthir xx^s. The forsaid dene of the gyld gif it to Schir Andro Quyth.

xxvij die mensis Octobris anno Domini j^m v^c xxxiij yeiris per Petrium [sic] Hackat decanum gilde et confratres.

The quhilk day Johnn Pattounsoune enterit gild be resoune of John Pattounsoun his em and was suorne tharto.

[Fo. 35v]

Curia tenta in pretorio burgj de Dunfermlyn per Patricium Hacheid decanum gilde et confratres etc. xx^{mo} die mensis Decembris anno Domini j^{mo} v^c xxxiij^o.

The quhilk day Villiem Donaldsone enterit gild brodir and was suorne tharto for xl^s and pait to the straucht [skaucht?].

The quhilk day Johne Karnis grantit in jugsment that he was avand thre yeiris to the Haly Bluyd quhilk cumis to xxxiij^s to pay betuix this and Pasch day.

The quhilk day Johne Burne grantit avand vij^s to pay on Pasch.

The quhilk day Villiem Wallud grantit thre yeiris quhilk cumis to vij^s vj^d, [addition: pait.]

The quhilk day Henry Bad and Johne Mltray grantit in jugsment to pay Schir Andro Pacok betuix this and Pasch xl^s [addition: and pait to the forsaid Schir Andro Pacok sen syne.]

The quhilk day Dauid Blak was maid gild brodir for xl^s and enterit tharto apone Al Hallow evin and to pay quhen is chargit.

    Curia tenta per Petrium [sic] Hacheid decanum gilde confratres etc. xviij^o die mensis Decembris anno Domini j^{mo} v^c xxxiiij^{to}.

The quhilk day Villiem Wallud was maid dene of the gyld for ane yeir and was sworne tharto.
The quhilk day the dene of the gyld and the laif of the gyld bredir for the tym that nayine of the gyldbredir sal rafuis the gaddering of the lycht as the kyrkmastir giffis thaim in byll and failyeand tharof thaj sal pay as the monetht cumis to estimat as the monetht gaddirit of befor in quhom the falt is fund.

[Fo. 36]

    Curia tenta per Vilelmum Wallud decanum de gilde et confratres eiusdem quinto die mensis Februarij anno Domini j^{mo} v^c xxxv^{to}.

The quhilk day Villieme Blacot was maid gild brodir and was suorne tharto for xiiij^s and the laif gevin quit be the gild bredir and the said gild bredir ordand the said Villiem ansuer Schir Andro Quhit of the xiiij^s.
The quhilk day Schir Andro Quhit hes tayne thair personis vndir writin in his fe bipast at Sanct Thomas day in the first in Dauid Blak hand xl^s and in Villiem Blacot hand xiiij^s, and sua restis avand to the said Schir Andro of the yeir forsaid xj^s iiij^d.
The quhilk the nychtbouris maid price witht Robert Gray for his ferme of the Haly Blud akyr of this yeir bipast, price of the boll xiiij^s and the half boll for vj^s viij^d, and sua he was ordand to pay Dauid Blak xiij^s and to Lovre Fergusone and Allan Covpir x^s and Adam Blacot v^s, and swa is the tabirnekles of the Haly Blud and Sanct Margret pait excep xxij^s to Dauid Blak.

    Curia gilde tenta in pretorio de Dunfermling per Vilmum Vallud decanum gilde et confratres eiusdem quinto die mensis Augustj anno Domini j^m v^c xxxvj.

The quhilk day Andro Reid was maid gild brodir and suorne thar to for xl^s.

    Curia tenta gilde in pretorio de Dunfermling per Vilmum Wallud decanum gilde et confratres eiusdem xxvj die mensis Augustj anno Domini j^m v^c xxxvj.

The quhill [sic] day that the nychtboris fyndis that Dauid Blak has forfaltit his fredome becaus he has dissobeyit the den of gild diuers tymis and dischargis

the said Dauid that he occupij it nocht in tymis cummyng
quhill thaj be fordar awisit. [addition: the said Dauid
maid a mendis tharfor the actis war adnullit and he rest-
orit agane to his fredome.]

[deleted: The quhilk day the nychtboris findis that
Williem Nichell sall bryng hayme to James Fergusone the
xix markis Spruce weill warit in Danskyne and the said
Williem sal bayr the aventor of it quhill he bring it
in Scotland to ony port betuix Disart and Leytht in the
first schippie that gangis to Danskyn or ellis betuyx
this and the fest of Sant Peter callit Aduincula. And
failyeand tharof the said Williem sall pay to the said
James for ilk mark x^s and the said James sal pay the
fracht and oncostis that the said Williem malkis apone
the forsaid xix markis [.... ?] et eque.]

[Fo. 36v]

The quhilk day the nychtboris fandis that Johne Hwtoune
sall caus Williem Nicholl tilbe ansuerit and get in
Danskyn xix markis that the said Johne left behind hyme
in Danskyn, and the said Johne sall gyf to the said
Williem Nicholl his obligacione tilbe ansuerit of the said
soume and failyeand thairof the said Johne sall pay to
the said Williem for ilk markis Spruce x^s Scotis.

Vigilia Sanct Thome.

 Curia tenta Villelmum Wallud decanum gilde et
 confratres eiusdem xx^{mo} die mensis Decembris anno
 Domini j^m v^c xxxvj^{to}.

 The littis to be dayne of the gild.
Ro. Stevart L. Fergusone To. Davgles M.D. Stevart Ja.
Murray V. Wallud
The quhilk day Thomas Davglis was maid dene of the gild
for ane yeir and suorne tharto.
The quhilk day the gild bredir maid Patrik Wemis kyrk
mastir.
The quhilk day the dene of the gild hes assignit Andro
Reid to pay Schir Andro Quhit xl^s for his fe that is to
say xx^s at Vitsonday and xx^s at Lammes and hes assignit
Schir Johne Cristisone to pay to Schir Andro x^s of the
cors.

 Curia tenta per Thomas Dawgless decanum gilde
 et confratres eiusdem octauo die mensis Februarij
 anno Domini millesimo quingentesimo xxxvij.
The quhilk day Johnn Karnis plumber was enterit gild
brodir be resoun of his fadir John of Karnis and suorne
thairto.

Curia gilde tenta in pretorio de Dunfermlyn xxvj die mensis Octobris anno Domini j^m v^c xxxviij per Johannem Hackat aldirmanum Thomas Davgles decanum gilde et confratres dicte gilde.

The quhilk day James Hovtoune enterit gild and was suorne tharto for fiftye s the spice and the wyne, and sal cum to Dunfermlyn and mak thair residens betuix this and the Purificatioune of Our Lade nixt and immediat falloand failland tharof to pay to the gildis x lib and to be dischargit of the fredome.

The quhilk day Johnn Pattoune enterit gild for fiftie s and suorne tharto. He sall cum to Dumfermling and mak his residens as the forsaid James Hovtoune oblist him to do vndir sek lik pan and dischargeit.

Till daye Williem Malcum enterit gild and was enterit thar to referrand him to the will of gildis. It was fund at John Malcum fadir to Williem Malcum vas gyld and he enterit tharto be rycht of his fadir.

[Fo. 37]

In vig natiuitatis Domini anno Domini j^m v^c xxxviij.

Curia tenta per Thomas Dawgles decanum gilde et confratres eiusdem die et anno prenotatis.

The quhilk day the said Thomas Dawgles was maid den of gild for a yeir and suorne tharto and Lovrens Ferguison kirk mastir.

The samyne day Gavin Lawsoun was chosyn to lycht the candillis lamp baitht to lycht and put it out and to keip the wax of the kirk opyn and steik the kirk duir and suorne thairto.

Vigilia Sancti Thome.

Curia tenta per Vilemum Blacot decanum et confrates eiusdem xix mensis Decembris anno Domini millesimo v^c xxxix.

The quhilk day Schir Thomas Malcum maid his compt of the offerand of the Haly Blud altar and the gild cors and all pait and thar for the gildis exonerit and dischargit him of all bigane to this daye.

The quhilk day the gild bredir hes sald to Robert Gray x firlotis of malt pertenand to the Haly Bluyd altar for xiij^s iiij^d the boll, and to pay the sacristane vj^s viij^d and sal answer for xx $^{tj s}$ viij^d to the altar quhen he is requirit.

The quhilk daye Dauid Dewar enterit gild for xl^s and suorne tharto.

The samyn day Robert Ferguisone enterit gild sik lik and suorne thairto.

> Curia gilde tenta in communitatie per Villelmum
> Blakuod decanum gilde et confratres eiusdem
> ix die mensis Octobris anno Domini j^m v^c xl.

The quhilk day ane venerable religius man Dene James
Crechton sacristan of Dunfermlyne the den of gild and
gild bredir wytht ane consent and assent, thai ratefiit
affermit and apprevit ane instrument vndir Mastir Nicholl
Bulle signe and subscriptioune manuall coroborat vyt the
appensioune of the commone seill of the burch of the
dait the xxiiij day of the monetht of Merch the yeir of
God j^m [deleted: v^c] iiij^c thre scoir and nyne in all
puntis and actis. And eftir the redyne of the samyn thaj
commandit the Lady preist chaplanis of Sanct Margret
altar the morne preist and all vthiris infeft be the
communite and the parochis clerkis to be in the habit
in the queir at evinsangis hie mess all solempt dais
halie and festivall dais vndir the paine of sequestryne
thair maillis and annuellis and vthir deviteis pertenyng
to the altaris.

> Curia gilde burgj de Dunfermlyne tenta infra
> burgum eiusdem per decanum gilde Thoma
> Dawgles et confratres eiusdem xxvj mensis
> Februarij anno Domini j^m v^c xl.

The quhilk daye the forsaid den of gild and gild bredir
dischargit Williem Cochrane litstar of the bying of ony
skynnis wythtin the fredome of Dumfermling vndir the
pane of xl^s, and the said Villiem oblist him of his avune
fre will to obserf the samyn and to purg him four tymmis
in yeir of the premis[sis ? text obscured]

The quhilk daye Elezabet Howtoune the spovs of Williem
Vilson enterit to the gild fredome be resoune of vmquhill
Johnn Hovtoune hir fadir and suorne thairto.

The quhilk daye the gild bredir has sald to Robert Graye
x firlot of malt pertenand to the Haly Blud altar for
xiii^s iiij^d the boll, and to paye the sacristane
vj^s viij^d and sall ansuer for xxvj^s viij^d to the den of
gild quhen he is raquirit.

[Fo. 37v]

Vigilia Sancti Thome

Curia tenta per Vilmum Blakwod decanum gilde xxj^o Decembris anno Domini j^{mo} v^c xlij^o.

xxvij^o Januarij anno Domini j^{mo} v^c xxlij^o.

Curia tenta per Villelmum Blakwod decanum gilde et
confratres eiusdem xxvij^o Januarij anno Domini j^{mo} v^{c}xlij^o.

The quhilk day the gild bredir hes ordand Villeme Blakwod Petir Hacheid Villeme Vallud and Schir Thomas Malcum tutoris to the Haly Bluyd altar and to persew and bringin all the profitis and deviteis perteinyn to the samyn, and in specialle to persew ane akyr that Villeme Smytht hes [*deleted* : tayn] intromittit witht at his avin hand and sal tak the expens of the samyn of all the gyld siluir and failyeng tharof to scot and lot amangis thaim for the weill of the altar, baith befor the spirituall jugis and temporall.

The quhilk day the dene of the gyld and the bredir hes ordand Gavane Lauson to bringin vattir in ane stop in the mornyn to mes and lycht to the samyn and he sal haf x^s by his fee for the lychtting of the candillis.

The quhilk day Williem Cowpar enterit to his gildfredome be resone of Dauid Cowpar his fadir brodir for the spice and the wyne and sworne thar to.

[*Fo. 38*]

    Curia tenta gilde per Villemum Blakwod decanum et confratres eiusdem xxvj Maij anno j^m v^c xliij.

The quhilk day Willieme Wilsone enterit to the gildfredome be resone of his wif Elizabeth Hutone his wif as air to [*deleted*: his] hir fadir Johne Hutone for the spice and the wyne and sworne tharto.

The quhilk day Andro Raid hes promittit to mak ane sufficient merchand bill agane this day viij dais to gif Alexander Stewart of his xxx lib. wareynne in Danskyne and for the wrangus intromytting tharwytht to tak the said Alexanderis monye becaus he is nocht ane fremane the said Andro is put hyme in the dene of gildis will and the bredyr.

    x^o Junij anno Domini v^c xliij curia tenta in pretorio burgj de Dunfermling per Vilemum Blakwod decanum etc.

The quhilk day Alexander Stevart and Andro Reyd wes baytht svorne to bid at the deliuerans of the merchandis and gildbrethir concernyng the some of the said xxx lib. to be warit in Danskyne is it is contenit in the saidis Andro Reidis obligatioune markit wyt his merchand mark.

The quhilk day the gildbredir and merchandis hes deliuerit be thar conuencience that Andro Rayd sall gif to Alexander Stewart for his monye ilk mark Spruce lent in Danskyne haymwert to be pait to the said Alexander in Scotland x^s Scotis the some of his monye in Danskyne

extendis to lxxv markis Spruce and delivis the said
Andro to pay to the said Alexander xxxvij lib x^S alanerlie
and this our deliuerans and finall sentens al in ane
woc and findis the saidis Andro his merchandis billis
of na effect.

> Curia gilde tenta per Vilemum Blakwod decanum
> et confratres xx^{mo} die mensis Octobris anno
> Domini j^{mo} v^c xliij^o.

The quhilk Jame Skynner and Marke Leichman was accusit
for the biing of roch scheip skynnis, quhilk thai put
thaim in wil and thai war remittit, and to forbeir in
tymmis tocum vndir the payne of ane vnlaw of x^S and
to escheit the gair tharby, excepand that thai by the
skynis for viij^d.
The quhilk day Johne Pavtoune was dischargit of
xxix^S ix^d of his [deleted: gild siluir] for his enteres,
quhilk was allovit for Gavan Lausone in anno xlj^o.

[Fo. 38v]

The quhilk day Villeme Fergusoune enterit gild brodir be
resoune of James Fergusone his fadir and suorne tharto
and to gif the spice and wyne was he beis requirit.

The quhilk Laurens Davgles enterit gild brodir for 1^S and
pait tharof x^S and to pay the laiff at the wil of the dene
and bredir and tharapone was suorne thairto.

The quhilk day Dauid Blakwod was licient to ws to by
and sell Danskyne wair for ane yeir, he giffand ane
pund of wax to the Haly Blud altar.

The quhilk day Tome Hwtoune was accusit for bying of
hidis and occupying of the gild fredome [deleted: the dene]
and he confessit this sammyn. The dene of gild and the
bredir hes forgevyn hym this falt and in tymmis tocum
he hes bund hyme to forbeir and gif he beis fundyng
occupying the fredome he sall pay xl^S vn forgevyne.

> Vigilia Sancti Tome.
>
> Curia gilde tenta in pretorio burgi de Dunferm-
> ling per Villelmum Blakwod decanum xx^o die
> mensis Decembris anno j^m v^c xliij.

The quhilk day Tome Dalglesh wes maid dene of gild and
svorne tharto for ane yeir and Lourens Fergusone kirk-
mastir for ane yeir and svorne thairto.

> Curia gylde tenta in pretorio burgi de Dun-
> fermlyn per Jhonne Patone decanum xxviij day
> mensys Maij anno Domini j^m v^c xlix.

The quhilk day the dayne off gyld and gyld brether

quitclamys and dischargis Maistir Johne Spens and Valtir Baxstar off thayr haill gyld sylvers and the said Jhonne Patone daynie off gyld grantis me veill content and payet off the said Maistir Jhone Spens and Valtir Baxstar gyld sylvers and the said Maistir Jhone and Valtir Baxstar bendis thayne to inbryng all the gyld sylvers restand one payet, and that the dayne off gyld sall poynd the saidis persons abone vrityne faylyeand that the said gyld syluer beis not payet withtin v owks eftir the dait heir off.

[*Fo. 39*]

The gáddiris of the kirk lycht anno j^m v^c xliij.

Januar
V Wallud
Jo Smyt
Februar
Lo Fergusone
Ro Wilsone
Marche
David Devar
Robert Spens
Aprill
Jo Paltoun ?
Jo Duncane ? Smytht
Maye
V Blakwod elder
Jo Keyr
Junij
V Blakwod
Ja Morray
Julij
Jo Moltrar
Jo Burne ? in the Corss
August
Ro Fergusone
Ja Dulye
September
V Wilsone
Da Vakar
Octobir
To Dalgliesh
Jo Pottar
Nouember
V Cowpar
Riche Quhitsone
December
To Gourlay
R Gray

It is statut that quha absentis thame selfis and gaddiris nocht in thar moneth sal pay v^s sa that thai be lauchfully varnit and gif he that gadirit afor warnis hym nocht and gafin the bill fra hym quhen his moneth is done sal pay v^s and quhen the lycht is gaddirit and the moneth is done sal [*deleted* : pay] put in his siluir in the box and ane tykkat wytht it vndir the pane of v^s.

[*Fo. 39v*]

Vigilia Sancte Thome viz. xxiij Decembris anno Domini j^m v^c xl quarto.
The quhilk day Mastir Andro Stevart vas maid dene of the gyld for ane yeir and suorne.
The quhilk day Villeme Blakwod was maid kyrk mastir and suorn tharto.

[*in margin* : nota] The quhilk day the aldirmane Johne Hacheid the deyne of the gyld and the laiff of the gild breidir hes statut and ordanit that nan mane be enterit gild brodir bot he sal pay fyf markis.

The quhilk it is statut that na man occupy thair fredome bot thai that is fre, and gif ony occupiis that is nocht qualifeit he sal pay yeirly to the deyn of the gild and the bredir xiij^s iiij^d, and he sal nocht by hyd skyne nor woll nor stapill gud vndir the payne of eschating of thair gudis.

[*in margin*: gild-brodir] The quhilk Adam Blakwod was maiid gyld brodir for fyf markis and suorne tharto and pait the samyn in hand gevin to the kyrk in vax.

The quhilk day the dene and the gildbrethir hes gevin xl^s to the kyrk for lycht becaus the offerent is fevir.

[*Fo. 40*]

[*deleted* : Vigilia Sancte Tho] Sabbato viz Decembris anno Domini j^{mo} v^c xl quinto.
Curia tenta per Magistrum Andream Stevart decanum de gilde.
The quhilk day Markye Leisman grantit in jugisment that he bocht thre scheip skynnis opinlie at the market cors and grantit he had maid ane falt and put hym in will and oblist him nocht to do the samyn vndir the payne of eschating of the samyn that happinnis to be bocht withtin our fredome.

Thir ar the naymes that hes occupiit the fredome as eftir follovis quhilk suld pay xiij^s iiij^d ilk persone eftir the tenor of ane act maid tharapon.
James Nevman–xiij^s iiij^d pait in wax to Johne Multray.
Gilbert Martynne–xiij^s iiij^d pait to the dene and the bredir in wax to Jo Multray.
Peter Movbray–xiij^s iiij^d pait to the dene of the gild and the bredir.

The lycht gaddiris that hes brocht in the samyn.

James Duly } xxiij^s vj^d.
Villeme Covpir
Adam Brand iiij^s v^d.
Robert Spens vij^s.
James Balfour xxvij^s.
Schir Thomas Malcum for Schir Johne Cristisone v^s iij^d.
Jo. Pottar ij^s ix.
Johne Multray [deleted: restis his yet] quhilk is iij^s pait.
Jo. Duncane half ane pund of vax.
Johne Multray in the Nevraw for ane land of his iij^s.

[Fo. 40v]

The gild court haldin in the tolbutht of Dunfermlyn be Mastir Andro Stevart dene of the gild and the laif of the gild bredir the xxiij day of December the yeir of God j^m v^c xlv yeiris.

The quhilk day Johne Keyr was maid gild brodir for fyf markis and pait twa markis in hand, and to pay the tothir xl^s quhen he is requirit. And attour the said Johne sal nocht vs merchandis vtoutht the burg nor his airis bot as the laif of the brodir dois, and giff he dois the contrar he is contentit and his airis to be dischargit of the fredome and apone this hes maid faitht.

The quhilk Johne Keyr was maid kyrk mastir and suorne thairto.

The quhilk day Schir Villeme Mason was maid [deleted:child] to lycht the kyrk and [deleted: and opyn the dur] steik the dur and lycht the lamp and put furtht the samyn and lycht the samyn at evinsang all tymmis as vs and wont is and keip the candillis. For the quhilkis he sal haif xviij^s of fe for ane yeir. And attour thai haf gevin hym v^s of the lycht siluir. And attour thai haif ordand hym to pas nyxt the queyr in all processees and to haif messis.

xv^{to} die mensis Nouembris anno etc. xlvj^{to}.

The quhilk day Thomas Davgles was maid dene of the gyld for ane yeir and suorne tharto.

The quhilk day Adam Blakwod put hyme in will to the dene off gyld and bredir of his wrangus that hes dovne in resauing of one framenis gudis and vthir faltis that he hes dovne.

[Fo. 41]

xxiij die mensis Junij anno j^m v^c xlvij.

Curia gilde tenta per Dauid Dewar decanum et confratres etc.

The quhilk day Gilbert Martyne cum in to will to the gildbredir for the occupying of the fredome for thir twa yeris bipast for the quhilk thai declarit thair will and hes ordant hyme to pay ij markis and in tymmys to cum thai haif ordand hyme to desist wndir the pane of xl^s.

The quhilk day James Newman James Schortus Villiame Andirsone ilk ane of thame xiij^s iiij^d for thar occupying of the fredom and to desist in tymis to cum vndir the pane of xl^s, but apone the mercat day. And siclik thai ordand Williame Wilsoune to desist fra occupying of the fredome bot thai will ourse hyme quhill Lammes nyxtocum.

xxvj day of Octobar anno j^m v^c xlvij.

Curia gilde tenta per Dauid Dewar decanum et confratres.

The quhylk day dane of gyld and gyldbredir hes decretit and ordand Welyem Nockhal and Lowrens Daugles to pay ilk of thaim xiij^s iiij^d for the entrometting wytht onfremen gudis and fra syne fourtht gyf ony gylbredir entrometis wytht ony onfreman gudis he sall be disschargit of his fredom of gyldre.

[Fo. 41v]

Vigilia Sancti Thome viz die mensis Decembris anno Domini j^{m}v^{c}xlvij^o.

The quhilk day Johne Pavtoune was chosin dene of gilde be the bredir of the tovne for ane yeir and suorne.
The quhilk day Alexander Stevinsone was enterit gild brodir be resone of Andro Gerwes his grantschir and suorne thairto, and to pay the spice and the wynne.
The quhilk day Jonet Martyne deliuerit to Johne Pavtoune dene of the gild four [deleted: lib] for [deleted: hyr fadir] Gilbert Martyne hyr fadir gild siluir.
The quhilk day Jonet Martyne i[d est] dochtir to vmquhill Gilbert Martyn was enterit to hyr fadiris fredome.
The quhilk day Johne Cristy enterit gild brodir be resone of Jonet Martyne his vif and was suorne thairto.
The quhilk day James Shorthus [deleted : Vilsone] was enterit gild brodir for fif markis and to pay the samyn quhen he beis requirit.
The quhilk day the dene of the gild and the gild bredir decernit that na man resait Peter Movbry nor his gayr

withtin the tovne ay and quhill he mak amendis for the missaving [sic] of Robert Ferguson balye sayand in jugsment that and he had hym at the tovne and he wald nocht deny na thing he said quhilk was preiffit that he wald nocht gif ij peccis of draf for thair fredome of gildre and dispicit the haill gild bredir at his collatione and vthiris plaicis, and wald nocht mak amendis till nathir of thame bot to [deleted: Robert] Laurens Fergusone.

The quhilk day Villeme Vilsone was maid gild brodir for four markis and tothir xiij^s iiij^d gevin quit for resonable causs and to pay the saidis four markis quhen he beis requirat at thair will.

[Fo. 42]

The court haldin be Johne Pavtoune dene of the gild witht the gild bredir the xxviij day of the monetht of Januar the yeir of God j^m v^c xlvij yeiris.

The quhilk day the actioune persevit be Villeme Vilsone youngar aganis Villeme Vilsone eldar anent vj stane of and ane halff of Spruice stanis of lynt, the quhilk was put to the knavleige of the said bredir the parteis beand present and put the samyn to thame quhat suld be dovne thairintill thai removit furtht of court. The said dene of the gild and the bredir decernit that Villeme Vilsoune eldar sall deliuer to the said Villeme Vilsone youngar vj Spruice stanis and ane half as it was markit to hym in Danskyn withtin aucht dais, failyeand thairof that he deliuer nocht the samyn lynt he sal pay als mekill mony for euirilk stane as he the said Villeme eldar sald his avin and vthiris nychtbouris and the payment to be maid in Dunfermlyn as said is.

[Fo. 42v]

The gyld court haldin be Johne Pavtoun dene of the gyld the xxvij day of the monetht of October the yeir of God j^m v^c xlviij yeiris witht the laif of the gyld bredir.

The quhilk day Patrik Hacheid was maid gyld brodir be resone of Johne Hacheid his fadir and suorne tharto for the spice and the wyne.

The quhilk day comperit in jugisment Mastir Johne Spens and was maid gyld brodir for iiij lib and of the samyn xl^{tjs} pait in hand and suorne thairto.

The quhilk day Thomas Stevart was maid gyld brodir for iiij lib and pait thairof xl^s and suorne tharto and to pay the samyn betuix this and Candilmes.

The quhilk day the dene of the gyld and the laif of the bredir hes [deleted: consentit] decernit and decretit that nay mane sal be enterit fra this day furt gyld brodir withtout he haf heretaige and [deleted: gudis and] at he haif at the leist j c lib in land and gudis and siluir qualifeit in his persone. And gif ony pass of the tovne and wil nocht remayne he sal pay [deleted: x lib] to the profit of the tovne as the bredir thinkis expedient and the nychtbouris hes dischargit the said x lib bot he that pass furtht sal tyne his fredome and quhen he cumis agane to be fre.

The quhilk day Waltir Baxster enterit gyld brodir for iiij lib and suorne thairto, and of that pait xl^s in hand and to pay the tothir xl^s quhen he beis requirat.

The quhilk day Johne Vilsone enterit gyld brodir be resone of his fadir Robert Vilsone his fadir for the spice and the wyne and suorne thairto.

[Fo. 43]

The gyld court haldine be Jhonne Patone daine of gyld Mastir Jhonne Spens Valtir Baxstar bailyes in yere off God j^m v^c xlviij and the xxiij day of December [deleted: witht the] laiff off the gild brether.

The quhilk day the dane off gild the baylyes and gild brether hes statuite ordinet x off the gild brethere to be sworne jlk ane for thayme self that is maist convenient thayr for to ws consult and set opone all ecsyons baytht for the weill off the gildys and commond weill off the towne, that js to say Patry[k ? folio obscured] Hecket prov- est Jhonne Patone dene off the gild Maistir Jhonne Spens Valtir Baxstar bailyes Williem Cwpir hed dekyne Jhonne Keir kerk maistir Thomas Stewart Robert Fergeson Thomas Dowgleis Larence Dowglis Larence Fergesone.

The court haldin be Johne Pavtoune dene of the gild and the laif of the bredir the xxvj day of Januar the yeir of God j^m v^s xlviij yeiris.

The quhilk day the dene of the gild and the laif of the bredir thai ar to say Master Johne Spens Valtir Baxster balyeis Thomas Stevart Robert Fergusone Laurens Fergusone Dauid Devar Johne Cristy and diuers vthiris hes thocht expedient that euiry gild brodir that enteres fre sal pay for the spice and the wyne vj^s viij^d. And thai haif fund thair sovmis vndir writin restand avand. Item in the first for the gild brethir that ar enterit befor extendis to the sovme of tuenty thre pundis ix^s. And for thame that is enterit fre cumis to xlvj ^{s} viij^d. Item in vnlais avand as eftir follovis, in the first Andro Burne for vsing of the fredoume of the said gildis sal pay xiij^s iiij^d. [deleted: and] Item Adam Blakwod Villeme Nicholl and [deleted: Thoma] Laurens Davgles jlkane of thame in ane vnlaw of xiij ^{s} iiij ^{d} for the occuping and bringin hame of on fre menis gudis. The hail sovme of all togyddir xxviij lib ix^s.

The quhilk day Andro Valcar was enterit gild brodir be resoune of Villeme Valcar his fadir and suorne thairto.

[Fo. 43v]

The quhilk day Jhone Keyr kerkmastir maid his count befor the bailyes and lycht gatherrys in the yere of God j^m v^c xlvij and xlviij and he restis awne to the towne xij^s and ane hepne.

> Curia gilde tenta in pretorio burgi de Dunfermling ix die mensis Februarij anno Domini j^m v^c xlviij^o quo die per Patricium [deleted: Johne] Pavtoune decanum de gilde [deleted: Johannem] Hacheid prepositum Magistrum Johannem Spens Valterum Baxster balliuos et ceteri confratres etc.

The quhilk day comperit in jugsment Villeme Hwyme enterit gild brodir for v lib and suorne thairto.
The quhilk day comperit in jugsment James Loich and was maid gil brodir for fif pundis quhen he beis requirit and suorne tharto.
The quhilk day James Berkar was maid gyld brodir for fif pundis and suorne thairto.

> Curia gyld tenta in pretorio burgi de Dunfermeling the secund day off Marche anno Domini j^m v^c xlviij yeris.

The quhilk day comperit in jugisment James Hwyme enteryt gild brother for v lib and suorne tharto.
The quhilk comperyt in jugsment Androwne Sandis enteryt gyld brother for v lib and suorne tharto.

> Curia gilde tenta in pretorio burgi de Dunfermling per Johannem decanum de gilde xxiij^o die mensis anno Domini j^{mo} v^c xlviij^o.

The quhilk day Patrik Loch was maid gild brodir and suorne thairto for v lib.

> Curia gilde tenta in pretorio burgi de Dunfermlyng per Johannem Pawittan decanum de gilde Julii mensis anno Domini j^{mo} v^c xlviij^o.

[Fo. 44]

The compereyt in jugment Vattir Baxter baylye one the taine part and Thomas Dowgleys one the owdir part anent the byeine of sertene wud bocht be the said Vattir fray the said Thomas. It was fownd be the dene of gyld and gyld brethur that the said Wattir faylleyt in hys day the quhylk was refferyt to Thomas Dawgles richt and say the said Thomas mecht dyspoine one hys wald to quhome he playssyt.

Curia [deleted: tenta] gilde tenta in pretorio burgi de Dunfermling per Thomas Stevart decanum de gilde xx^o die mensis Decembris anno Domini j^m v^c xlix^o.

The quhilk day Thomas Stevart was maid dene of gyld be ane interlocutour of the court and suorne thairto.

Curia gilde tenta in pretorio burgi de Dunfermlyn per Thomas Stevart decanum de gilde xxiij^o die mensis Decembris anno Domini j^m v^c xlix^o.

The quhilk day Thome Stevinsone was maid [deleted: den] gild brodir for v lib and Thomas Davgles and Laurens Davgles coniunctly and seueraly that he sal pay the samyn quhen euir the dene of the gyld requirit the samyn withtin aucht dais apon the quhilkis was suorne tharto and payit of this c^s. Restis 1^s and pay to Johne Bosuell and lent to the bygyn of the towbutht.

[Fo. 44v]

Curia gilde tenta pretorio Dunfermling per Thomas Stewart decanum de gilde xxiiij die mensis Decembris anno Domini j^m v^c xlix^o.

The quhilk day comperit in jugement Waltir Baxtar to answer to the clame of Lowrens Fergesone anent certan wad the said Wattir bocht fra the said Lowrens drawand to the sovme of xj lib xiij^s vj^d the quhilk was gifin to the said Lowrens preif quhyll gif the said Wattir suld haif payit the said Lowrens the said sovme or nocht at Sanct Andros day passit. The quhilk day it wes found be honest men that is say Jhone Pattoun Lawrens Dawgles James Schortoris Thomas Dawgles that the said Wattir suld pay the said sovme to Lawrens Fergeson. The same day answerit Wattir Baxtar to Thomas Dawgles clame anent ane quarter pak of wod than the said Thomas [deleted: alyegit] referrit to the said Wattiris aith quhydder the said quartir pak pertenit to the said Thomas and wes coft be the said Thomas awn money or nocht and the said

Wattir tuk ane day to be adwysit witht his aytht.

The quhilk day wes found be the dene of gild and gild brethir that Willyam Wilsone schew the consaill done and said in the court eftir he passit furtht of the tolbutht and the said Willyam is in wode for the said falt.

The quhilk day it is acit be the dene and gildbrethir that in tymes to cum na gild brothir sall reweill thar consaill vndir the pane of tynsaile of thar fredome for ane yeyr.

[Fo. 45]

Item Wille Andirsone for vsing of the fredome xxvj^s viij^s payit.
Item Moris Pacok [deleted: xiij^s iiij^d] vj^s viij^d to Jhone Keyr.
Item Georg Werkman vj^s viij^d to Jhone Keyr.
Item Nycholl Hendresone xiij^s iiij^d to Jhone Keyr.
Item Sande Nycoll and Nycoll Bad iiij^s iiij^d payit to Jhone Keyr.
Item Rechmont ij^s payit xvj^d.

  Curia gilde tenta pretorio Dunfermlyng per Thomas Stewart decanum de gilde xvij^o die mensis Januarij in anno j^m v^c xlix yeyris.

The quhilk day Waltir Baxtar wald nocht swere bot the quarter pok of wald pertenit to Thomas Dawgles quharfor it wes fund that the said Waltir suld pay the said Thomas for the said wald extending to the sovme of xxx^s and the said sovme payit.

The quhilk day Laurens Fergusone and Waltir Baxtar maid compt and reking of all thingis betwex thaim to that day and the said Waltir hes maid payment to the said Laurens of all dettis by passit and dischargis the said Waltir as said before the dait heyrof.

[Fo. 45v]

  The court haldin in the tolbuth of Dunfermlyng the xxij day of Januar the yeyre of God j^m v^c xlix yeris be dene of gild and gild brethir.

The quhilk day comperit Willyam Makcum cordynar and wes found be the brethir that he bocht hydis by the statutis and akis maid of befor and his said hydis maid eschet and the said Willyam cum in will of the brethir and thair will declarit that the said Willyam sall pay xiij^s iiij^d the quhilk is payit be him.

[*in margin*: nota] The quhilk day all the cordynaris of the burgh wes warnit to compere and wald nocht obey be ressone thaj were gilty and brokin the actis afor mayd. Tharfor it wes found be the brethir that the bark pottis of the cordynaris suld be condemnyt and closit on to the tyme thaj compere afor the brethir and the falt punyst.
The quhilk day Waltir Baxtar clamet Lawrens Dowglas of ane barell of ass and was found be the brethir that the said Lawrens awit nane to the said Waltir and be ressone that Thomas Stewinsone was i.e. merchant to the said Waltir and found thirto the said Thomas suld mak rekin of the said ass to Waltir Baxtar and contynewit quhill the cumming of Thomas Wallat afor the dene and brethir.

> The court haldyne be Thomas Stevart den off the gyld Patrik Hacheid prowest and the laif of the gild brethir the [*blank*] day of Januar the yeir of God j^m v^c xlix yeiris.

[*Fo. 46*]

The quhilk day it is decernit be the said dene of the gild and all the laif of the bredir, that all the suttaris and cordinaris withtin the said burg that ony of thaim to presuyme to by ony rouch hydis and syne to sel thaim vndir the payne of eschaeting of the samyn, nor yet bertour thame, bot throw tollerans to berk samony to staik thame selffis to sel withtin the tovne [*addition*: for ane yeir] and that becaus thair is na gild bredir berkaris now presently in the tovne.

The quhilk day it is decernit be the forsaid dene of the gild prowest [*?text obscured*] and gyld bredir that na flessour sal by ony hyd or skyne nor yit to sel ony bot to [*deleted*: offer] fremen that is gildis, and to offer the samyn to thame or thai sel thaim furtht of the tovne and sufficient vitnes tayne thairapone that thai refuess the samyn, vndir the payne of eschaitting of the samyn.

The quhilk day it is decernit be the dene of the gild prowest and bredir forsaid that na landward man cum to the mercat wytht ony carrhaige or best withtout he bring the hyd and skyn witht the best vndir the payne fforr the first tyme of ane vnlaw, the secund tym to pay ane muttoune bowik and to be punyst vthiris wais at the wil of the den of the gild, and that [*deleted*: is] becaus it is murmurit that the bestis ar stovin.

The quhilk day is decernyt that [*deleted*: Willyem] Nychell

Hendersone sall pay for his unlaw vj^s viij^d.

[*Fo. 46v*]

The court haldin in the tolbuth of Dunfermling the yeir of God j^m v^c xlix yeiris the xv day of [*deleted*: Januar] Februar be Thomas Stewart dene of gild witht the laift of the gild brethir.

The quhilk day Jhone Pattoun gaif ane claym of certane hydis to the nomer of vij daikar iij hydis apone Robert Fergesone.

The same day Robert Fergesone grantit that he wes merchant to the said Jhone and sald and schipit waris for the said geyr in Flandreiss in the toun of Handwart as he allegeit.

The quhilk day Robert Fergusone tuk to preif that the forsaid gudis and gayr was schippit in the tyme he lay in Flanderis in presoune and thareftir that the empriour dovaris intromittit witht the said gair and rovpit the samyn in the tovne of Handwerp to the vs and profit of the empriour quhilk thai disponit tharapone.

The quhilk day Robert Fergusone grantit in the jugsment that he sald fife dakerris of hydis and schippit the samyn to Villeme Vilsone behuff in likwis and tuk to preif the samyn that it was rovpit and dysponit in Handwerp to the empriour vss and thair markis wes apon the samyn gudis and gayr.

The court haldyne in the tolbuitht of Dunfermling be Patrik Haicheid prowest and the den of the gild brethren the awcht day of Julij j^m v^c and fyftye yeiris. [*in margin*: and be Thomas Stevart den of gild and Robert Murray bailye].

The quhilk day it is conprommittit betwix Maister Johne Spens and Thomas Stewart on the tanepart and Jhone Criste on the tothir part in maner as followis. The said parteis hes equaly chosin in all debettable materis concernyng the wayage maid be the said Johne Cristye in the esteir seyis the said parteis hes chosyne four men to aggre thaim wytht in a xv dayis the fowr men to deliuer and failyeand that thaj can nocht agre to haif power to cheiss ane owrman and to prolonge the day one vthir xv dayis gif nid be.

[*Fo. 47*]

The said parteis hes chosyne for the part of Maister Johne Spens and Thomas Stewart Thomas Daugleiss and Dawid Dewar for thair part. And Johne Crystye hes chosyne for

his part Lore Fargisoun and Vilyem Coupir the fowr men
beand sworn befor the prowest and Robert Murray bailye
till deliuer trewly as sayid is and als the said parteis
sik lyik ar sworne to abyid at the four menis deliuerans.

  The [*deleted*: quhilk day] court haldin in the
tolbut of Dunfermlyng be the dene of gild and
Maister Jhone Spens bailye witht the laif of gild
brethir in the yeyre of God j^m v^c l yeyris.

The quhilk day wes dissyrnyt be the gild brethir that
Wattir Baxtar suld pay to Robert Fergesonis wyf for
cont and reknyn wes betwex the said Robert and Wattir
the sovme of fyfty v^s to be payit jnstantlie. And gif the
said Wattir hes ony thing to lay to the said Robertis wyf
scho sall ansver afor the dene of gild and brethir as law
wil.

The quhilk day was found be the dene of gild and bruthir
that Dauid Brandis wif James Newmans wyf that thaj haif
done wrang in sellyng of wyne and hes condemnyt jlk ane
of thaim in xx^s of ane vnlaw for the fyrst falt and
xl^s the nyxt and the thryd the ponychone aschet. Gif ony
vthiris vss saklyk fredome as pertenyis the gilde [*deleted* :
fredom] sall vndirly the same wnlawis.

[*Fo. 47v*]

  The court haldan in the tolbuth of Dunfermlyn the
viij day Novembere the yeyr of God j^m v^c l yeyris
be the provest dene of gild and bailyeis witht
the gild brethir.

The quhilk day Dene Jhone Bosvell sacrestane of Dun-
frmlyng enterit gild brothir for the spis and the wyne be
ressone of his predessour [*sic*] and sworne tharto.

The quhilk day the provest dene of gild and bailyeis
witht consent of the haill brethir hes chusing Schir
Alexandere Aitkyne gild prest and to gif him yeirlie for
his fe tene markis and to be payit at four termes in the
yeyr, that is to say Candillmes ij markis and half at
Beltane ij markis and half Lammes ij markis and half at
Hallowmes ij markis and half and this enduring our will
eftir his gud seruice. And siklyk the provest hes
prom[est ? *folio torn*] him ane mark and the secrestane
ane vthir mark to be payit a[t ? *folio torn*] sam termes.

The quhilk day James Daly wes enterit gild brothir for
v lib and sworne tharto Maister Jhone Spens souerte for
the sowne quhen he is requyirit and the said James to
releif him payit of this 1^s.

[Fo. 48]

The court haldin in the tolbuth of Dunfermling be the provest dene of gild bailyeis witht the gild brethir the xxvij day of Januare the yeyre of God j^m v^c fifty yeyris.

[*in margin* : nota] The quhilk day it is statut and ordanit be the provest dene of gild and balyes witht the haile gild brethir that na merchand by nothir hyd nore skyn of thairis that is slane in the olk that the four gild brothir fallis to haif ondir the pane of escheting of the hyd and skyne that he byis and gifin to thaim that hes the olk as is specefeit in the act maid of befor. And attour gif ony flessour saltis his hidis and makis his skynis thaj sall be coft fra the said flessouris be the dene of gild and payrtit equaly amang the gild brethir as euiry man debursis his money, and siklyk quhat persone that bryngis othir hyd or skyne to the toun that na man by thaim bot thaj that hes thair olk, and siklyk that na man withtin the borch that takis ony merchandis to landwart to sell and thaj by ony skynis or hydis [*deleted*: thai sall] witht-in a myl or maris thaj sall br[? *folio torn*] thaim to the ane that hes the olk ondir the pane of escheing of the same.

The quhilk day Dauid Wilsone wes enterit gild brothir for v lib and sworne thairto payit 1^s. Restis 1^s.

The gild court halding in the tolbuth of Dunfermling be dene of gild and bailyes witht the gild brethir the xiiij day of Februar the yeyr j^m v^c l yeris.

[Fo. 48v]

The quhilk day it is found be the dene of gild and bruthir that Willyam Wilson sall haif four lib ij^s for thre cronis of the some that the said Willyam deliuerit to Jhone Somerwell to haif wairit conformand to his merchant bill fond witht him in Danskyne the quhilk the said Jhone warit nocht as the said Willyam ordanit him. And for that causs it is ordanit that the said Jhone sall gif x^s for the mark to the said Willyam as vs is.

The quhilk day it is decernit be the dene of gild and brethir that Willyam Cowpire sall pay to Jhone [*deleted*: Willyam] Wilsone for the lynt the said Willyam coft fra him quhilk extendis to v lib xvj^s vj^d, iij lib in hand and the rest betwex this and mydsummir, and siklyk to pay to the said Jhone for fraucht xlj^s to be payit now instantlie.

The gild court haldin in the tolbuth of Dunfermlyne the [*blank*] day of Aprill be the dene of gild and balyeis witht the laif of the brethir.

The quhilk day Thomas Dawgles wes found be the brethir
that he faltit to the dene of gild in his speking in jugement and be interloquitour cum in will [deleted: of] to the
dene of gild and hes declarit his will that gif the said
Thomas dois sik ane falt in tyme to cum to the dene of
gild he sall pay the gret unlaw oneforgifine.

[Fo. 49]

The quhilk day the dene of gild balyeis and gild brethir
hes gafin to my lord Robene Hud all the prewelegis and
wnlawis that fallis in his tyme witht the the [sic] gild siluir that entres in the said tyme.

The quhilk day Maister Georg Hakat enterit gild brethir
be ressune of his Robene Hud schip and put in the
commone purs xxiij^S, and is sworne tharto.

The gild court haldin in the tolbuth of Dunfermling be the
dene of gild and bailyeis witht the gild brethir the
[blank] day of Aprill the yeyr of God j^m v^c lj yeyris.

The quhilk day Jhone Prateris wes enterit gildbrothir fe
fyv lib and sworne tharto, payit to Robyne Hud.
The quhilk day Jhone Cowane wes enterit gild brothir fyv
lib and sworne tharto, payit to l[deleted: Roben Hud.]
The quhilk day Jhone Andersone wes enterit gild brothir
for fyv lib and sworne thairto payit to
And siklyk Jone oblyst him self that he sall nocht vs na
slauchttir of scheip nor cattell nor na vthir handling of
flesch except the brekin and takin of the skyne and gif
he dois the contrare he sall tyne his fredome.
The quhilk day James Balfour wes enterit gildbrothir
for fyf lib and sworne tharto and payit tharfor.
The quhilk day Andro Horne wes enterit gild brothir for
fyf lib. and sworne tharto, and payit tharfor.

[Fo. 49v]

The quhilk day Alexandere Kellok wes enterit gild bruthir
for fyv lib and sworne tharto, and payit tharfor.
The quhilk day Robert Spens wes enterit gild brothir for
fyf lib and sworne tharto, and payit tharfor.
The quhilk day Jhone Smytht wes enterit gild brothir for
fyv lib and sworne tharto, and payit tharfor.
The quhilk day Jhone Pottar wes enterit gild brothir for
fyv lib and sworne tharto, and payit tharfor.

The gild [deleted: brethir] court haldin in the tolbuth of
Dunfermling be the provest dene of gild and bailyeis,
witht certane of the gild brethir the xxiij day of May

the yeyre of God j^m v^c lj yeire.
The quhilk day Jhone Peyrsone wes enterit gild brothir for fyv lib and sworne tharto, and payit tharfor.
The quhilk Jhone Aslone wes enterit gild brothir for fyv lib and sworne tharto, and payit tharfor.
The quhilk day the provest dene of gild and bailyeis affermiis and ratefeis all thir gild brethir that is enterit heyre togiddir and to defend the same in thair prewalegis of gildschip, thaj vsaid thaim self as honeste gild brethir sauld do, eftir the statut and actis onand of befor.

[Fo. 50]

The gild court haldin in the tolbuth of Dunfermling be the dene of gild witht the laif of the gild brethir the x day of Octobere the yeyr of God j^m v^c lj yeyr.

The quhilk day Jhone Bosvell wes enterit gild brothir for v lib, and sworne tharto. Payit to the dene of gild [? text obscured] payit 1^s. Rastis 1^s.

The gild court haldin in the tolbuth of Dunfermling be the dene of gild bailyeis and gild brethir the foirt day of Novembr [deleted: November October] the yeyr of God j^m v^c lj yeyre.

The quhilk day Robert Murray wes found ane vnlaw to pay ane pund of wax to the altar for his absens beand teichit witht the gild serieand.

The gild court of Dunfermlyng haldyne in the towbuytht of the same be Thomas Stewart dene of the gild brethyr the fift day of December the yeir of God j^m v^c fifty ane yeir.

The quhilk day Johne Boswell was attechit and acclamyt for 1^s for the makyng of James Hwtone gild at wmquhill Robert Fergussone become suurte for the said dene of gild assignit the said John the xx day of Youll nixt tocum, othyr to pay the same or ellis to preiff it pait to the dene of gild and gild brethyr, to the quhilk the said John grantit.

[Fo. 50v]

The gild court hadin in the tolbutht of Dunfermling the xv day of Decembere the yeyre of God j^m v^c lj yeyre be the dene of gild and brethir.

The quhilk day Jhone Cristeson actit to Willyam Nycoll that he sall deliuer to the said Willyam in Danskin xij

faddome of tow and xvj ellis of pakin canwes or to ony
in his name the fyrst that passi[s? *text obscured*] thair or
ellis the awaile tharoff quhilk is xxiiij ^{S}. And this to be
payit to the said Willyam gif the said Jhone deliu[eris?:*text
obscured*] nocht the towis and pakin claytht or caus it
be deliuerit to him of his factouris.

      Sanct Thomas ewin.
The lytis chosine and set furtht be the provest bailyeis
and gild brethir thaj ar to say

   Watir Baxtar   Willyam Fergesone
   Jjhone Boswell
   Lawrens Dawgles
   Jhone Patting

The quhilk day Jhone Bosvell wes chosine dene of the
gild for ane yeyre sworne tharto.

The geld cort hadin in the tolbothe of Dunfer[lyng ?
text obscured] be the prowest Johne Bosuell dene of the
geld and balyeis witht the laif of the gyld brethir the
xvij day of December the yeir of God j^m v^c fyftie and ane
yeir.

The quhilk day the dene of the geld and brether hes
statut and ordenit that euiry gyld brothir beand in the
towne and warniit to the gyld cort and beis absent sall
pay xvj^d of ownlay and thaim that vas obsent this day
thar onlayis to tain oneforgein.

[*Fo. 51*]

The quhilk day the dene of the gyld and gyld brethir be
interlocutour of hes ordand Lorrens Fargesone to pay
to Johne Andersone x^S for [? *text obscured*] the hert of
ane best be the serwandis of the said Lowrens.

  The gyld cort haldin in the towboutht of Dunfermlyng be Johne Bosuell dene of the gyld Thomas
  Stewart balye witht the laif of the gyld brethir
  the secund day of Januar in the yeir of God
  j^m v^c lj yeir.

The quhilk day Johne Keir keirkmaister hes maid his
cowmpt of the keirk lycht and all expens allouit to hym
maid one the kerk wax and all othir expens. Restis awand
to the said Johne the sowme off xvij^S [? *text obscured*] de-
claro etc.

  The gyld cort haldin in the towlboutht of Dunfermlyng be the deine of the gyld and balyeis and
  gyld brothir the xv day of Janewar in the yeir

of God j^m v^c lj yeir.

The quhilk day William Cowpir and James Schorthus wes put in agreence for ewill wordis elk ane to othir fund be the brethir quhat brethir misperssonis othir in tyme cumyng the iniuri [?] of ewill wordis sall pay ij pund of wax to the altar one forgawin.

> The gyld cort haldin in the tolbuotht of Dunfermlyng be Johne Bosuell dene of the gyld Thomas Stewart and Wilyeame Walwod balyeis witht the laif of gyld brethir the xv day of Januar in the yeir of God j^m v^c lj yeir.

The quhilk day Thomas Stewart gaif in his cowmpt of the gyld schiluir gyld anwellis and all thyngis alowit to hym deporsit be the said Thomas. Restis awand to the gylbrethir the sowme of xxviij lib xiij^s viij^d. And the said Thomas and Waltir Baxter hes promest to bryng in the said mony instandlie or thame to pay the gret onlaw.

[Fo. 51v]

The quhilk day Johne Cowane oblest him to pay Thome Stewart or preif hym payit betuex this and this day xv day and seik lyk to pay Thomas Dalglesche the mony the quhilk is awand hyme.

> The gyld cort haldin in the tolbowtht be the dene of the gyld and gyldbrethir the xij day of Fabravar in the yeir of God j^m v^c lj yeir etc.

The quhilk day Henry Glas come in will of the brethir for the wrangus occuhpeyng of the fredowme withtin the towne and in tyme to come that he occupeyng na fredone ondir the pane of the aickis contenet in the buk.

The quhilk day Johne Cowane come dettur to Thomas Dalgles for xxxj^s ix^d to pay hym one the ferst Sounday in Lentrowyn withtout ony proses [deleted: or pundis.]

> The gyld cort haildin in the tolbutht of Dunfermlyng be the dene of the gyld the balyeis gyld brothir the xij day of Marce in the yeir of God j^m v^c lj yeir.

The quhilk day Schir Andro Quhit chapland of Sanct Margretis altar byndis hym self for ane yeir to uphald the sowng mass euiry Mununday at the forsaid altar and he to haif the offarand tharfor.

> The gyld cort haldyne in the tolbuotht of Dunfermlyng be the dene of the gyld and balyeis and gyld brethir the xxvij day of Maij in the yeir of God

j^m v^c lij yeiris.

The quhilk day William Blakcat interit gyld brothir be resonne of his fader William Blakcat for the spyce and the wyne and sworne tharto and Thomas Dalglesche suerte tharfor.

The quhilk day the dene of the gyld and gyld brothir to the nomer of xv brothir condesendit that thair suld nocht na gyld soune nor na othir one fre men tap wyne nor wax nor na othir stapill gudis ondir the pane of the gret onlaw contenet in or acis withtout thai haif lassience of prowest and balyeis and dene of the gyld and xv gyld brethir in tyme to cum eftir the day of this dait.

  The gyld cort haldyne in the towbothe of Dunfermlyng be the dene of the gyld balyeis and gyld brethir the v day of Nowember in the yeir of God j^m v^v lij yeiris.

[Fo. 52]

The quhilk day James Burne enterit gyld brothir for v lib. Payit tharof 1^s. Restis 1^s and to be payit betwex this and Yowll and swarne tharto.

  The gyld cort haldin in the towbothe of Dunfermlyng be the dene of the gyld and gyld brethir the xvij day of Febrear.

The quhilk day Lowrens Dalglische grantit in jugment that he resauit fra Thomas Stewinsoune in name and behauf of Waltir Baxtar iiij lib of ais and dischirgis the said Thomas of the said ass.

  The gyld cort haldyne in the towbuthe of Dunfermlyne be Johne Bosuell den of the gyld and the balyeis ther at Sant Tomas ewin in the yeir of God j^m v^c lij yeiris.

The quhilk day Johne Bosuell gaif in his compt of the gyld schiluir gyld anwellis and all othir thyngis, and that same day he deluerit to Waltir Baxtar to the wpbigyne of the towbowthe for James Burne 1^s for Thomas Stewinsoune 1^s for Dauid Dewer xl^s.

  The vj day of Octobir in the yeir of God j^m v^c lijj yeiris.

The quhilk day Johne Keir gaif in his cowmpt of bredir schiluir and all othiris cowmptis and swa is he awand to ws ij^s x^d, and all othiris cowmptis of befor dischergit to this day.

  The gyld cort hadyne in the towbutht of Dunfermlyne be the dane of gyld and balyeis the xxij day of October in the yeir of God j^m v^c liij yeir.

The gyld cort haldin in the towbutht of Dunfermlyn be Johne Bosuell dene of gyld and gyld brethir apone Sant Thomas ewin.

The quhilk day Johne Bosuell dene of gyld gaif in his cowmpt of gyld schiluir and alwellis and swa is the sad Johne restand awand to the said the brethir vij^s j^d teynless and in the cros ix^s and in the bust viij^s. The some is xxiiij^s iij^d.

[Fo. 52v]

The gyld cort haldin in the towbuthe of Dunfermlyne be the dane of gyld and gyld brether the sacund day of Janower in the yeir of God j^m v^c liij.

The samen day Johne Keir kerkmaister gaif in his cowmpt and bred schiluir keirk anwellis and all othir thingis resauit be hym and depursit and of the rest that he wes awin of the yeir of befor and swa is he awand to ws xv^s vj^d.

The geild kowrt hadine ine the towbucht of Dunfarmaling ine the yeir of God j^m v^c liiij yeiris the viij day of Junj.

The sam day Vilyem Rogar and Vilyem Schurtus yungar was maid be the dein of geild and geild brudar to pay to James Bowrn for the mone that thaj ar awand to him skin and and [sic] hyd, and all vthair penevorthis as he haid befor quhyll he be payit his mune.

[Fo. 53]

Curia fratrum gildorum [sic] tenta in pretorio burgi de Dunfermlyne per Joannem Boswell decanum gilde eiusdem xij^o die mensis Julij anno Domini j^m v^c quinquagesimo quarto in presencia Patricij Haikheid de Pitfurane aldirmanum dicti burgi confratribus gildorum [sic] congregatis et presentibus acetiam ad subsequentia consensientibus.

The quhilk day Schyr Johne Cowpar capellane was enterit gild brethir be the hall consent of the gild brethyr fre and maid faitht.

[in margin: fre manis douthir] The quhilk day Dauid Aitkyne was enterit gilde brothyr for v lib. Tharof pait iij lib. Restis xl^s to be pait quhene he is requirit be the dene of gild togiddyr witht the wyne and spis and maid faitht as efferis. Xx^S wes gewin quit becaus he mareit one fre manis douthir. Payit et eque.

    The gild court haldyne in the towbugh of Dunfermlyng the xxviij day of Julij the yeir of God j^m v^c l four yeiris be Johne Boswell dene of gild.

The quhilk day Thomas Stewynsone come in will for the merchant beand for Robert Fresar quhilk was nocht ane freman at this last salyng at he sall pay to the gild brethtyr at this tyme vj^s viij^d. The remanent wes forgewin hyme for certane causis and attour gif it sall happyne him in tyme tocum at he sall pay to the said gild brethyr for ilk falt xl^s.

[*in margin*: payit] The quhilk day Robert Fresar was enterit gild for xl^S, and maid faitht, and thre poundis forgewne hyme be request of the provest to mak the banket the morne witht the heilp of the dene of gyld.

The quhilk Johne Hwtoune was maid gild brothir and enterit tharto and maid faitht for v lib tharof iij lib forgewyne. And the remanent xl^S sall pay quhen he is requirit tharwitht. Payit.

The quhilk day it was grantit at [*deleted*: Johne] Robert Fillane sald be enterit gild brothir for v lib, tharof gewin quitance quit iij lib. And the remanent viz. xl^S he sall pay quhene he beis requirit tharwitht.

    The gyld cort hadyne in the towbutht of Dunfelyng be Johne Bosuell dane of gyld and the balyeis and gyld brothir the xiij day of October in the yeir of God j^m v^c liiij yeris.

[*Fo. 53v*]

    The quhilk day Wilyeme Wilsone disobeiand the deine of gyld command in not bydand in the tolbotht bot yeid furth of the sam but lycens for the said disiobediens he come in the deine of gyld will as plesit hym to charge.

    The gyld cort haldyne in the twbuthe of Dunfermlyne be Johne Bosuell dene of gyld and gyld brether the xij day of Desembir in the yeir of God j^m v^c liiij yeir.

The quhilk day Harye Mwrray wes maid gyld brothir be rasoune of his fadar James Mwrray and wes sworne thar to for the spece and the wyne.

    The gyld cowrt haldyn in the tobbotht of Dunferm-

lyng be Johne Boiswell den of gild and gyld brethir apone Sant Thomas ewin the xx Decembris anno Domini j^m v^c l tercio.
The quhilk day Jhone Boiswell gaif in his compt of gild annuellis and all wthir thyngis and swa he restis awand to the gyld bredir iiij^s vij^d.

The lyttis chosyn in chesyng deine of gild Jhone Pawtone Thomas Davglis Lawrens Dawglis Robert Dawgles Jams Burne James Schortovs.

[*Fo. 54*]

The quhilk day Johne Patoune wes maid dene of gyld for ane yeir be the hell interlocotur of the nychtbowris and wes sworne thar to.

The gyld cort hadyne in the towbowtht of Dunfermlyn be Johne Patoune dene of gyld and gyld brethir the same day.

The quhilk Thome Stewinsoune and Lowrens Dalglasche rafarit to the interlocutor ane b[*oll ?*] of as quhilk wes in pley betwex the said partteis and the heill interloctur fand that Thomas Stewinsoune was fre of the said b[*oll ?*] be resune becauss he deliuerit to Lowrens in name of Waltir Baxtar.

xxix^o Decembris anno Domini j^m v^c l quarto.

The quhilk day Johne Keir kyrk maister gaiff his compt of the kyrklycht resauit be hyme and disponit as eftir followis. Fra the [*deleted*: xj day] ij day of [*deleted*: December] Januar inclusiue anno Domini j^m v^c l tercio usque ad dictum xxix die mensis Decembris inclusiue anno Domini j^m v^c l quarto.

Oneratio dicti Joannis.

In primis onerat se cum xv^s vj^d per arreragia vltima suj computare de dici apud Dunfermlyng secundo die mensis Januarij anno Domini j^m v^c quenquegesimo tertio ut partem ibidem.

xv^s vj^d.

Item idem Joannes onerat se recepisse a congregantibus infra ecclesiam parrochialem de Dunfermlyng a secundo Januarij inclusiue anno Domini j^m v^c l tercio usque ad xxix^{mo} Decembris inclusiue anno Domini j^m v^c l quarto extenden ad summam x lib xv^s iiij^d.

Item pro anno redditu inprimis de terra seu vacca quondam Joannis Duncan in Monyrodis ij^s de terris

Joannis Mowtray iij^s.

  Summa omnium oneracionis
   xj lib iij^d.

Summa totalis oneracionis cum arreragiis – xj lib xv^s ix^d.

[*Fo. 54v*]

     Expense dicti Joannis.

Inprimis allocantur computanti in x lib x^s v^d pro cera empta per computantem in candelis et factura earundem ac pro ceris aliis ministris expensis factis a 2º Januarij anno Domini j^m v^c quinquagesimo tercio usque ad xxix^{mo} Decembris inclusiue anno Domini j^m v^c l quarto particulariter exonerat super computum – x lib x^s v^d et eidem in sex solidis solutis Willelmo Angus pro custodia ecclesie ad detendum pauperes extra ecclesiam infra dictum tempum hac vice tantum – vj^s.

  Summa totalis expensarum – x lib xvj^s v^d.
Et sic restant super computantem – xix^s iiij^d tenet.

  The gyld cort hadyne the towbutht of Dunfermlyng be Johne Patoune dene of gyld and brethir the xvij day of Janewerij the yeir of God j^m v^c liiij yeiris.

The quhilk day Johne Cowene comperit befor the dene of gyld and brethir and aclemit Robert Murray of lj^s. The quhilk the said Robert denyit and the said Johne Cowene rafarit the said lj^s to his aitht. And the sad Robert wes sworne and diserit xv dayis to be acwysit thar witht. And the said Robert maid aitht that he wes awin nathyng to the said Johne Cowene and wis discherge tharof.

  Primo die mensis Februarij anno Domini j^m v^c l quinto.

The quhilk day it was statut and ordanit that James Dwly was the causar of the ewill langagis betuix hyme and Thomas Dalgles dene of gild becaus the said James come till the buycht of the said Thomas and thar gaif the iniuorius vordis at vas thar pronuncit and said and tharfor ordanit to ask the said Thomas forgewynes, and to pay to the Hally Blud altar ane pound of wax, and to forbeyr siclik thingis in tyme cummyne wndyr the pane of tynsall of his fredome.

[*Fo. 55*]

  Curia fratrum gildorum [*sic*] tenta in pretorio burgi de Dunfermlyng per Thome Dalgles decanum in presentia Robertj Fressall et Joannis Boswell balliuorum Joannis Keyr Joannis Pawtone Joannis Hwttone Walteri Baxtar Joannis Andersone carnefecis Dauid Aitkyne Jacobj Schurtus Willelmj Walcar Joannis Fillane et Joannis Cowane fratrum primo die mensis Februarij anno Domini j^m v^c quinquagesimo quinto.

The quhilk day Johne [deleted: Pautoun] Keir gaif his compt of the gild siluyr. And restis of the fut of his last compt maid at Dunfermlyng the xxix day of December last anno Domini j^m v^c quinquagesimo quarto.

Oneracio.

Inprimis the said Johne Keir [deleted: chargis] hyme witht xix^s iiij^d for the rest of his last compt maid the said xxix day of December anno l quinto ut patet ibidem. Item idem Joannes onerat se cum iiij^s vij^d for the rest of Johne Boswellis compt maid be hyme the xx day of December the yeir of God j^m v^c l thre yeiris as the compt tharof preportis.

The quhilk day Jhone Boiswell declarit his will apone Wilyeme Wilsone that quhen the said Jhone Boisuell wes den of gyld and for ane ressonabill caws chargit and said Wilyeme to remane in the tolbuitht, quhilk charge the said Wilyeme disobeit. For the quhilk he com in to the said Johne will the quhilk is declarit that the said Wilyeme sall pay and delyuer in the handis of Thomas Dalgles the soume of iij lib to be distribuit apone the Haly Bluid altar.

The quhilk day Robert Fillane was enterit gyld brethir and sworne thairto and sall pay conforme to the act befor writtyne.

[Fo. 55v]

Curia fratrum gide [sic] de Dunfermlyng tenta in pretorio eiusdem per Thomas Dalgles decanum dicte gilde xiiij^o die mensis Augusti anno Domini j^m v^c l sexto in presenciis Roberti Fressar balliuj Waltir Baxter Joannis Huttone Jacobi Burne Joannis Cowane Dauid Brand Roberti Wilsone Dauidis Aitkyne Joannis Pawtone Jacobi Schourtus et Robertj Fillane.

[deleted: The quhilk day Robert Fressall grantit to gif the reparatioune and wphaldyne of the Hally Blud alter ay and quhill he or his airis gif stait and possessioune of samekill yeirly annuell as ij^s of annuel rent.

Thomas Dalgles grant siclik ij^s
Walter Baxtar grantit siclik ij^s
Johne Hwtone   siclik xij^d
James Burne   siclik xij^d
Johne Cowane   xij^d
Dauid Brand   xij^d ['pait' *in left*
Alexander Kellik   siclik xij^d *margin*]
Dauid Aitkyne   xij^d
Williame Wilsone   xij^d
Robert Fillane   siclik xij^d
James Schourtus   xij^d
Johne Pawtone   xij^d
Johne Andersone   xij^d]

[*Fo. 56*]

Curia fratrum gilde de Dunfermlyng tenta in pretorio eiusdem per Thomas Dalglesch decanum dicte gilde quinto die mensis Decembris anno Domini j^m v^c l sexto in presentiis Patricii Hakheid de Pitfirran [*deleted*: Roberti Frasar] Joannis Bosuell Laurencii Dalglesch Robertj Frasor Valterj Baxtar Joannis Pautoun Jacobj Schorthous Jacobj Burne Villelmj Vilsone Dauidis Aitkyne Thome Stewynsone Joannis Hutoun Villelmj Nycholl and Robertj Fillan fratrum dicte gilde.

> Curia fratrum gilde de Dunfermlyne tenta in pretorio eiusdem per Thomas Dalgles decanum dicte gilde vigesimo die mensis Decembris anno Domini j^m v^c l sexto in presentiis ceterorum gildorum ibidem congregat.

The quhilk day John Persone was maid gild brothir for v lib [*deleted*: fiftie] and found William Couper souertie for payment of fyftie withtin yeir and day and maid faytht as efferis.

The quhilk day Thomas Dalglesch witht consent of the laif of the gild brethir was continuit dene of gild for ane yeir tocum and maid faytht for ministratioune as efferis etc.

> Curia fratrum gilde de Dunfermlyn tenta in pretorio eiusdem per Patricium Hakheid de Pitfirrane prepositum Thomas Dalglesche decanum dicte gilde nono die mensis Octobris anno Domini 1557° etc.

Quo die computum Joannis Keir custodis templi factum in

dicto pretorio de receptis in anno lv°. Inprimis dictus Joannes onerat se cum xix^s iiij^d de resta computj annj liiij. Item
And siclyk the said Johnne chargis hyme of the lvj yeir witht vij lib xx^d gaddirit in the kirk and kirk annuellis and siclyk his discharge and expenssis extendis to viij lib xx^d. And swa restis awand to the said John kirk annuallis and all thyng beand allovit of the lv and lvj yeiris – xj^{s}vj^d.

[Fo. 56v]

> Curia burgi de Dunfermlyne fratrum gilde eiusdem tenta in pretorio dictj burgi per Thomas Dalglesche decanum dicte gylde et quosdam alio[rum ? text obscured] fratres gildos [sic] xxiij° die Octobris anno Domini j^m v^c l septimo etc.

The quhilk day Johnne Cristye callit Laurence Dalglesche for ane berrall of jrne coft in Danskyne. Quhilk Laurence comperit and referrit hes part of the matir to the nychtbouris gild brethyr of the said burght all or four or tua, quhilk John refusit to do the samyne, and tharfor the forsaid Laurence protestit for remeid conforme to the ws of gild brethir fand grantit that he had the syluir of ane barrell of jrne kepand to vtilite and profitt of ane mane in Danskyne gif he requiris the samyne at thar next metyng.

The quhilk day it is ordanit be the dene of gild and gild bredir that all the gildis at ar enterit and nocht payt thar gild syluir bryng it in withtin xiiij days nixt cumyis vndir the pane of dischargyne of thar fredome and lokyne wp of thar butht durris in tym cumyne etc.

> Curia burgj de Dunfermlyne fratrum gilde eiusdem tenta in pretorio dictj burgi per Thomam Dalgleische decanum dicte gilde et quosdam aliorum fratres gildos [sic] xviij° die mensis Decembris anno Domini j^m v^c l septimo.

The quhilk day it is statut and ordanit be the dene of gild and gild brethir at Johnne Bosuell caus the gild brethir that enterit in his tyme to bryng in thair gild [deleted: brethir] syluer vpoune Sanct Thomas ewine nixt cumis vndir the pane of tynsell of his fredome.

The quhilk day Thomas Stewynsoune promittit in jugement to preif at he hes payt and maid rakyne to Valtir Baxtar of ane berrall of ays vpoun Monday nixt cumis [deleted: and failyeing tharof sall refer it to the aitht of the said Valtir.]

[Fo. 57]

[in margin : compromissio] The quhilk day ar compromittit in jugement Robert Fraser quh[ay? text obscured] chesis for hime Dauid Aitkyne one tha tane part, and Johnne Pawtoune quhay chesis for him Johnne Bosuell one the vthir part jugis arbitroris and amicable compositoris tueching certane compt and rakyne restand betuix the saidis parteis of the slawchtir hydis and skynnis of Dene William Lumisdene sald be the said Robert to the forsaid John Pawtoune quhilkis jugis sall conuene the morne and deliuer withtin vj dayis nixt thareftir. And the said jugis ar obligit and suorne to deliuer lelelie and trewchtlie in the said matir, and the saidis parteis sic lyk ar suorne to byd at thar deliuerance etc.

The quhilk day Johnne Bosuell was decernit be interlocutor of the court to pay to Valtir Baxtar the sovme of fywe poundis xiij^s vj^d money betuix this and Monoday nixt cumis etc. and payit et eque.

The quhilk day the said John Bosuell offerit pennyworthtis extendyne to the sowme aboune expremitt to releif hime of the samin and protestit he be fra safar as his pennyworthtis is awaill etc.

The quhilk day comperit in jugement Laurence Dalgleische.

> Curia fratrum gilde de Dunfermlyne tenta in pretorio eiusdem per Patricium Hakheid de Pitfirrane prepositum [deleted: decanum] Thomam Dalgleische decanum dicte gilde xx^o die mensis Decembris anno Domini j^m v^c l septimo.

The quhilk day Dauid Aitkyne was chosine dene of gild for ane yeir tocum.

> Curia gilde de Dunfermlyng tenta in pretorio eiusdem par [sic] Dauidem Atkyn decanum gyld the xxviij^o die mensis Decembris anno Domini j^m v^c lvij^o.

The quhilk day Thomas Dalglesche maid his cowmpt of the annuellis and offirandis of the Halye Blowd altar of thir twa yeiris presidint and restis he awand to the brothir viij^s.

[Fo. 57v]

[deleted: Curia] Curia gilde de Dunfermline tenta in

pretorio eiusdem per Dauid Aitkine decanum gilde xxij die mensis Merchye anno Domini 1558.

xxvij die mensis Augustj anno Domini 1558.

The quhilk day Thomas Dalgleysche befor the Patrik Hakheid provest Dauid Aitkyne dene of gyld and nychtboris vnder writtin protestit for expensis costis and skaythis to be obtenit of Robert Fillane alanerlie gif Laurence Dalgleysche his sone beis langar haldyne in captiue lyand in Ingland becaus the laif of the merchandis has maid thar ranssonis and expensis reddye and the said Robert will nocht fulfill his part of the samin.

And the samin day Johnne Bosuell protestit gif ony skayt or damnag happynnis to him at passis agane to releif Laurence Dalgleysche quhilk lyis in wed of the expensis of him self and the said Robert for remeid of law becaus the said Robert aucht to pas and bryng hayme the said Laurence as is allegit etc. and as in the dene of gild and gild brethir hes decernit etc. Testibus Roberto Murray Andrea Walcar Alexandro Myllar Jacobo Schorthous diuersis multis etc.

[*Fo. 58*]

Curia in pretorio gylde eiusdem per Dauide Aitkine decanus [*sic*] gylde die mensis xxijj Septemberis [*sic*] 1558.

The quhilk day Robert Fyllane grantit that Jhone Bosuall payit his toll for him in Elsone vre the quhilk toll of fyf last of geir and ane half and the haill schip was vj dolloris and als grantit xxx ^{d}.

Curia fratrum gilde de Dunfermlyne tenta in pretorio eiusdem per Dauide Aitkyne decanum dicte gilde Joannem Bosuell ballivum et ceteros fratres prefate gilde xxiij^o die mensis Decembris anno Domini 1558 etc.

The quhilk day Laurence Dalgleische youngar wes jnterit gild brudir to the fredoume of vmquhill Thomas Dalgleische his fathyr to pay tharfor vj^s viij^d for the spyce and vyne.

The quhilk day Abraham Waluod wes jnterit gild brethyr and maid faytht as efferis payit xx to Robert Dawgles.

The quhilk day Dauid Aitkyne wes continuit dene of gild for ane yeir tocum and maid faitht to minister justice etc.

The quhilk day Robert Fillan allegit at the dene of gild haid nocht ado to decreit in the actioune betuix him and Johnne Bosuell becaus the provest hes dischargit to molestit him quhill he be present him self etc.

[Fo. 58v]

  The gyld court haldine in the towbutht of Dunfermling be Dauid Aitkin dene of gyld and gyld brethir of the same the yeir of God j^m v^{ct} fyfte aucht yeiris wretin the xviij day of Febrewar.

The quhilk day Jhone Boswall deponit the aitht that he was nocht awin [deleted: him na thing] to Robert Fillane nathing of the xxx gros and vij mark and an half for the recompens of Jemis Burne and Thomas Steinsone of thair cuning skyngis. The brethir hes opsolwit him thairof.

The quhilk day Jhone Keir kerk mester geif in his count of the keirk lycht and kyrk anvalis of the lvij and lviij yeiris all thing seine and hard and all thingis considerit and we ar restand awand him xviij^{s}vj^d.

  The gyld cort haldyne in the towbutht off Dunfermlyng be Dauid Aitkyn dene of gyld and brethir of the same the xxiiij day of Nouembir in the yeir of God j^m v^c lix yeiris.

The qlk day Waltir Crystye enterit to the fredome of the gyld brethir and sall pay tharfor v lib. The tane xl^s wes forgewin and the vthir l^s to be payit quhene euir the dene of gyld requiris hym thar witht and mad faitht tharto. Payt to Robert Dowglesche xxx^s.

The quhilk day William Mechall beand acuhist be ane brothir fund be Robert Dawglesche that quhar the said William cowft the peneworth that is skynis and hyddis the nychtbouris fyndis ane falt witht the said William the ownlaw of x^s and gaif he or[? *text obscured*] dois seklyk in tym cuming tharof sall pay xl^s oneforgewin.

[Fo. 59]

We Waltir Baxtar William Cowpir James Burne James Schortus Dauid Aitkyn and John Bosuell [in margin: and Lowrens Daugless] gyld brethir and burgessis of Dunfermlyng the vij men befor nemit grantis ws euiry ane of ws respektewe to half rasauit fra Dauid Aitkyn dene of gyld viij ownc of schiluir scharp wayit of the owcryst and challence of the Haly Blud alter and be caus of the trublus warld batht of the Congregatione and the Frenche men becaus we thowcht it nocht expedeante to put it all

in ane hand and for the releif of the dan of gild we bend ws and ylk ane of ws be this present wret to hald it furt cumand to the gyld brethir subcryvit witht our hand and our mercheand markis set to at Dunfermlyng the last day of Nouember in the yeir of God j^m v^c lix yeiris.
Waltir Baxtar wytht my hand. Jhames Bwrn witht my hand.
William Coupir witht my hand at pane led be John Bosuell.
Dauid Atkyn witht my hand at the pene led be John Bosuell.
James Schortus witht my hand at the pene led be John Bosuell.
Lowrens Dalglesche witht my hand at the pene led be John Bosuell.
John Bosuell witht my hand.
[*subscribed : JB and six merchant marks*]

Item quhen it wes wayit sindrey Dauid Aitkyn part wantit ½ ownce.

[*Fos. 59v and 60 - blank*]

[*Fo. 60v*]

[*This folio was originally folded in four. One side was left blank. The other has text on three quarters and is blank on the fourth.*]

[*Top-left hand corner*]
My lord dene of gild and gild brither I Wilyeme Boswall humlie compleinis apone Jhone Lowdiene our brother that quhar he allegit that I missaie him and promist to preifit tharfor I am content to submit me to the gild brither and lat our mater be tryit beseikim herto to preifit.

        The wn lawis
Robart Fallane	xvj^d
Wa Wricht	xvj^d
Alexander Necholl	xvj^d
Johne Walcar	xxxij^d
John Cawone for his	xlj^s sall pay viij^d.

[*Bottom-left hand corner*]
   The x day of August the yeir of God 1566.

The quhilk day Sanders Nicoll was fund in ane onlay of xl^s in the bretheris will becaus that he promist withtin ane xiiij dais to bringe ane probassioune the quhilk he did nocht at the day.

The quhilk day Wilyeme Wilsone was fund in ane merciament for the ganging and bying of the pennyworth apertainng to Sanders Nicoll quhilk the probassioune tesstifeit the quhilk merciament in xl^s to be payit at the bretheiris will.

[*Bottom-right hand corner*]
Wilyeme Walkar
James Schortus
Robert Fallene
Waltir Crysty

The listis of the dene of the gild.

Robart Wilsone
Sanders Nicoll
Jhone Mowbray
James Schortous

[*Fo. 61*]

The gyld cort haldyne in the towbuthe be Dauid Aitkyn dene of gyld and the brethir the xij day of Juinij anno Domini lx yeiris.

The quhilk the dene of gyld gaif in his cowmptis of his reset and dispositioune of the lviij and lix yeiris of all cowmptis and the brethir restis awand to the dene of gyld xij ^{s} iij^d and he hes nocht maid rakknyne of the lix yeiris anwell becaus he hes nocht gottin it in as yet and the brethir ordanis hym to do vttir delegence to the ingettyng of the same.

The gyld court haldyn in the tolbutht of Dunfermling the xx day of December the yere of God j^m v^c lx be Dauid Aitkyn dene of gyld and Robert Fresser bailey and conwenit of gyld brether abone.

[*in margin*: Pattrik Mvray peyit the spys and the wyne.]
The quhilk day Robert Dawglesche and Patryk Mu[rray ? *text obscured*] dissyrit to be interit be the den of gild to thar fathiris fredomeis and it wes grantit be the den of gyld bailye and gyld brether stud sworne and ressauit payand t[hair ? *text obscured*] for the spyce and wyne accordyng to the awldross, and the said wyne and spyce to be payit at the den charg.
The quhilk day William Nycoll persewit Androw Walka[r ? *text obscured*] for certan slawchter skynnis. Andro denyit the sam and the said William offerit to preif that he coft Andro haill slaw[chter ? *text obscured*]

[Fo. 61v]

> The gyld cort haldyne in the towbuthot of Dunfermlyne the fort day of Janewor in the yeir of God j^{m}v^c lx yeiris.

The quhilk day Robert Dawglesche wes maid dain of gyld for ane yeir and maid faitht to do justece.

The quhilk day Johne Wemis of Pittincreff wes maid gyld brothir be rasoune of Patrik Wemis his fader and maid fatht as afferris for the spece and the wyne.

The quhilk day James Mowbray interit gyld brothir for the banket and maid fatht that he sall do his wter delegens to set furt the dene of gyld and brethir of resoune.

The quhilk day it is statute and ordanyt be the dane of gyld and gyld breydryne that Dauid Aaking sall haif his cownttis rady agane this day fowrtyne day wt all maner of dawattytis belangand to the saming.

> The gyld court haldyne in the tolbutht of Dunfermlyne be Robert Dawgleische dene of gyld and the rest of the gyld brether xviij Januarij anno 1561.

The quhilk day it is dewysit and ordanit be the dene of gyld and gyld brether that all the money dettis and geir pertenand to the gyldrye sall be brocht in betuix this and viij dayis nixtcumis to be put and kepit in ane kyst to the vtilitie and proffitt of the haill brether as it salbe dewysit and thocht maist expedient. Ilk mane that hes ony of the said money and geir to bryng in his awyne part vnder the pane of tene poundis of vnlaw at the day forsaid and thareftir to be laid vpoune proffitt one cautioune or securitie of land as said is etc.

[Fo. 62]

The quhilk day it wes decernit be the dene of gyld and gyld brethir that Johnne Hwtoune sall by ane cott to ane pwyr bairne callit Marane Barklay, for the quhilk thaj sall allowe to the said Johnne x^s of his gyld syluer.

The quhilk day Dauid Aitkyne producit in the tolbutht of ane kyst pertenand to the gyld brether, in the quhilk wes liand in kepyng this gair followand. Viz twa abbis ij altar claythtis and 1 ½ of lynnyng v altar towellis iij chaissaippis ane of thame of blew walvet, ane gylt croce of brais, ane fronetell of yawills walvat and

ane stoill. Upoune the delyuerance of the said kyst and
geir the said Dauid tuk act at he be fre of the samyne.
Item twa braissyne chanedelaris etc.

> The gyld court haldin be Robert Dawgles dene
> of gyld and the rest of the gyld briddir the xxvj
> day of Jenuar anno Domini 1561.

The quhilk day the gyld bryddir box requirit be the
dene of gyld for the siluir that thai ar awand and the
said gyld briddir requerit the dene of gyld to continw
quhill the heme cuming of the prowest and the rest of
gyld briddir and to compeir witht the said mony quhene
thei be requirit.

> The gyld cowrt haldayne in the tobutht of Dunfarm-
> alyne be the profest and the dane of gyld and the
> rest of the gyld brydring the vij day of Februar
> anno Domini 1561.

The sowme beand laid in the tobutht of the [? *folio torn*]
gyld sylwair be the prowyst and the dane of gyld the
sowme is iij xx of lib and ix lib and xvj^s.

The quhilk day it is statuit and ordanyt be the pro[west ?
folio torn] and the dene of gyld and gyld brydryne that
some as haif the gyld sylwair to cowme in betuix this
day and the day acht dayis and gyf sasyne of landis
for the mony that is in thair handis or elys to delywer it
to the dane of gyld onder the paint of tying of thair
frydowme.

[*Fo. 62v.*]

The quhilk day Robairt Patowme wace ettreit to the faderis
frydowme for the spyce and the wyme [*sic*].

The quhilk day Wylyam Wrycht wast etteryt ane gyld
breder four fowrtye s to pay withtin tue yeyre.

> The kyld court haldin in the tolbuit of Dunferm-
> ling haldin be the dene of gild and gild brethir
> the xxv day of Februar the yeir of God j^m v^c and
> lx yeris.

The quhilk day the gild bredir viz. Dauid Aitkyne James
Mowbray Robert Fresser Robert Gray William Nicholl Waltir
Crystie Johne Boisuell Alexander Kellok Johne Smytht
youngar John Hutoune Robert Pawtone and Thomas Steuisoune consentit and grantit that the haill money gudis
and gair pertenand to the gildbrethir salbe collectit and
gadderit togiddir and put in ane kist.

The quhilk day Dauid Aitkyne deluirit to Robert Dalgleis
dene of gild sevine vnce and ane half vnce of syluer

unkewnyeit to be put in the kist foirsaid in kepine quhilk the said Dauid Aitkyne askit to be actit and this was done in presence of the said brethir.

The quhilk day Robert Dalgleis dene of gild grantit him ressauit fra the relictis of vmquhile Lourence Dalgleis aucht vnce vnkevnyeit siluer siclyk scharp wayit to be put siclyk in the said kist quhilk the haill brethir askit to be actit and this in presence of the said brethir.

The quhilk day James Burne deliuerit to the said Robert dene of gild aucht vnce siclyk wayit of vnkewnyeit siluer to be kepit as said is quhilk the said James askit to be actit in presence of the said brethir.

The quhilk James Schortus have dalyweryt to Robart Dawgleche vij lib and x^s in presence of the balye James Mowbra Jhone Howtene Watye Cryste and this the said James askyt to be wretting for his dyscharge.

    The gild court haldin in the tolbuit of Dunfarmling hal[din ? *text obscured*] be the dene of gild Robert Dalgleis and the gildbreth[ir ? *text obscured*] the xiiij day of Merche the yeir of God j^{m}v^c lx yeris.

The quhilk day Robert Dalgleis dene of gild at the plesour of God to pas to his vaige hes deput Johne Boiswell his deput to execute justice in his absence and that witht consent of certane gild brothir beand present and that quhill the said Robertis returing fra his said vaige.

[*Fo. 63*]

and the nyxt falt thai sall payit x lib quhat sowme euir thai be that occupyis sylk lyk.

    The gyld cowrt halyne in the tobuthe be the dayne of gyld and gyld brydryne the yir of God j^m v^c iiixx of yeiryis the xxiij day of September.

The quhilk day the dane of gyld and gyld brydryne haie decrytit that Dauid Dawaris wyf omquhyll sall pay xiij^s iiij^d for occupying of one fry w[orn ? *folio torn*] or frydome and scha sall be descharigit hir frydome ey and quhyll scho eccepe.

    The quhilk day the gyld cowrt haldyne in the tobutcht be the provist and dane of gyld and gyld- bryderyne the yir of God j^m v^c iij xx of yiris and the v day of October.

The quhilk day the dane of gyld and bredir of the saym have dasernit and ordand conforme to the ald ackis that na mane sell na wayne in to this towne dar ma viiij^d now- der in the howce nor owt of the howce and Ja[? *folio torn*] Carmur be and callyt be for the dane of gyld and breder

of the saming for salling of saxtyne p[? *folio torn*] wyne be
and nocht fre to the towne the breder dasarnis is onlay
to be tane jnstantlie xx ᔆ and ey quhen oft he sallis this
onlay to be [? *folio torn*]ey and qhyll he be entteryt.
The quhilk day James Carmur cowme in will and and as[kit? *folio torn*] for his gyld schip and enteryt gyld broder.

[*Fo. 63v*]

      The gild court haldin within the tolbuith be Rob[? *text obscured*] Dalgles dene of gild and the brethir the penul[tima ? *text obscured*] of Januar anno 156j⁰.

The quhilk day is electit and chosin James Mowbray
dene of gild Waltir Baxter in his absence to execute the
office trewlie jndu[ring ? *text obscured*] this yeir ay
and quhill thaj be removit and the saidis James [and ?
text obscured] Waltir ar sworne de fidelj administratione
quhilk is actit.

      ix Februarij anno 156j⁰.

The quhilk day the gildbrothir decernis James Carmur
and his sp[ous ? *text obscured*] to pay for the falt
committit xvjᔆ and the fredome of his gild to be [in ? *text obscured*] the dene of gildis will for ane yeir quhilk is
actit.

      xij Februarij anno 156j⁰.

The quhilk day Waltir Baxter in presence of the prouest
and gildbrider hais the powar vndir the dene of gild
for the tyme in his absence decernis that James Carmur
sall heif the kyr of his taviroune agane to sell punscioune
of claret wyne pruiftit and to desist fra forder occupying of wyne ay and quhill forder cognitioun be had in
this mater, that in presence of thir gildbrithiris Johne
Wems of Pittincreif pr[ouest ? *text obscured*] Waltir Baxtir Andro Walcar Johne Cowane Waltir Crystie Robert
Fyl[lane ? *text obscured*] Johne Hutoune merchand Johne
Peirsone William Nichell William Meikiljohne Abrahame
Waluod Johne Smytht youngar William Boissuell James
Schort[us ? *text obscured*] Robert Pawtoune Johne Boiss-
uell and Williem Wrycht.

      The xxiij of Merce 156j.

The quhilk day the dene of gild and brethir hes des-
cernitt that thaj that sa hed onfre menis gair sall pay
for the bygane falt xvjᔆ instantlye one forgawin. That
is to say John Pairsoune William Mekkyljohn Wat Crestye
John Hutoune John Schara and gaif thaj or ony othir
gyld brethir takis ony onfre menis gair in tyme cumyng
sall pay for ylk falt x lib tascente cossience.

[*in margin*: [? *text worn*] 1562] The quhilk day John Lowdeene wes maid gyld brothir for iiij lib be the haill introloquitour and maid fait as afferis.

The same day John Loudeene hes tane one hand to raleif William Mekkyjohn of his onlaw for the furtht havynt of the said Johne gair.

The same day Lowrens Pairsoune wes interit for iiij lib and maid fayth as aferris.

[*Fo. 64*]

xviij° Mercij anno 1560 vel 61 alij scributur 1561.

The quhilk day Johnne Peirsoune hes payit the rest of his gyld syluer extendin to x^s to Robert Dalgleische dene of gyld in compleit payment of his gyld syluer etc.

The quhilk day it is condesendit be the said dene of gyld and the rest of the gyld brether that thair gyld kist stand still in the dene of gyldis butht, and the keyis of the samyne be deliuerit ane to James Mowbray ane to James Schortous and ane to William Nycholl.

> The gilt [*sic*] court haldine in the tolbuit of Dunfarmling be Robert Dalgleis dein of gyld witht the rest of the bretherine the x day of Maij anno 1561°.

[*in margin*: Williaime Boussuell] The quhilk day William Boisuell was enterit gild for payment of the sowme of fyff pundis money. Tharof defasit be the bretherine thre pundis for certane ressonabill causis movand thaim tharto and to pay the sowme of xl^s, as for the rest of the saidis v lib in compleit payment of the samyn quhone it sall pleis the dene of gild and brethrene to require the samyn, quhilk is actit.

[*in margin*: William Meiklejohn] The quhilk day William Meikiljohn was enterit gild bruthir conforme to the said Williem Boisuell and hes deponit conforme to the samyn and peit.

[*in margin*: Andro Andirson] The quhilk day Andro Andersoune was enterit gild bruthir for payment of the sowme of fyff pundis tharof defaissit thre pundis for certane ressonabill caus and to pay the sowme of xl^s in compleit payment of the said haill sowme and hes deponit the aith conforme to samyn quhilk is actit.

The quhilk day the dene of gild witht consent of the haill bretherine hes decernit that thair salbe byggit ane sufficient seit in the kirk to the hail bretherine apone thair expens quhair at sall pleis the said dean witht consent of the four of the saiddis bretherne.

>The gild court haldine withtin the tolbuit of Dunfarmling be Robert Dalgleis dene of gyld and the bretherin the xxiij day of Maij anno 1561.

The quhilk day the dene of gild prouest baillies and the rest of the bretherin haiffand consideratioune that Robert Gray is ane bruthir of the gildis and as sumthing faillit quhairfoir thaj be ressoune foirsaid hes grantit and consentis to gif to the said Robert Gray four pundis of thair gild syluer to be deliverit instantlie to the said Robert and that fre.

The quhilk day it is fundine that Johne Keir is restand awand of the bell xlj^s v^d $\frac{1}{2}$, as for the rest of the parte of the samyn.

[*Fo. 64v*]

>Penultimo Maij anno 1561°.

The quhilk day Walter Cristie confessit that he had vnfremannis gair sc[hippit ? *text obscured*] and to be merchand to the samyn hayme and afeild.

>The gilde court of the burt of Dunfarmling hal[din ? *text obscured*] witin the tolbuit of the samyn be Robert Dalgl[esche ? *text obscured*] dene of the samyn the xiiij day of Junij anno 1561.

The quhilk day the dene of gild provest witht the rest of the gild dischargeis Johne Louthiane that he by not nor vs nane of thair fredome siclyk as skyne and hid vndir the pane of the greit vnlaw as actit.

The quhilk day Johne Louthiane askitis of the dene of gild and g[ild ? *text obscured*] brethir gif he occupyit ony mair of thair fredome be in to tha[ir ? *text obscured*] will quhane thaj requir him.

>Tertio Julij anno 1561°.

The quhilk day comperit in jugement Katherine Sym relict of vmquhile Laurence Dalgleis and desyris licence of the dene of gild bailye and gild brethir to marye quhilk was grantit and is ac[tit ? *text obscured*]

The quhilk Robert Dalgleis dene of gild God willing to pas to h[is ? *text obscured*] vaiage hes deput Johne Boisuell his deput to execute his off[ice ? *text obscured*] and justice amangis the gildbrethir vnto the said Robert returnis.

The gyld court haldyne in the tob[outh *? text obscured*] the xij day of Septymber.
The quhilk day Jhone Scharep grantyt in jugment th[at *?
text obscured*] he haid one frymanes gair and was
merchand thair for.
The quhilk day Johne Hautone grantyt the saimyn that he
haid one frymanis gair and was merchand fra thairfore.
The quhilk day Jhone Persone grantyt the saimyn.
The quhilk day the dane of gyld witht the rast [of *?
text obscured*] the gild brydering that Jhone Hwtone and
Jhone Scher[ap *? text obscured*] and Jhon Person sall pay
for the occupying of one frymarch[anis *? text obscured*] sall
pay xvj ˢ, and the tothir twa ylk ane [v *? text obscured*].

[*Fo. 65*]

The quhilk day Robart Dalglesche hes maid his cowmpt
of all his rasait of the haill gyld schiluir and anwellis
and all othir thyng pertenand to the gylbrethir and he
restis awand na thyng restand in his hand and hes
deliuerit the kyst to James Mowbray the same day and the
brethir descharges hym of all intromissione.

  Penultimo mensis Aprilis anno 1562 in pretorio de
  Dunfarmling in presencia Jacobj Mowbray decanj
  gilde Willelmo Baxter Joanne Keir Roberto Gray
  Waltero Crystie Abrahamo Waluod Joanne Hutoune
  Joanne Mowtray Alexandre Kellok Thoma Steuisoune
  Joanne Smytht juniore Willelmo Nicholl Willelmo
  Cowpir et Joanne Boissuell.

The quhilk day James Mowbray dene of gild becaus James
Carmour tweching his fredome for ane yeir refarrit in the
dene of gildis will conforme to the act maid ixº Februarij
vltimj dischargeis the said James Carmour of his fredome
amangis the gild brethir for ane yeir, quhilk is actit.

  Nono die mensis Maij anno 1562 in pretorio ante-
  dictarum.

Quhilk day the dene of gyld witht adwys of the prowest
and the maist part of the gyld brether being present
for the tyme ratifeit and apprewit the actis aboune
writtin anent the dischorgeyng of James Carmour and his
spous fredome for ane yeir to cum amangis the gyld
brethir, admittand thaim onelye to seill thair pvnsioune
of vyne ves parzsit and na forthyr withtout licence
etc, quhilk is actit.

  The aucht day of August the yeir of God 1562
  the court haldine be James Mowbray daine of gild
  and gild brither.

The quhilk day Wilyeme Wrycht beand chargit be the
deine of gild to pay his gild siluir and for othir chargis
as fund be the brither that he hes nocht obeyit the deine
of gild and for thir causis sall pay viij^s one forgyfing
togiddir witht his gild siluir or he pas out of the
towbutht and gif he or ony orther dissibeyis in tyme
cuming sall tyne his fredom and als that na danes of
gild gyf na charg to ony gyld brothir withtout the con-
sultatione of [deleted: brether] sertane brither witht
him.

    The [deleted: quhilk day] gild court halding in
the towburtht be Water Baxter deine of gild deput
xiij day of August the yeir of God 1562.
The quhilk day the deine of gild and gild brither hes
reformit the heill weychtis of the towne and markit
the saming witht the townis stamp and for that caus the
said deine of gild and gildbrither hes ordinit that ne
othir weychtis be weyit excep thai be of the same stamp
ondir the paine of tynsell of thair fridum and peying
of ane onlay of xx^s[deleted: to the townis].

[Fo. 65v]

Item it is ordnit that na craftis mane haif na weychtis
excep thai be stampit of the said townis mark onder the
said penis continit in the actk of befor and that the
deine of gild warne thame that occupyis dur by dur or
thar be opin proclamatione.
The quhilk day the deine of gild and gild brither retifiis
ane actk maid of befor that na one frie meine sell nor
tak na landwart mane nor one fre meinis geir witht
thame onder the panis continit in the buk of befor.
The quhilk day John Robsoune was maid gyld brothir
for iiij lib and to be payit quhene euir he beis raquiret
and maid faytht as afferis.
The same day Hendre Red was enterit gyld brothir for
iiij lib and to be payit quhene euir he beis raquirit and
maid fayt as afferis.
The samen day John Scharay beand callet for sallyng
beand nocht fre man and haifand one fremenis gair to
the saill sall pay xiij^s iiij^d and in tyme cumyng sall
nocht occupe in tyme cumyng witht he be lescheand be
the nychtboris nothir to sell nor na othir fredoume.

    The gild court haldyne in the tolbutht the xxv
day of August the yeir of God 1562 be Valter
Baxter haifand the power of James Mowbray dene
of gyld and the rest of the gyld brythyr etc.

[*in margin*: solvit] Quhilk day Abraham Waluod wes decernit be the dene of gyld and gyld brethir to paye to Robert Fillane x^d for ilk grote of xxiiij gris. Summa xx ^{s} quhilkis the said Robert waryit in Danskyne to the vtilite of the said Abraham withtin terme of law etc.

  The gyld court of the burcht of Dunfarmling haldin be James Mowbray dene of gild and the gild brethir the nynt day of October the yeir of God j^m v^c thre scoir twa yeris.

The quhilk day the dene of gyld and gildbrethir decernis that Johne Louthiane sall pay viij ^{s} for ane vnlaw and that becaus that he dischargeit ane maltman to mak William Waluoddis malt quhilk is actit.

     xxiiij^o Octobris anno 1562.

[*in margin*: solvit] The quhilk day Johne Scheraris enterit gild bruthir and hes payit thar foir iiij lib and hes maid the aith de usu et consuetudine.

[*Fo.* 66]

  The court halding in the towbutht be James Mowbray deine of gilde and gild brither the xviij day of September and the yeir of God 1562.

The quhilk day the gild brither hes ordinit Robert Daugless Abrame Wallat and Jhone Boswall to pay ane ollay continit in the buk for obsente fra the court quhane thai wars warnit.

[*deleted*: The quhilk day comperit Jhone Keir Wilyeme Wilsone Robert Fillane Wilyeme Boswald Jhone Cowane Hendry Reid Johne Persone Johne Huttone Jhone Mowtray Robert Fillane James Schortius Robert Patoune and hes ordinit that Jhone Lowdiene sall pay xx^s for desobeying of the deine of gildis command.]

  The gild court of the burcht of Dunfarmling haldine withtin the tobut be the gild brethir and dene of gild the fyft day of Nouember anno 1562.

The quhilk day William Cowpir and Thomas Steinsoune hes offirit viij markis be yeir of proiffeit for the [*deleted*:haill] hundretht markis of the gild syluer and sall gif strait gude and sufficent of feild landis for swir payment of the samyn yeirlie.

  The gild cowrt of the burcht of Dunnfa[mline *? text obscured*] halding withtin the tobuit be the gild breth[er *? text obscured*] and dane of gild apone Sanct Tamas day foroto Yewll

[*Fo.* 66v – *blank*]

[Fo. 67]

The gild court of the burt of Dunfarmlyne haldin be the gild brethir the xxiiij day of December anno 1563.
The quhilk day the gildbrethir continewis the dene of gild ellis electit and chosin and in his absence Waltir Baxter as of befoir.
The quhilk day William Nicoll allegit that Robert Dalglas had tane poundis fra his sonis and disponit apone thame the tyme he was dene of gild quhilk the said Robert askt to be actit.
The quhilk day William Wrycht confessit in jugement that he had vnfremannis gair witht him at the saile this yeir, quhilk is actit.

The gild court of Dunferling halding be the provest and the gild brithiring the xxij day of Desember the yeir of God 1564.
The quhilk day the provest and the gild brither hes choesing Robart Pattoune dene of gild and gild and suorne as affeiris.

The gild court halding be the daine of gild the 4 day of Jenewar the yeir of God 1564.
The quhilk day Robart Willsone entret freman for xiij^s iiij^d and payit to the bankat.
The quhilk day Sanders Nicoll enterit to his faiders fredome for the spys and the wyne.
The quhilk day Wilyeme Wallat enterit fre mane [deleted: for causis] wit consent of the gild brither and payit to the bankat and maid faytht as aferris.

The xij day of Nouember the yeir of God 1565 in the toubuthe be the dene of gild and gildbrith[er ? text obscured]
The quhilk day the daine of geild and gild brether grantit lecence to [deleted: marry] Bessie Spettell the relict of Robart Mvrray to mary and occupy her friddom of as becumis ane gild brither wyf durryng hir liff.

[Fo. 67v]

[deleted: The gyld court haldyne in the tolbutht of Dunfermlyng be Robert Paittoune dene of gyld and the rest of the gyld brethir the xj⁰ day of September the yeir of God 1565.]

The gild court haldyne in the towbutht of Dunfermlyng be Robert Patoune dane of gyld and gyld brether the the xx day of Nouember the yeir of

God 1565 yeiris.

The quhilk day it is constitut and ordanit be the dane of gyld and gyld brether that Wilyeme Wilsone James Schortus Walter Crysty Wilyeme Wallat ar schossing to by the heill slautter of the landwart fleschoris of one ilk Sonday and that ne glyld [sic] brothir gang in landwart to by ony of the forsaidis fleschoris slautter in onder the pane of tynsell of his fredune for ane yeir and that the for said four mene sall occupy and by the heill slautter to the vtillite and proffit of the rest of the brether for ane yeir fre this day furtht.

   In pretorio burgi de Dunfermlyne ix die mensis Marcij anno 1565.
The quhilk day it is statute and ordanit be the said dene of gyld and gyld brethir that the forsaidis William Wilsoune James Schorthous Valter Cristye and William Waluod in name and behalf of the remanent gyld brethir to thair vtilite and proffit as said is sall by the haill slauchter and intromett tharwitht of hyddis and skynnis of quhat sumewer kynde or sort of skynnis fra all and syndry flescheris and handillaris wthtin this burcht or outwitht and fra all vthiris that offeris the samyne to be sauld withtin this thar fredome and jurisdictioune induring the space of ane yeir nixtocum. And that it sall nocht be lesum to ony vthir of the brethir of gyldis to by or intromitt witht ony of the forsaid slauchter induring the space forsaid nor to pas to landwart to seirche seik or forstar the saidis slauchter be ony manir of way vndir the pane of tynsall of thar fredoume.

The quhilk Robert Dawgleische disconsentit fra the foirsaid act and all vthiris actis that ar mad in this jnstant yeir by the auld actis and plegis for his fredoume and priuelege in tym cumying as afor and vpone askit act.

The quhilk day William Wrycht come in the dene of gyld and brethiris will for brekyne of the dene of gyldis comand and tharfor witht the adwys of the said brethir jnstantlye declarit the said will that the said William sall pay tene s. vnlaw and gif he be fondyne diobedient stubburne or ewill wordy in tyme cumyng to tyne his fredome during the dene of gyld and gyld brethiris will, quhilk is actit.

[Fo. 68]

   Penultimo Octobris anno 1566.
[in margin: John Reid] The quhilk day in presence of

the dene of gild and the beilye and the brethrene Jhone Reid was enterit to be gild brether for iij lib and xl^S forgyfing him and maid faitht to keip the aictis as affeiris.

   The gild court halding be Robert Pattoune dene of gild the xvij day of Nowember anno 1567.

The quhilk day Robert Pattone geif our the offic of dene of gildry.

The quhilk day Wilye Wallot was schossing dene of gild for ane yeir and maid faitht.

   The gyld court haldyne be William Waluod dene of gyld the thryd day of December 1567.

[*in margin*: dome] The quhilk day Johne Bosuell mad faytht that he payit Robert Johnsoune in Leytht the sowme of xix lib for the fraucht of certane geir of Robert Dawgleische and got na thing thairof and is restand awand of the said Robertis clame iiij lib ix^S quhilk the said dene of gyld ordanis to be payit the said Johnis expenis to be deducit.

   The gyld court of the burcht of Dunfermlyne haldine in the tolbuit of the samyn be William Waluod dene of gild and gild brethir the aucht of Januar anno 1567.

The quhilk day in the actioune and caus persewit be William Boissuell aganis Robert Dalgleis in the terme assignit to the said Robert quha hes the clame of the said William to ansuer tharto.

The samyn day comperit the said Robert and allegit that the clame gyvine in is in Edinburgh and tharfoir aucht nocht not tane ansuer tharto and also allegit that the dene of gyld is na juge competent to sit apone siclyk actionis and dettis the prouest and baillies becaus it is withtin ane brocht of justice and protistis gyf thaj proceid forder for remeid of law cost skaytht and dampnage and appellis befoir the prouest and baillies of this burcht.

The quhilk day the said William Boisuell offeris him reddye to stand and vnderlye the jugement of the dene and gild brothir concerning the contents of this actioun and desyris proces.

[*Fo. 68v*]

The quhilk day William Waluod dene of gyld protistit solemplie in jugement that gyf ony gildbruthir comperis in jugement and appellis fra the jugement and justice of the dene of gild and gildbrethir quhatsumeuir that thaj tyne thair fredome and desyrit the samyn to be actit.

1568 the feirt of December.

The quhilk day Gilbart Kennedy enterit gildbrothir for fifte s. quhilk thaj forgaif him for the banket and he maid fath to keip thair actis.

[*deleted*: The quhilk] daye Jhone Valkar enterit gild brothir [*deleted*: for fifty] sillingis quhen the gild brethir requirit it at his hand. And he maid faytht to keip thair actis.

The gild court haldin be Villeam Valwod dein of the gild and gild brethrine hald thair gild court the xxij day of Disember the yeir of 1568.

The lytis

Villeam Valwod   James Schorttus
Villeam Mekiljhon   Robert Willson

[*in margin*: Robert Patone] The quhilk day Villeam Valuod den of gild hes protestit for the x^s quhilk is restand of ane banket quhilk is maid it the gild brethrine.

The quhilk day James Schorttus is chosin dein of the gild be the gild brethren vitht this restriksion that he sall gathir in the gild annuellis.

[*Fo. 69*]

The gyld cort haldin in the towthebuthe of Dunfermlyne be James Schortus dene of gyld the prowest and bailyeis and the brethir the iij day of Janewar 1568.

The quhilk day Robert Fellane cum in the well of the prowest for the dissobedeence of the dene of gyld and his officer and the toune officeris the quhilk wes prowin be Gylbart Kanetye William Bosuell and John Bosuell and for evill wordis gewin be the said Robert to the dene of gyld befor the said witnes.

The gyld cort haldyne in the towthbothe of Dunfermlyng the secund day of September be James Schortus dene of gyld and gylbrothir.

[*in margin*: George Barnat enterit ane gildbruther, payit] The quhilk day Gorge Barnat enterit gyld brothir for v lib and becaus he is ane byrges soune the bruthir hes forgewin him the ane half the othir half to be payit quhene he be requirit and maid the gret atht tharapone. [*addition*: payit 1^s.]

The quhelk day Johne Cowane sall pay xvj^S for the
first half of one fre menis geir and that wes decernit
be the dene of gyld and brethir the gair of [instant ?
folio worn]

    The court haldine in the thowbotht of Donfarmylyng
be the den of geild and geildbreder the xxj day
of Octobeir that quhair Welyeme Wrycht is
sworne to gyf he eitht apone the pount of Welyeme
Wallatis beill.

    The geild court haldine in thowboutht of
Denfarmy[ling ? *text obscured*] be the dein of
geild and geildbredeir the xxii day of Octobeir
the yeir of God ane thouisand v hun[? *text obscured*] thre^{xx} ix yeiris.

The quhilk day the deine of geild and beilyeis and the
bredir heis deisayneit and akit thame seilis that ewere
Sowinday efter the renking and saisayine of the hemmaist
beill renk to the preishyne that na beithow dour sall
be opein ondir the pane of viij^S the feirst falt and xvi^S
the naix fat and thre falt xxxij^S tell the precheine be
endit.

[*Fo. 69v*]

The court haldeine in the thowboutht of Denfermlyng
quinto Nouembris 1569 be the prowst and the den of
geild witht the bredeir and balleyeist that quhair Welyeme
Walat and Welyeme Mekeiljhone and one the tene peirt
and Welyeme Wreicht one the todir peirt that quhair thai
ar compeirmeitit and obleist and sowrne [*sic*] to byd at
the delewirins of fowr mane the quhilk fowr mane is
sowrne [*sic*] in to deleweir thair namis Wateir Carste
and Sander Neikeill for the peirt of Welyeme Walat and
Welyeme Mekeiljhone and Thomas Bourne and Jhone Couane
for the toider peirt of Welyeme Wreicht, and the quhailk
peirteis is swornt to byd at the delewarns of the fowr
mane for the sairtane maircheneris that is be tewex
theis peirteis and the said fowr mane saill delawer be
tewx theis and the day viij dayis trewle apone thair
[?] and gaif thair fowr man cane nocht gre apone
mateir thai sall sand to Edbrocht apone the pairtes
expence to fand the teirkane [*sic*] thairof.

    The gyld cortt haldyne be James Schorthous dene
of gyld and the rest of the gyld brethir the
xiiij day of Nouember 1569.

The quhilk day the actioun and caus persewit be William

Waluod and William Meklejohne aganis William Wrycht
the dene of gyld and gyld brethir present for the tyme
do awoid and put away murmeris decernis and ordanis
that the said William Wrycht sall content and thankfully
pay to the saidis William Waluod and William Meklejohne
for ilk dolor xxvj^s viij^d to be payit jnstantlie and that
fre withtout ony merchandis cost or expenss to be sus-
tennit be the saidis persewaris.

[*Fo. 70*]

   The gyld curt haldyne in the towbuthe of Dunfermlyng be James Schortous dene of gyld the xvj
   day of Decembar 1569.
     The lyttis for the chesyne of the dene
     of gyld

     James Schortus
     William Mvkkilihone
     Williame Wallat
     Robert Fellane
     Robert Welsone
     James Burne

The quhilk day William Mvkyihone wes maid dene of the
gyld for ane yeir and maid faytht to minister justece.

The quhilk day the dene of gyldbrether hes decernit
that William Wricht to pay vj^s viij for the sellyng gair
darrar nor the four halfabout.

   The gyld curt haldyn in the towbutht of Dunfermlyne be Williame Mwkkiliohne dene of gyld and
   the brethir the xxv day of Maij 1570.

The quhilk day the dene of gyld and the brethir hes
decernit that Andro Pacok sall pay for the sellyng of
stapill gud for the twa yeiris last by past xiij iiij^d and
gaif he proseidis langar he sall ylk yeir xxx^s.

Item fra Robert Necholl for the spece forsaid [*deleted*: viij^s.]
vj^s viij^d.

   The gild court haldin in the towbutht of Dunferlin
   be Wilyeme Mikkilihone dene of gild the 24 day
   of September anno 1570.

[*Fo: 70v*]

   The gyld courtt haldyne in the tolbutht of Dunfermlyne the x day of October 1570 be William
   Mekkeljohne dene of gyld the rest of the gyld
   brethir beand present.

[*in margin*: Johne Cowpir] The quhilk day Johne Cowpir wes enterit gyld brothir and to the fredome tharof to vmquhill Schir Johne Cowpir his fader and maid the brothirlie aith to pay tharfor the bankat quhene the gyld brethir requiris, quhilk is actit etc.

The quhilk day the dene of gyld and gyld brether decernit and ordanit that nane be interit in tymes cuming to the fredome of gylddrye vnder the payment of the sowme of tene pundis withtout he be interit to the samyn be airschippe. And quhay procuris in the contrare tharof to pay hyme self v lib gif he be ane gyld brothir, quhilk is actit.

The samyn day it is decernit be the saidis brethir that William Ray sall pay for this jnstant yeir xx^S for his handilling of merchandice and Robert Andirsone vthir xx^S and that thaj sall nocht seill in tymes cumyng withtout thaj be fre othyr witht the gyld brethir of this bur or ellis of sum, vthir quhilk is actit etc. And bayth the said parsonis refarit thame to the gild bretheris will and said brether desernis that the for said aict sall stand the x day of December anno 1570.

[*Fo. 71*]

    The gyld courtt haldin in the tolbutht of Dunfermlyne the xx day of December the yeir of God 1570 be William Meklejohne dene of gyld and the rest of the gyld brethir present for the tym.

The quhilk day Robert Pautoune wes electit dene of gyld for ane yeir and maid faytht tharto.

[*in margin*: gyld brothir] The quhilk day Schir Dauj Stewart baillie wes jnterit gyld brothir as nest and laufull air to umquhill M. Andro Stewart his fader to pay the spice and vyne and maid faytht tharto.

The quhilk day the dene of the gyld forsaid and gyld brethir ratefeis the actis maid of befor the tene day of October lastbypast anent the intereing of vnfremenis sones to the fredoum of gyldrye in all poyntis witht this additioune that the gyld brethiris first sone intere for the spice and vyne conforme to the auld ordor and the secunde sones of gyld brethir be in the will of the dene of gyld and gyld brethir for thair intre etc.

    The gild court haldin in the towbuth of Dumferling be the deine of gild and gild breder the penvlt day of Januer anno 1571.

The quhilk day Robart Fillane was conwictit be resone that he coft not sic seip to Jhone Walkar as he coft to to him self and desernis the said Robar to gyf to the said Jhone half ane barrall of his seip becaus that the said Jhonis baill specifecit that he suld by to him as he bocht to him self.

[Fo. 71v]

  The 5 day of June anno 1571.

The quhilk day Jhone Keir entreit to his gucheris [sic] fridume and come in the bretheris will of xl^s that his qucher was awand for his entere and is suorne to ws the handill of merchandris and to obserf the statutis of gildry payand thairfor the spyce and the win.

  The court of gilddry halding be the dein of gild
  and gild bryder the 5 day of October the yeir of
  God 1571.

The quhilk day Wilyeme Meikilijhone maid his count of his gild siluir that he hes referrit and hes delywerit to Sanders Nicoll tresor[ar ? *text obscured*]

The quhilk day Robart Nicoll the brider hes desernit thair will on the said Robbart haifand respec in he is ane unfre manis sone decernis him to pay for his vnlay x^s.

The quhilk day the breder hes decernit thar will one Wilyame Waswat for his handdilling beand onfre to pay xx^s.

[*deleted*: The quhilk day]
  The gyld court haldin be the dene of gyld and
  gyld brethir the x day of October 1571.

The quhilk day Dauid Tod wes interit gyld brothir and maid the aitht tharto and to paye tharfor the sowme of tene pundis money conforme to the act maid thar annent. And gif vthir beis interit bettir chaipe than he handillit thareftir at the will of the dene of gyld and brethir quhilk is actit.

  The gyld cort haudin in the towbwthe of Dunfermlyng the x day of Nouember 1571 be the dene
  of gyld and brethir.

[*in margin*: payit] The quhilk day the daine of gyld and brethir hes dec[ernit ? *text obscured*] that Williame Gaij sall pay for his falt xl^s for the wp making of his bowtht doore eftir the dene had tane the kye fra him for the sailling of his geir with[tout ? *text obscured*] licence of the gyld brethir, the quhilk is acit.

[*Fo. 72*]

The gyld cort of the burcht of Dunfermlyne haldyne in the tolbucht tharof the xij day of December 1571.

The quhilk day in the actioune and caus persewit be James Burne and Alexander Nycoll aganis Johne Covane comperit the said Johne Cowane and maid fayt that he onelie remanit and scheippit the silver upoune the incravying of certane copper syluer pertenand to the saidis thre personis equalie and thairby wes put to greit expenss.

The quhilk day Wilyeme Steinsone come in will of the brether for the occupying of the fredome in landwart and gif that handill ony mair in tyme to cume he sall pay tene lib quhilk he hes asent to quhilk will the brether hes declerit to the soume of xx ^{s} to be payit at the dene of gildis will and Jhone Cowane souerty for the same.

The gild court halding in the towbuth be the deine of gild and the gild breither the 20 day of December anno 1571 one Sant Tomas ewin.

The quhilk day it is dessernit be the brethir that Lowrens Persone and Jhone Persone bretheir saill pay to the brether xx lib gyf it sall happin the ane offendand to the tothir the offender sall pey the forsaid soume and the said Lowrens is cume in will of the dene of gild and the gild breither for his onreverand speikun and gyf he happin to do the lyk he sall tyne his fridome, quhilk is aictit.

The quhilk day Androw Pakcok come in will for his handelling. The gild brethir hes decernit thar will for his handilling of ij yeiris bygein xiij ^{s} iiij^d.

The quhilk day Robart Patone wes chosin dane of for ane yeir to cum be the brethir and to mak ane gud cowmpt of the gyld schiluir and owlawis and maid faytht as afferis.

[*Fo. 72v*]

The gild court haldine in the towbuthe the 24 day of December be the deine of gild and gild breithr anno 1571.

The quhilk day it is staittut be the deine of gild and

gild breither all in ane mynd that quhene it sall happin ony tua breither to discord the falt beand tryit that the offender sall mak the bankat to his broder that he offendit and he that the bankat is meid to he sull mak the bankat to him agane that feilyeand of the same the offender sall pey for the same xvj^S, quhilk is aicit.

> The gyld cortt haldyne be Robert Pautoune dene of gyld of this burt xiiij Augustj anno 1572 and the rest of the gyld brethir eftir specifeit viz William Waluod ane of the baillies and Dauy Stewart James Schortous James Burn Johne Multray Gylbert Kelnedye William Mekolejohne Johne Lowthyane Johne Peirsone Laurence Peirsoune Johne Cowane Alexander Nycoll Johne Robertsoune merchand Johne Cowpir.

The quhilk day the dene of gyld and brethir forsaid beand patronis and haifand power to dispoune the annuell vndirwrittin for certane gud caussis moving thame gaif and disponit ane annuell rent of xx^S of ane tenement of land of Henry Stewart Laurence Turnbull liand one the northt syd of the troune to the said Henry for all the dayis termes and yeiris of the said Henryis lyftyme, provyding that eftir his deceis the said annuell returne and be at the gift and disposicioun of the dene of gyld and gyld brethir for the tym. And thairapoune the said Henry and Robert Pautoune dene of gyld forsaid requirit actis and instrumentis hinc inde.

> Ita est Joannes Cwnynghame notarius publicus manu propria.

[*Fo. 73*]

The ii day of Junij anno 1573.

The quhilk day the deine of gild and gild breither gyfis lechent to Dauid Tod to pay his gild siluir the ane half presentlie and the tothir [*deleted*: fyf] half in ij yeiris quhilk half is v lib and the tothir ij partis l^S yeirlie to be payit heir efter withtout farder deleij, payit v^S this v lib.

> The gyld cortt haldyne be Robert Pautoune dene of gyld of this burcht the xxiij day of September 1573 and the remanent gyld brethir.

[*in margin*: payit Andro Cristye] The quhilk day Androu Cristy wes interit gyld brether and to the fredome tharof and maid his aith tharto and to pay tharfor conforme to the actis payit vs this v lib.

[*in margin*: payit William Cristye] The samyne William Cristye wes interit gyld brothir to the fredoume tharof and maid faytht as efferis and to pay tharfor conforme to the actis viz. v lib in hand and the vthir v withtin twa yeiris viz 1^s yeirlie [*addition*: payit the penult day of Septermber anno 157[3 ? *text obscured*] the summa of v lib.]

    The gild court haldin be Robart Patoune deine of gildis and the rest of the gild breider the 9 day of October anno 1573.

[*in margin*: payit] The quhilk day Robart Nicoll come in will of the breider for his formar handillin to this instant yeir and the breider desernis thar will to the said Robart to pay xxvj^s viij^d instantlie and grantand lecience to him to sell his geir for this yeir, quhilk is actit.

    The nemis of the counsell.

    Hendry Reid
    Wilyem Meikiljhone
    Robart Filleine
    Jhone Mowtray
    James Schortus
    Wilyeme Waluod

[*Fo. 73v*]

    The gild court of Sant Tomas alfor Yull haldin in the towbuth the 22 day of December anno 1573 be Robart Patone dene of gild and the rest of the gild brether.

    The lytis of the ellectione fyr dene of gild.

    Jhone Mwtray
    Jemes Burne
    Jemes Schortus
    Hendry Reid
    Robart Pattone

    The gild court haldin in the towbutht be the prowest the deine of gild witht the beilyeis and the rest of the gild brether the 25 day of Jenuer anno 1573.

The quhilk day Robart Patoune was ellectit and chossing deine of gild for ane yeir.

DUNFERMLINE GILD

The xvj° October anno 1574.
The quhilk day James Schorthous become caution and souertie for the entres of Patrik Irwane befoir the brethir quhen he beis chargit.
The quhilk day Jhone Cowpir become catione and sowerty for the entres of Tomas Cowper biffor the breither quhen he beis chargeit.

> The 21 day of October anno 1574 the gild court haldin be Robert Pattounn dene of gild witht the rest of the gild brether.

The quhilk day Wilyeme Waluod was chossing beilye for ane yeir.

> The court haldin the 29 September be Robart Patone deine of gild and Wilyeme Waluod bailye witht the rest of the gild brither anno 1574.

The quhilk day Tomas Cowper was entreit to the fridome of gildrie be resone that he is hes fatheris air payand tharfor xl^s in the bretheris will and the spice and the wyne and maid faitht as affeiris.

[Fo. 74]

The quhilk day Robart Trowmbill was entrit to the fredume of gildrie acordin to the aict and meid faith as afferis payand tharfor teyne pond of the quhilk payit vij lib x^s.
The quhilk day Robart Nicoll was entrit to the fridume of gildrie for v lib in will of the brither be caus he was ane fremanis sone and mad faith as affeiris.

The samyn day it wes grantit permittit and frelie gevin to William Cowpir sone to William be the haill consent of the dene of gyld and gyld brethir that the said William Cowpir youngar haue ane annuell rent of xxiiij^s yeirlie frie of the tenement of land of William Turnbull and Henry Steuart witht the yairdis and pertinentis for all the dayis of his liftyme begynand his intre tharto at the deceis of the said Henry Stewart. And this forsaid annuell at the deceis of the said William Cowpir to be at the distributioune and gift of the dene of gyld as patroune appoyntit and nominat tharto conforme to the first foundatioun withtout impediment.

> The gild court haldin the 22 day of December be Robart Pattoune dene of gild in anno 1575.
>
> The lytis to be ellecht to be dene of gild for the nixt yeir.
>   Robart Patoune

Wilyeme Meikiljhone
Hendry Reid
Jemes Schortus
Jhone Mowbray
Wilyeme Waluod

The quhilk day Wilyeme Meikiljhone was chossing dene of gild for ane yeir.

[Fo. 74v]

The quhilk dai ane cort haldyng be Wellyem Meikilljhone dyng of gyld and the balyeis witht the gyld bredir in in the towbowtht on the xvij dai of Janewar lxxv yeris.

The quhilk dai it wes ordynit be the hell consant of the prowest and balyes and dyne of gild and the mast pert of the bredryng that the deyn of gyld and ane of the bredryng abowt the Bowlyeon [?] saill pas to the town of Adnbro[? *text obscured*] to the consaill one the xx dai of Janawar lxxv yeir.

> The gyld cortt of the burcht of Dunfermlyne haldyne in the tolbutht tharof be William Meklejohne dene of gyld and gyld brethir of the samyne the xx day of Februar the yeir of God 1575.

The quhilk day Robert Pantoun maid his compt of the gild syluir receivit in his tyme quha restit of his haill receit vj lib vj ^{s} ais the ticket beris.

The same day Johne Multray be commoun consent of the said dene of gild and gildbrethir wes chosein collector to gather and vplift the haill sowmes of money pertenand to the gildrie for the space of ane yeir and to mak compt tharof.

[*in margin*: Patrik Durye payit] The quhilk day the den of gyld and brethar haifand consideratioun of ane bankcat maid of before be Patrik Durye to the prowest and baillies for the tyme and nochtwithtstanding tharof the said Patrik come in will for his fredoune of gyldrie and tharfor resauit him to broderheid of gyldrie and maid the aitht tharto and this withtout preudice of the actis maid of befor anent the intre of gyld brethir etc.

[Fo. 75]

> The gyld cortt haldyne in the tobbutht be William Meklejohne dene of gyld the thrid day of Merche the yeir of God 1575 yeiris.

The quhilk day Andro [*deleted*: Wilyam] Cristye maid payment to Johne Multurar collector of the sowme of fyve pundis in compleit payment of tene pundis for his gyld syluer and dischargit tharof simpliciter etc.

The samyn day the said William Meklejohne dene of gyld beand reddye to pas gud vaiage witht adwyis of the brethir depute Johne Bosuell dene of gyld in his absence quhay acceptit the samyn vpoune him for doing of justice.

> The gyld cortt of the burcht of Dunfermlyne haldyne in the tolbutht of the samyne be John Bosuell deput dene of gyld the xvj day of Merche 1575.

The samyne day James Burne merchand wes ordanit to mak ane amendiment to Robert Pautoune for the mispersonyng of him in jugement. And gif he or ony vthir gyld brodir dois the lyk offence in tymes cuming to tyne his fredoune. [subscipti ?]

> The gyld court of the said burcht haldin be Johne Bosvell dene of gyld depute and gyldbrethir the sevint day of Aprile the yeir of God 1576.

The quhilk day anent the bill gevin in be Lourence Burn and Patrik Cowane aganis Thomas Cowper for inlaik of certane stanes of lang irne coft in Danskin amangis thame as partinaris it being confessit be the saidis Lourence and Patrik that thay brek bouk at thair awin hand the said Thomas nocht beand present the said dene of gild and brethir ffindis that thaj did wrang tharintill. And tharefore ordanes the saidis Lourence and Patrik sall tyne the tua part of the inlaik and the said Thomas the thrid part according to the quantitie of thar geir eftir calculatioun beand maid and that na brothir beand partinar witht ane vthir brek bouk in tymes cuming withtout consent of his partinar vndir the pane of tinsall of the haill inlaik and ane vnlaw to the brethir.

[*Fo. 75v*]

> The gyld court haldin be the prowest and Wilyeme Meikiljhone dene of gild and the rest of the brether the 20 day of Appryll anno 1576.

> The gyld cortt haldin in the tolbutht of Dunfermlyn be William Meklejohne dene of gyld and gyld brethir the xj day of Maij anno 1576.

The quhilk day Robert Pautoune maid his compt of the

rest of vj lib vj^S restit lij^S to be payit to the collectouris
and the said Robert Pautoune dischargit tharof and of
all othir comptis precedand this det.

[*in margin* [*caret sign*] lib] The quhilk day Robert Turnbull payit of his gyld syluer v lib and dischargit tharof
and to pay the vthir v [*caret sign*] withtin twa yeiris nixt-
tocum.

[*in margin*: Fillane and Alexander Nycoll] The quhilk day
it wes foundyne that Robert Fillane hes miscallit and mis-
personatit Alexander Nycoll aganis the ordour of brithir-
heid and thairfor ordanis the said Robert to mak amend-
ment to the said Alexander at the sycht of the prowest
and gyld brethir to pay the bankat to thaim and the
xl^S to be payit to the pure, and gif ather of the saidis
parteis or ony vthiris dois the lyk offence to ane gyld
brothir in tymes cumyng to be dischargit of the fredoume
at the will of the prowest baillies dene of gyld and gyld
brethr and quhilk is actit. [subscriptit ?]

   The gild cowrt haldin in the towbuth of
   Dunfermlin be William Mekiljhone dene of gild and
   gild brither the 9 day of August anno 1576.

The quhilk day the dene of gyld and brither chargit
Pattrik Dury that he sell na wyne darrar nor iij^S iiij^d
the pynt and that he sell nane bot with the guge meit
heir efter.

[*Fo.* 76]

   The gyld cortt haldyne in the tolbutht of Dunfermlyn xxij Septembris 1576 be William Meklejohne
   dene of gyld and gyld brethir. [subscripti ?]

The quhilk day it wes statut be the dene of gyld and gyld
brethir that brothir tak vnfremene in thair companye to
fraucht witht thame as partinaris quhilk is to the preiudice of the kingis custume and priuilege of our libertye
vnder the pane ane vnlaw of - lib to be payit be the
resauer of the vnfremanis and his geir toties quoties
sal viz tynsell of fredoume. [subscripsit ?]

   The gyld courtt haldin in the tolbuth of Dunfermling the xj day of October the yeir of God 1576
   be William Meklejohne dene of gyld and gyldbrethir.

The quhilk day Androu Chrystie come in will of den of
gyld and gyldbrethir for taking witht him of vnfremenis
geir the breither desernis thair will to the ij markis of
onla.

The quhilk day Robart Wilsone come in will of the dene of gild for the takin of wnfrimenis geir the breither desernis thair will to be ij markis of unla. [*addition* : and peit the saym.]

> The 19 day of Nouember anno 1576.

The quhilk day the breither desernis the will of Robart Nicoll entres to be v lib and nane to be entrit to the fridoume of gildrie if the secund sonis and docteris beter chepe and that to be peyit presentlie.

The quhilk day Jhone Reid hes payit the rest of his entres siluir

[*in margin*: fremane payit] The quhilk day Jemes Culbart was entreit to the fridome of gildrie for v lib. and be resone of his wyf beand ane fre manis docter and meid faith as affeiris and peyit the same presentle.

[*Fo. 76v*]

> The gild court haldin in the towbuth of Dunferm-
> ling be Wilyem Meikiljhon dene of gild and gild
> brether the xxij day of Dec[ember ? *text obscured*]
> anno 1576.

The quhilk day the dene of gild witht the beilyeis and the rest of the gild breither consederand the innormetiis that is throwth the entres of samony to the fridome of gildris hes stattut and ordenit that jlk ane that enteris in tyme cume sall pey jmedietlie at ther entres the souma of tuanty markis mony and quha procuris in the contrar beand ane brother sall pey the souma of tene markis mony onfregewin.

The quhilk day William Waluod was chossin dene of gild for a year.

> The 23 day of Januer 1576.

The quhilk Gillie Wilsone was permittit to mary Pattrik Cawane and to ws the fridome durein the said Gille lyftym.

The quhilk day the prouest dene of gild and brither decernis Tomas Couper to pey to the pur xiij^s iiij^d and that for the mispersoning of James Culbert and to ask the said James forgiufe and this aict to be extiunit in the forme of the aldis auctis at mair lenth.

> The gild court haldin be Williame Waldwod dene
> of gild of Dunfermling the xxvij of August anno
> 1577.

The quhilk day Alexander Nicoll collector maid compt of his colleccioune restis awand viij^d off all comptis dis-

chairgand the said Alexander of all sowmis preceiding this day and dait heirof.
The quhilk day George Andirsoune wes conwictit in any wnlay for the handline and tapping of irne and lint contrair our previlege to pay xiij^s iiij^d.

    The gild cortt haldin in the tolbuith of Dunfermling be William Waluod den of gild and gildbrethir the xxiij day of September 1577.

[*in margin*: fredome] The quhilk day Robert Fargussone sone and air to vmquhile Robert Fargussone was interit to his said vmquhile fathiris fredome of gildbrethir and maid faytht as vse is.

[*Fo. 77*]

The quhilk day William Burn and Laurence Adesone come in will of the den of gild and gildbrethir for the selling of certane lint irne and hemp and wer ordanit to sell na mare withtin this burcht vndir the pane of confiscatioune of the hail ware.

    The gild court haldin in the towbuth of Dunfermlin the xix day of December anno 1577 be William Waluod deine of gild and gildbreither.

The quhilk day Robart Pattone was chossing dene of gild for ane yeir.

    The gild cortt haldin in the tolbuth of Dunfermling the xxiiij day of Merche 1577 be Robert Pautoun den of gild and gildbrethir.

The quhilk day the den of gild baillie and gild brethir decernis Robert Fillane to be the first movear of Robert Nycole and Robert Nycole the last molestar of him vpone the Saboth day, decernis ilkane of thame to pay xx^s [*deleted*: of thaime to pay ane unlaw of viij] to the pure togidder that Robert Fillane to pay vther xx^s of vnlaw that he wes auchtand of before, and gif ather of the saidis pairteis beis fund molesting or turbuling vtheris in tymes cuming the offendar to tynt his fredome of gildrie. And attour giff ony of the saidis Robertis bagbyttis or sclanderis ather of vther owthir in word or deid the pairtie offendand to pay v lib uneforgivin and this decernit be decreit of arbotrie Johne Boswell Robert Pattoune for the pairt of Robert Fillane and James Burne and Johne Cowane for the pairt of Robert Nicoll.

    The [*deleted*: toilbuith] gild court haldin in the toilbuith of Dunfermling the xxiij day of Appryle 1578 be Robert Patoune dene of gild and gild

brethir.
The quhilk day the gildbrethir findis Thomas Cupar dissobeyand the dene of gild in vsing his office decernis him according to the actis befor.

[Fo. 77v]

The gild court haldin in Dunfermling the xx day of December 1578 be Robert Pantoune dene of gild and gild brethir.
The quhilk day the dene of gild and gild brethir contenowis this cortt to the day aucht dayis.

The gild court haldin in Dunfermling in tolbucth thairof the xxvij day of December 1578 be Robert Pantoune dene of gild and geildbrethir.
The quhilk day Robert Pautoune was chossin dene of gild for ane yeir.

The gild cortt haldin in the tolbuitht of Dunfermling the last day of Junij 1579 be Robert Pawtoune dene of gild and gildbrethir Johne Bosuale baillie.

[in margin: Ritchart Walker enterit, payit] The quhilk day Ritchart Walkar was enterit ane gildbruthir and to pay thairfoir conforme to the last act and maid his aith to vse himselff as ane honest merchand [deleted: quhill is actit] according to the auld actis [addition: and peit thair for xx mark to the den of geild Robert Wylsoune dein of geild.]

The gild cortt haldin in the tolbuitht of Dunfermling the xxj day of September the yeir of God j^m v^c lxxix yeiris be Robert Patoune dene of gild and gildbrethir Johne Bosuale and Patrik Murray baillies.

[in margin: Williame Aisoim enterit. payit]
The quhilk day Williame Aisoune was enterit ane gildbrothir and to pay thairfoir conforme to the last act and maid his aith to vse him self as ane honest merchand according to the auld actis quhilk is actit. [addition: and pait thair for xx markis to the den of geild Robert Wylsoune den of geold.]

The gild courtt haldine in the tolbutht of Dunfermling the xix day of December anno j^m v^c lxxix yeiris be Robert Pautoune dene of gild and gildbrether, and Gilbert Kennidy ballie.

[in margin: George Persoune enterit] The quhilk day George Persoune was enterit [deleted: ane] gild bruther

to his fathiris fredome and to pay thairfoir the spyce and the wyne and maid his aith to vse him selff as ane honest merchand according to the auld actis.
The quhilk day Robert Wilsoune was chossin dene of gild for ane yeir to cum.

[*in margin*: being in the toun] The quhilk day the dene of gild and gildbrithir constitud and ordanis that gif ony framanis sone entir nocht withtin yeir and day that he sall cum in the dene of gild and gildbrethiris will for ane on freman of his entres quhilk is actit.

[*in margin*: Robert Friser enterit] The quhilk day Robert Friser wes enterit gildbrother to his fatheris fredome for the spyce and the wyne and maid faith and effeiris quhilk is actit.

> The gild courte haldin in the tolbuth of Dunfermling the xxvj day of December the yeir of God j^m v ^{c} lxxix yeiris be Robert Wilsoune and the gild brether witht the baillies.

[*in margin*: statut] The quhilk day it is statut and ordanit be the dane of gild and gild brethir that all one freman that enteris ane gildbruthir fra this furth sall pay for his entres and to be fre witht the gildbrothir the sowme of xx lib money instantlie to be delyuerit eftir his entres and quhatsumuvir of the gildbruthir procuris in the fauouris of ony thai entres and disyris to haue dome of the said.

[*Fo. 78*]

> The gild court haldin in the toilbuith of Dunfermling be Alexander Nicoll dene of gild and William Meklejohn bailyie and remanent of the gildbrethir the xv Appryll 1581 yeiris.

The quhilk day the dene of gild with consent of the gildbrethir ordanis Robert Wilsoune to deluir agane to James Dowgall the croune takin fra him in plege in Appryll lastbypast in respect of his unfortunat wayage prowyding that the said James vse na handling of merchandice heireftir withtin this burgh acttit.

The quhilk day Robert Wilsoune maid his compt of his resett being dene of gild in the four scoir yeir and delyuirit to Alexander Nicoll dene of gild for this yeir the sowme of xvj lib xiij ^{s} iiij ^{d} in compleit payment of all sowmis of money resauit be him duiring his office. And the said Alexander Nicoll dene of gild grantit the ressett thairof and dischargit the said Robert of the samen.

The gild cowrt haldin in the tolbuth of Dunfermling be Allexander Nicole dene of gild and William Meiklejohnne bailyie and remanent of the gildbrethir viz. Johnne Vemys of Pittyncreff George Bothuell Johnne Lawdiane James Burne Allexander Kellok Androw Crystie Valtir Crystie Villiam Valuod Patrik Cowan Richart Valcar and remanent gildbrethir vpoun the xxviij of Junij anno j^m v^c lxxxj yeiris.

The quhilk day the dane of gild and gild brethir decernis and ordanis James Schortes to sell his wyne fra this furth for ii^d darreir nor it is in Leyth and Edinburgh and na derar nothir to nychtbouris nor straingearis vndir the pain of xvj^d for the first fault and tinsale of his fredone for ane yeir for the secund fault, and this act to be extendit to all and sindrie hawing or sall haif vyne to sell vithin this brucht in tymes cuming. And in respect the said James contrauett the dane of gild and gild brethiris command be selling his wyne for four schillingis decernis him to pay ane half galloune of wyne vitht the pertinentis instantlie to the dane of gild and gild brethir, quhilk is actit.

[*deleted*: The gild court haldin in the toilbuith of Dumfermling be Robert]

[*Fo. 78v*]

The gild court haldin in the toilbuith of Dumfermling be Alexander Nicoll dene of gild and William Meklejohn and Gilbert Kennydy bailyeis of the bur[cht ? *text obscured*] of Dunfermling and the remanent of the gild brethir the xxiij day of September anno 1581 yeiris.

The quhilk day it is statut be dene of gild and gildbrethir that n[a ? *text obscured*] fleschour fra this day furtht by ony woll hyid or skinne withtin the toune or mak pryce of ony hyid or skynne that thai slay to vthir m[en ? *text obscured*] withtin the burghe wnder na les pane nor tynsall of thair fredo[me ? *text obscured*] and paying of tene pundis giff thai have geir and giff thai h[ave ? *text obscured*] nocht the said sowme of tene pundis to be pinnyschit at the sycht of of the prowest bailyeis den of gild and gild brethir and the said bailyeis interponit thair authoritie thairto.

The gild cowrt haldin in the tolbuth of Dunfermling be Alle[xander ? *text obscured*] Nicole dane of gild and Villiam Meiklejohnne bailyie of the said brucht witht the remanent of the gild brethirine the xxvj of September 1581.

[*in margin*: William Mowtray enterit] The quhilk day William Mowtray sone and appeirand air to Johne Mowtray merchand was enterit gild bruthir in his fathiris place he payand thairfoir the spyce and wyne and maid his aith to vse and behaiff him self in all tymes cuming lyk ane honest gild bruthir conforme [to ? *text obscured*] the auld actis maid tharanent. Payit.

>The gild court haldin in the toilbuith of Dunfermling be Alexander Nicoll dene of gild and John Bosuell Thomas Cupar bailyeis of the burghe of Dumfrmling and the remanent of the gildbrethir the xxviij day of December anno 1581 yeiris.

The quhilk day the dene of gild and gild brethir statutis and or[danis ? *text obscured*] that na wyne be sauld fra this [*deleted*: day] our furth bot for iij^s viij^d[the ? *text obscured*] pynt wndir na les pane nor tynsall of thair fredome and dinging out of the pounctioune heid.
The quhilk day William Pattoune was electit and chosine be the gild bre[thir ? *text obscured*] dene of gild for ane yeir quha exceptit the office and maid faytht for dew ministratione therof.

[*Fo. 79*]

>The gild court haldin in the toilbuith of Dunfermling be Robert Pattoune dene of gild John Wemis proweist John Bosuell and Thomas Cupir bailyeis of the burghe of Dumfermling and the remanent of the gildbrethir the thrid day of Februar anno 1581 yeiris.

The quhilk day Alexander Nicoll last dene of gild maid his compt of the gildsilvir quhairwitht he intromettit during his office of the quhilk he hes debursit vj lib. xix s allowit to him swa restis ix lib xiij^s iiij^d and that delyuirit to Robert Pattoune now dene of gild and the said Alexander dischargit.

[*in margin*: Johne Andirsone enterit] The quhilk day anent the supplicatioune giwen in be John Andirsoune sone and air to wmquhill Johne Andirsoune at the croce desyring him to be enterit gildbrothir to his wmquhill fatheris fredome the dene of gild witht consent and assent of the proweist bailyeis and hail gild brethir repellis the petitioune of the said John Andirsoune and refus simpliciter to entir him to [*deleted*: his fathiris] the fredome of gildrie throuche his father in respect of ane act maid aganis the same, and thaireftir the said John refering him selff in the willis of the dene and gildbrethir tuiching his entres renuncand all tytle that he may have be his father tharto was enterit gildbrothir conforme to the last act maid anent the entres of onfremene. And the said John maid his aith to vse and behaiff him selff decentlie in all thingis as effeiris.

 The gild court haldin in the toilbuith of Dumfermling be Robert Pattoune dene of gild Johne Bosuell bailye of the said burghe and the remanent of the gildbrethir the xxvij day of December anno 1582 yeiris.

The quhilk day Robert Pattoune wes electit and chosin dene of gild be consent of the gildbrethir for ane yeir quha exceptit the office and maid faith for dewe [*deleted*: ad] ministratione thairof.

The quhilk day the dene of gild and gildbrethir statutis and ordanis that na wyne be sauld fra this day furth bot for iij^s iiij^d the pynt.

[*Fo. 79v*]

 The nynt day of November anno 1583 yeiris Robert Patoune den of gild and the gildbrethir.

The quhilk day the dene of gild in presence of the gildbrethir resauit fra Robert Edisoune the sowme of x^s vj^d for his annuell rent awin to the said gildberthirn furtht of his tenement of land lyand in the sowth syid of the Nethirtoune extending yeirlie to vij^s in compleit payment of the Witsonday terme bypast and of all yeiris and termes preceiding the terme forsaid and wes dischargit simpliciter tharof prowyding he mak gud and thankfull payment of the said annuell rent yeirlie and humelie in tyme cuming.

 The nyntene day of Nouember anno 1583 yeiris in presens of Robert Pattoun dane of gild and gildbrethrin.

That day William Horne merchand and burges of Edinburgh personalie comp[erit *? text obscured*] and was absoluit fra the half barrell of soapp acclamit of him be Johne Mowtray merchant burges of the said brucht inrespect of his aith givin in presens of the brethrine that he causit delyuir the said half barrell soapp to camp in Campheir and haid ressauit na gratitud nor gud died thairfor.

The gild court of the gildbrethrine of Dunfermling haldin in the tolbuth thairof be Robert Pattoun dane of gild brethrin the xxj day of December anno j^{m}v^c lxxxiij yeiris.

The quhilk day Robert Pattoun was be wotis of the haile gildbrothrin was continewit dane of gild for ane yeir to cum quha acceptit the said office in and vpoun him and maid faytht for dew administratioun thairof.

The gild court haldin in the toilbuith of Dumfermling be Robert Pattoune dene of gild and the bailyies and the remanent of the gildbrethir the viij day of Januar anno j^{m}v^c lxxxiij yeiris.

[in margin: Alexander Stewin] The quhilk day Alexander Stewin wes enterit gildbruthir and to pay thairfor conforme to the last act and maid his faith as ane honest merchand according to the auld actis quhilk is actit and delyuerit the sowme to the dene of gild.

[Fo. 80]

The gyld court haldin in the tolbuth of Dunfrmling be Robert Pattoun dane of gild of the said brugh bailyies thairof and remanent gildbrethrine of the samin vpoun the xviij day of September the yeir of God j^{m}v^c and lxxxiiij yeiris.

The quhilk day the dene of gild and gildbrethrine grantit licence to Isobell Templeman relict of vmquhile William Crystie burges and gildbruther to marie in the Lord and to enioy hir fredome and handling nocht in this brucht conforme to the ordour vsat be thame in sack casis of befor.

The quhilk day Patrik Crystie of the Hoile laufull sone to vmquhile Walter Crystie burges and [deleted: dane of] gildbrethir of this bruch was enterit gildbrethir to his fatheris fridome and maid his aith to vse him self as ane honest merchand payand tharfoir the spyce and wyne conforme to the last actis provyding also that gif the said Patrikis eldest bruther or ony of his sonnis or airis happinnis to come heireftir and desyris to be enterit to the said vmquhile Walter [deleted: fadiris] fridome in that cace the said Patrik obliss him and his airis to pey for the said fridome as ane gildbrethiris secound sone according to the last actis that is fyve pundis.

The quhilk day Johne Andersoun at the croce vpoun his awin confessioune submittit him to the dane of gild and gildbrethrine and to thair decisioun and decreit for the mispersoning and iniuring of Allexander Nichole and

Thomas Cowpar baillies in the executioune of thair office. And the dane of gild be introloqutor of the haile brethrine ffindis the said Johne Andersoun in the wrang in mispersoning and iniuring the said Allexander Nichole sindrie tymes for the executioun of his office and also in mispersoning of the said Thomas Cowpar of Furisday last and thairfoir ordanis him to acknawlege his offence and mak amendis to the saidis baillies at the sytht and avyse of the dane of gild and gildbrethrine, and give the said Johne or ony wthir gildbruther withtin this brugh committis the lyk offence heireftir or iniuris the said baillies or ony wthir gild bruther ather in word or deid in tyme cuming that the offendar quhatsumevir sall tyne his fredome thairfor foirevir.

[*Fo. 80v*]

Thyre ar the gild brethir that sall haif all the hydis and skynis euiry ane as thair olk fallis iiij men to the ok and that na vthir prevene thaim withtin the tyme nathir in land nor borcht vndir the panie contenit in the act maid thairvpone of befor, thair names heyreftir is expremit and writting as thay sall use.

> The gild court of the gildbrethrine of Dunfermling haldin in the tolbuth of the said burcht be Robert Pattoun dane of gild the bailyeis and gild brethir of the said brugh the xx day of October anno j^m v^{c}lxxxiiij yeiris.

That day George Hachet of Pitfirren was enterit gildbruthir to the fridome of vmquhile Patrik Hachet of Pitfirren his father and was sworne thairto as effeirit.

> The gild court haldin be the dane of gild and gild brethr[ine *? text obscured*] of the brucht of Dunfermling in the tolbuith thairof be [*deleted* : dane of] Robert Pauttoun dane of gild baillies and remanent gilbrethrine of the said bructh the xxj day of Nouember the yeir of God j^m v^c lxxxiiij yeiris.

The quhilk day comperit Laurence Trumble and Dauid Stewart and delyuerit to the dane of gild and gildbrethrine the sowm of threttene pundis money for redemptioun of ane annuelrent of tuentie schillingis annualeit to vmquhile Schir John Coupar chaplane his assignais be vmquhile Johne Wrycht ffurth of his tenement of land lyand benyith the trone vnder reversioun contenand the said sowm with fyve yeiris takkis of the said tenement eftir the redemptioun and be the said Schir Johne Cowpar dotat to the Halie Blud altar and gildbrethrine of this brucht patronis thairto. [The ? text obscured] quhilk sowm witht threttie schillingis fra the said Dauid Stewart in compositioun of his part of the saidis fyve yeiris takkis the said [deleted: Dauid] Laurence maid faytht that he haid satisfeit alreadie the said vmquhile John Coupar in his lyftyme be delyuering to him fyfe hundretht schillingss for his part of the saidis takkis. The said dane of gild and gildbrethrine haldis thame weill content and peyit and for thame and thair successouris dischairgis the said Dauid and Laurence thair airis of the samin for evir grantis the said annuelrent laufullie redemit and renuncit the samyn and obliss thame to warrand the saidis Dauid and Laurence and thair forsaidis of the same for evir.

Robert Pattoune dene of gild
James Lowry John Bosuell

The quhilk day James Blaw spous to Cristiane Schortus dochtir and air of vmquhile James Schortus burges and gildbruther of this brucht was enterit gild bruther to the fridome of the said vmquhile James Schortus and maid fath to keipp thair actis, peyand thairfor the spy[ce ? text obscured] and wyne provyding alwayis that the said James Blawe vse nocht the priuilege of the said gildrie nor fredom of this brucht in Culross nor in na vthir partis outwith the jurisdicthoun of the br[ethir ? text obscured]

James Blaw witht my hand.

[Fo. 81]

      Prymis
Dauid Deware
Willyam Fergesone
Adam Blakwold
Jhone Brwne in the Nethirtoun
      Secundus
Lawrens Dawgles
Willyam Cowpere
Thomas Stewinsoune
James Dulie
      Tertius
Willyam Hume
Waltir Cristie
Robert Murray
Jhone Crystie
      Quartus
Jhone Keyre
Willyam [deleted: Willyam] Wilsone

Jhone Willsone
Jhone Mowtray
    Quintus
Patryk Hakat
Janot Dawgles
Willyam Walwod
James Schortus
    Sextus
Thomas Stewart
Thomas Dawgles
Dauy Stewart
Robert Gray
    Septymus
Alane Couttis
Willyam Nycoll
William Andersone
Dauid Wilsone

    Octavus
Maister Jhone Spens
Lawrens Fergesoun
Thomas Fyne
James Muray
    Nonus
Maister Andro Stewart
Jhone Pattoun
Waltir Baxtar
Andro Wakare

And Dauid Dewar to begyne one Gud Fryday afor Pass and endure to the nyxt Furisday at ewin, and the laif to follow eftir that the same manir.

[Fo. 81v]

    The gild court haldin in the toilbuith of Dunfermling be Robert Pattoune dene of gild bailyies and the remanent of the gildbrethir vpon the secund day of Januar anno j^m v^c four scoir four yeiris.

The quhilk day Robert Pattoune in presens of the gildbrethrine was chosin dane of gild for ane yeir to come quha acceptit the same office in and vpoun him and maid fayth for dewe and laufull administratioun tharof.
The

    The gild court haldin in the tolbuith of Dunfermling be Robert Pauttoun dane of gild and baillies with the remanent gildbrethrine vpoun the xxiij day of Januarij j^m v^c and foure scoir and foure yeiris.

[*in margin*: Henrie Turnbull enterit] The quhilk day Henrie Trumbill was enterit to the fridome of gildrye within this brucht be reassoun of Helene Mowtray his wyff being ane frie mannis [*deleted*: wyff] dochter peyand thairfoir fyve pundis instantlie and maid fayth to keipp thair statutis and ordinances.

    The gild court haldin in the tolbuith of Dunfermling be Robert Pautoun dane of gild provest and baillies of the said burcht and gildbrethrine of the samin vpoun the xviij day of Februarij anno j^m v^c four scoir and foure yeiris.

The quhilk day in presens of the provest bailiies and

gild brethrine Robert Pauttoun dane of gild maid his compt of the gild syluir and annuellis pertening thairto intrometit with be him sen his last entring dane of gild be the space of thrie yeiris bypast, his chairge extendis to xxx lib xiij^s ij^d, his dischairge thairof haid and allowit extendis to xvij lib vj^s vj^d. Sua restis in his hand xiii lib vj^s viij^d and was dischairgit of the rest.

[*deleted*: The 9 of Julij anno 1585.]

> The gild courte haldin in the tolbuith of Dunfermling be Robert Patoun dane of gild the baillais of the said burcht and gild bretherine of the samyn the xxij day of December the yeir of God j^m v^c four scoir and fyve yeir.

The quhilk day Robert Patoune in presens of the gildbrethrine was chosin dane of gild for ane yeir to cum quha acceptit the said office in and vpoune him and maid fayth for dew and lauchtfull administratioune thairoff.

[*Fo. 82.*]

The quhilk day the dene of gild and gildbrether ordanis that the fourttene pundis and ten schillingis pertening to vmquhile Schir John Coupir of ane annueill quhilk he hade yerlie of xx^s quhilk annuell was gevin to William Coupir sone to William Coupir in the Newraw ordanis the said sowme of xiiij lib and ten shillingis to be layd vpoune land for ane ressonible proffet be yeir, the said proffeit to be gevin to the boy yeirle during the said Williamis lyftyme and principall sowme to be furtht cuming to the dene of gild and gildbrether.

> The gild court haldin in the toilbuith of Dunfermling be the prowest dene of gyld bailyies and the remanent of the gildbrether vpone the xxiiij day of December anno 1585 yeiris.

That day anent the petitioun that Robert Dewgart and Katherin Porteous his spous desyring licence and privilege to vse handling withtin this brucht be vertew of ane licence grantit to thame be our souerane lord for vsing of of handling in all the burrovis withtin this realme. The provest dane of gild and haile gildbrethrine all in ane voce ffindis that na priuilege are to be grantit to thame be rassoun of the said licence. Because of thair priuileges and liberties grantit to the said brugh of befoir and that the samin is erectit ane frie brucht of regalitie quharvpoun the kingis ma may [sic] nocht justlie intrude uny persoun vpoun thame for hurting of thair liberties and thairfoir statutis and ordanis that na persoun nor person[is ? *folio worn*] be admittit heirefoir to bruik uny priuileigis withtin this bruch be vertew of siclyk priuileigis and licencis to be obtenit in tyme cuming. Quhilk ansuer the said Robert Dewgait acceptit as ressonable and passed fra the vsing of the benifite of his forsaid licence withtin this brucht and submitted him selff simpliciter to the will of the said Robert dane of gild and gildbrethrin. Quha vpoun his submissioun inrespect of this present plaige of pestilence quhar throw they may nocht guidlie travell in the countrie for vsing of the handling grantit thame tollerance and oversight to handle withtin this toun during thair pleasur allanerlie and ay and quhill they be dischargit be the dane of gild and gild brethrine tharfra.

The gild court

[*Fo. 82v - blank*]

[*Fo. 83*]

The rentaill of the annuallis awand to the Haly Blud altar yeirlie to be payit

Item Sanderis Blak landis in annuall – iij^s Lowrenc Hutton.
Item the landis of Willyam Wallat lyand one the north syd of the commone gatt in annuall – iij^s.
Item the landis of Dauid Blak in annuall lyand one the northt syd of the commone gait – v^s Symon Hair.
Item the lyandis of Dauid Dewar lyand one baksyd of the said land of Dauid Blak in annuall – xj^s.
Item the landis of Jhone Wrycht the buthe of the cros paying in annuall – xij^d Georg Trumbill.
Item the Braid Yard in the New Raw now pertening to Jhone Smytht eldar in annuall – xij^d Lowrent Smythtis ayrs.
Item the landis of Thomas Stewinsone lyand at the fuit of the New Raw one the est syd of commone gait in annuall – ij^s vj^d.
Item the landis of – Wawane lyand in the Nethertoun one the sovtht syd of the commone gait in annuall – xx^d Edward Burn.
Item the landis of James Kellok in the west end of Nethertoun in annuall – vij^s Jhon Adison.
Item the landis of Schir John Cowpir gewyne to the Halye Blud altar lyand one the northt sid of the Hie Gait at the

troune in annuall - xx^s.

[*Fo. 83v*]

    The gild cortt haldin in the tolbuith of Dunfermling be the dane of gild and gildbrether the xxij º December 1586 yeris.

The quhilk day Robert Pattoune wes chosin dene of gild for ane yeir and maid faith for administratioun of justice during his office.

The quhilk day it is ordanit be the dene of gild and gildbrether ordanis the sowme of xiiij lib x^s quhilk is in the handis of the den of gild to be delyuerit be him to Thomas Cuper and the said Thomas Cuper to mak sufficient securitie for the forsaid sowme to the brethrin and the profeit thairof quhilk is xx^s to be gevin yeirlie to William Cuper brother germane to the said Thomas during the said Williamis lyftyme conforme to the provisioune quhilk wes maid affoir to the said William.

The quhilk day Dauid Stewart fund in the wrang in dissobeying the dene of gildis offiser and thairfor the said Dauid submittis him in the will of the dene of gild and gild brethir. Quhilk will the den of gild and gildbrethir conwickis him in xxvj^s viij^d. And giff the said Dauid Stewart be stubburne or speikis ewill langage the said Dauid Stewart sall tyne his handling of fredome and that na vther in tyme cuming dissobey the offiser vnder the pane of tynning of thair fredome according the former actis.

    The gild court haldin in the tolbuith of Dunfermling be the dane of gild baillies and gildbrethrine of the said brugh the xviij day of Februar 1586.

The quhilk the dane of gild witht auyse and consent of the provest and baillies and haill gildbrethrine of the said brugh vndirstanding them to be hurt and the ordour of gildrie abusit be frimennis wyffis mareing vnfrimene eftir the depairtur of thair first husband and bryuking of the priuileges of the gildrie and vsing the handling tharof withtout making ony satisfactioun or peyment tharfoir ffor remeid quhairof it is statut and ordanit be the dane of gild provest baillies and gildbrethrine that na widow fra this furth vse ony handling anent the said gildrie bot during hir widowhead allanerlie and that hir secound husband sall vse na handling eftir his mariaige vntill he be of new enterit witht the

gildbrethrine and pey tharfoir according to the actis and
discretioune of the dane of gild and gildbrethrin and
quhasoeuir procuris or solistis in the contrair heirof
to pey fyve pundis.

that day

[Fo. 84]

[in margin: Johne Dewar enterit] That day Johne Dewar
was enterit gildbrothir be reassoun of [Besse ? folio torn]
Waluod his wyf being ane frimannis dochter and ordanit
to pey thairfoir fyve pundis instantlie witht the space
and wyne and maid his aith as effeiris.

> The gild court haldin in the tolbuith of Dumiferm-
> ling be Robert Pattoune dene of gild and the
> remanent of the gildbrether xvij day of October
> anno j^m v^c fourscoir sewin yeiris.

[in margin: Johne Law enterit] That day Johne Lawe
wes enterit gild brother be reasoune of Barbara Stewart
his wyff being ane fremanis douchter and ordanit to pey
thairfoir five pundis instantlie with the spyce and the
wyne and maid his aith as effeiris.

> The gild court haldin in the tolbuith of Dunferm-
> ling be Robert Pautoun dane of gild and George
> Bothue ane of the baillies of the said bruch witht
> the remanent of the gildbrethrine the xix day of
> October the yeir of God j^m v^c lxxxvij yeiris.

The quhilk day the baillie dane of gild and gildbrethrine
all in ane voce having apprehendit certane lint brocht
fra Dysart to this toun be Henrie Rodger extending to
twentiefoure stane quhairof tuentie stane belangis to
James Mochrie bocht be him in Dysart as be deponit in
his consuence being sworne and examinit that the vthir
foure stane pertening to the said Henrie Rodger hame
bringar of the said lint and cum bound thairof weyand
v quarteris tua pund sauld be him to Isobell Huttoun
spous to George Cambell and weyit in the said James
Mochries houss the rest of the said four stane yet in
the said James Muchries handis according to his awn
confessioun quharthrocht the said Henre has contravenit
the actis and ordinance of the gildrie in bringin stable
gear to this toun and selling thairof withtin the samin
and [in margin: he having na priuilege nor fridome to
that effect being vnfrie witht the said gildbrethrine]
thairfoir decernis the said foure stanis lint appertening
to the said Henrie asweill sauld be him alredy as yit

restand vn sauld to be escheattit to the vse of the said
gild brethrine to conforme to thair actis and statutis maid
tharanent of befor.

[*in margin*: William Pratus enterit] The quhilk day William
Pratus was enterit gildbruther and referrit him in the
willis of the dane of gild and the gildbrethrine anent his
gild syluir and maid his aith thairto as effeiris.

[*Fo. 84v*]

The gild court haldin be the provest bailyeis and
gildbrethrine of Dunfermling in the tolbuith tharof
vpoun the nyntene day of December the yeir of God
j^m v^c lxxxvij yeiris in absence of Robert
Pauttoun last dane of gild being presentlie
furth of this realm.
Lyttis for electing of the dane of gild
William Meikiljohn
Henrie Reid
Thomas Coupar

The quhilk day Thomas Coupar was be the provest baillies
and maist pairt of the gild brethrine electit dane of gild
withtin the said brucht for ane yeir to cum quha acceptit
the said office and maid fayth tharto.

The gild court of the gilbrethrin of the brucht
of Dunfermling haldin be the baillies and dane
of gild and brethrine tharof in the tolbuth of the
said brucht the saxtene day of Februarij 1587.

[*in margin* : Johne Walker enterit] The quhilk day Johne
Walker eldest sone and appeirand air to Riche Walker
burges and gild bruthir of the said brucht was enterit
gild brethir and maid his aith thairto as effeirit
peya[nd ? *text obscured*] thairfoir fyve pundis conforme
to the former actis.

The quhilk day Robert Pattoune maid his compt in presence
of the hail gildbrethir all comptis be hard and sene
the tyme of his reseit sa restis in the said Robertis hand
the sowme of vij^s and

Vpoun the xxiiij of Februar anno Domini 1588
yeiris in presens of the dane of gild and gild
brethrine.
Robert Pauttoun maid his compt of his intromissioun
witht the gild syluir during the tyme he wes dane of gild
(except of the annuellis sen the foure scoir yeir of God)
his haill chairge and dischairge being hard and allovit
to him of all yeiris preceiding the dait heirof the dane

of gild and gild brethrine dischairgis the said Robert
of his intromissioun for euir.

[*Fo. 85*]

The gild court of the brugh of Dunfermling haldin [in *? text obscured*] the tolbuth tharof be the provest and baillies of the said brugh Thomas Coupar dane of gild and gildbrethrine withtin the said brugh vpoun the aucht day of Maij the yeir of God j^m v^c lxxx and aught yeiris.

[*in margin*: David Broun enterit] The quhilk day Dauid Broun clerk of the said brught was enterit gildbrethir be reassoun of Gelis Reid his spous eldest dochter of vmquhill Andro Reid hir father burges and gild brother withtin this bructh and succeidand to the said vmquhill Androis fridome of gildrie peyand tharfoir the spyce and wyne as vse is and was sworne thairto. [*addition*: peyit xl^s for spyce and wyne.]

[*in margin*: Johne Anderson enterit] That day Johne Andersoun laufull sone of Adam Andersoun burges of this brught was enterit gild bruther be reassoun of Besse Crystie his spous dochter to Patrik Crystie gild bruthir for peyment of fyv[e *? text obscured*] pundis conforme to the lait actis witht the space and the wyne and was sworne thairto. [*addition* : peyit all.]

[*in margin*: Edward Thamsoun enterit] That day Edward Thamsoun was enterit gild bruther for tuentie pundis witht the spyce and wyne conforme to the actis and was sworne thairto. [*addition*: peyit spyce and wyne.]

The gild court of the burgh of Dunfermling haldin in the tolbuith thairof be the [*deleted* : prov] baillies and dane of gild witht the gild brethrine the xiiij of June the yeir of God j^m v^c lxxxviij yeiris.

[*in margin*: Dauid Eldar enterit] The quhilk day Dauid Eldar was enterit gild bruthir for tuentie pundis witht the spyce and wyne conforme to the former actis and was sworne thairto. [*addition*: peyit spyce and wyne and all.]

[*in margin*: Act anent the [e *? text obscured*]ntring to the gildrie]

The quhilk day it is statut and ordanit be the dane of gild and gild brethrine all in voce that quhatsumeuir persoun heireftir strangear enterand to the fridome of gildrie withtin this toun sall pey for his entrie fourtie markis money witht the space and the wyne and ane

COURT BOOK, 1433-1597 143

gildbruthiris secund sonne and the persounis mariand frimennis dochteris to pey for thair entrie tene markis witht the space and the wyne. And nane to procure in the contrair heirof vnder the painis contenit in the former actis.

[Fo. 85v - blank.]

[Fo. 86]
   The gild court of the brucht of Dunfermling haldin be [Thomas ? *folio torn*] Coupar dane of gild baillies and gildbrethrine in the tolbuith thairof the twentie day of December the yeir of G[od ? *folio torn*] j^m v^c lxxxviij yeiris.

The quhilk day Thomas Coupar was be voitting of the brethrine electit and chosin dane of gild for ane yeir to cum quha acceptit the samin and maid fayth tharto.

[*in margin* : William Phillane enterit] That day William Phillane eldest sone and air of vmquhill Robert Phillane burges and gild bruther withtin this brucht was enterit gild bruther to his vmquhill fatheris fridome peyand thairfor the spyce and wyne at the discretioune of the [*deleted*: gild] dane of gild and gildbrethrine, peyit xl^s for spyce and vyne.

[*in margin*: act dischargenig James Allanne of bying leddir] The quhilk day anent the complant gevin in be the cordenaris aganis James Allanne for bying roch and barkit ledder withtin this brucht and cowppyng the samin to vthiris to the hurt and preiudice of the brethrine of the said craft he being na frimane etc. The dane of gild brethrine and bail[lies ? *folio torn*] dischairgis the said James Allanne fra all and sindrie sick handling in tyme cuming vnder the painis of eschaeting of all sick gear as he sall happin to be apprehendit athir bying or selling withtin this brucht heireftir becaus the said James Allane comperand personalie culd alleg na relevant cause in the contrar.

   The gild court of the brucht of Dunfermling haldin be Thomas Coupar dane of gild baillies and gilbrethrine in the tolbuith tharof the 27 of December anno 1588 yeiris.

[*in margin*: James Reid enterit] That day James Reid eldest sone and air of vmquhill Henrie Reid burges and gild bruther withtin this brugh was enterit gildbruther to his said vmquhill faderis fridome peyand tharfoir the

spyce and wyne at the discretioun of the dane of gild
and gildbrethrine and maid fayth thairto as effeirit.
[*addition*: peyet spyce and wyne.]

[*in margin*: James Kingorne enterit] That day James
Kingorne clerk of the regalitie of Dunfermling in re-
compence of the fauour schawin be him to the toune anent
thair customis and in hoipp of fauour at his handis in
tyme cuming quhan occasioun shew was enterit gild brethir
and was sworne thairto as efferit peyan[d ? *folio torn*] onlie thairfoir the spyce and wyne at the discretioun of the
dane of gild and gild brethrine.

[*in margin*: Laurence Huttoun enterit] That day Laurence
Huttoun was enterit gild bruther and was sworne thairto
peyand thairfoir fourtie markis money witht the spyce
and wyne conforme to the last actis. [*addition*: peyit spyce
and wyne.]

[*Fo. 86v*]

    The gild court of the brucht of Dunfermling haldin
in the tolbuth thairof be Thomas Coupar dane of
gild and gild brethrine the xxiij day of June the
yeir of God j^m v^c fourscoir and nyne yeiris.

[*in margin*: [a ? *text obscured*]bsoluitour [Nyc ? *text obscu-
red*]holl contra [C ? *text obscured*] udbert.] The quhilk day
the dane of gild and gildbrethrine absoluit [*deleted*: James]
Robert Nicholl fra the clame persewit aganis him be James
Cudbert anent the merchand fee acclamit of him be the
said James for selling and wairing of the said Robert
Nichollis gear in England in the yeiris of God j^m v^c fourescoir fyve and fourescoir sevin yeiris. Becaus the said
James tuik nocht his factor fe of the first end of the said
Robertis gear the tyme of his seruice and als becaus the
said James refusit to give his aith de calumpnia that he
was myndid to tak ony factor fee of the said Robertis gear
the tyme of his seruice.

[*in margin*: [Sy ? *text obscured*]mon Hair [e ? *text obscured*]nterit.] That day Symon Hair spous to Issobell Blak
laufull dochter to vmquhill Dauid Blak gild brethir was
be introloquitour and voitting of the brethrine enterit
gildbruther as ane that hes mareit ane friemannis secund
dochter peyand thairfoir tene markis with the spyce and
the wyne conforme to the last actis and maid fayth thairto. [*addition*: peyit spyce and wyne.]

[Fo. 87]

The gild court of Dunfermling haldin in the tolbuith th[arof ? text obscured] be Thomas Coupar dane of gild the brethrine thairof vpo[un ? text obscured] the penult of November anno 1589.

That day the gild brethrine finding falt witht James Reid that Dauid Reid hi[s ? text obscured] bruther being in his seruice brocht hame fra Danskin to Harie Mudie certa[ne ? text obscured] lint bocht be the said Dauid in Danskyn witht the said Haries awin syluir, he being ane vnfriemane contrar the tenur of the actis of the said gildrie, the said James comperand personalie allegit the said Dauid did the samen by his auyse and counsall and that he dischairgit the said Dauid to do samin befoir his passing to the saill alwayes he submittit him in the brethrinis will for the said fault in sa far as the samin may be extend[id ? text obscured] vpoun him and the brethrine convictit him in xxvj^s viij^d vnla[w ? text obscured] for the said fault.

That day the brethrine convictis James Cudbert comperand personalie in the wrang in bying lint witht Patrik with cartane pakking to him and selling the samin withtin this toune the said Patrik being ane vnfriemane in sa far as Bessie Nicholl spous to the said James for quhais deid he is hal[? text obscured] to ansuer sauld yisterday tua stane of the said lint withtin this brucht the ane half tharof pertening to the said Patrik extending to ane stan[e ? text obscured] of lint quhilk aucht and suld be escheatit, thairfoir the brethrin convic[tit ? text obscured] the said James in the half of the pryce of the said stane of lynt extending to.

The gild court of the burcht of Dunfermling haldin in the tolbui[th ? text obscured] thairof vpoun the xx day of December the yeir o[f God ? text obscured] j^m v^c fourescoir nyne yeiris be Thomas Coupar dene of gild baillies and remanent gildbrethir of the said brucht.

The quhilk day was nominat lyttis for chesing of the dane of gild.

Thomas Coupar ////////////////
George Peirsoun /////
Robert Pattoun //

William Meiklejohnn
//
James Cudbert
/////

That day Thomas Coupar be voitting of the maist part of the brethrine was electit and chosin dane of gild and contineuit it for ane ye[ir ? *text obscured*] to cume quha acceptit the said office and maid fayth for lauful administratioun thairof.

The quhilk day compeirit James Reid and vpoun his awin confessioune grantit that he haid offendit the haill gild brethrine in saying that certane of the brethrine haid na mair mercie vpoun his bruthir nor doggs beris towardis ane hair befoir thame tharby representting the saidis brethr[in ? *text obscured*] merciles doggs and lykwyse thaireftir saying to William Pratu[s ? *text obscured*] baillie that he knew nocht quhidder to call thame doggs or swyne and thair foir submittit him in the willis of the dane of gi[ld ? *text obscured*] and gildbrethrine for the said offence.

In lyk manir comperit Henrie Trumbill grantit that he haid offendit dane of gild and gild brethrine in mispersoning James Reid in thair presens and submittit him in will for the said of[fens ? *text obscured*]

8 Marcij 1590.

[*deleted*: The dane of gild and gild brethrine giv upoun James Reidis submissioun convictitit h[im ? *text obscured*] in fyve poundis in unlaw for first tymmis [*addition*: payit]

[*Fo. 87v*]

The gild court of the brucht of Dunfermling haldin in the tolbuith thairof be Thomas Coupar dane of gild and remanant gild brethrin withtin the said brucht the tuentie ane day of December the yeir of God j^m v^c lxxx ten yeiris.

The quhilk day Thomas Coupar be voitting of the gildbrethrine was contin[uit ? *folio torn*] daine of gild for ane yeir to cum quha acceptit and maid fayth tharto.

The gild court of the brucht of Dunfermling haldin in the tolbuith tharof be Thomas Coupar dane of gild and gildbrethrine withtin the said brucht the aughtene day of October anno Domini 1591 yeiris.

[*in margin*: Robert Bruce enterit] The quhilk day Robert Bruce of Baldrig was be introloquitour of the dane of gild and brethrine convenit enterit gild brother for the spyce and wyne and maid fayth tharto.

> The gild court of the brucht of Dunfermling haldin in the tolbuith thairof be Thomas Coupar dane of gild and gildbrethrine withtin the said brucht the tuentie tua day of Nouember the yeir of God j^m v^c fourescoir elevin yeiris.

The quhilk day anent the clame gevin in be George Peirsoun ane of the said brethrine aganis Johne Law brother alsua of the samin for no peyment to the said George of fourtie foure pundis [ib?] money delyuerit to him be the said George in Februar or tharby last bypast for certane angell nobles quhilkis war nocht delyuerit according to the conditi[oun *? folio torn*] maid betuix thame tharanent. The said Johne Law comperand and perso[nalie *? folio torn*] and als the said George Peirsoun quha vpoun thair awin confessi[oun *? folio torn*] submittit thame amiable to the decisioun of the saidis dane of gild and gild brethrine presentlie convenit anent the saidis actioun and oblished thame to stand at the delyuerance of the said brethrine, and the saidis gildbrethrine having acceptit the decisioun thairof vpoun thame and having hard the allegeancis and clamis of bayth the said parties decernis the said Johne Law content and pey to the said George Peirsoun fyvtene pundis at Pasche nixtocum and tuentie pundis money at Lambes nixt thaireftir quhilk witht nyne pundis awin be the said George to the said Johne Law for ane quarter hundreth daillis extendis to the said sovm of fourtie foure pundis and that becaus the said Johne grantit the ressait of the said sovm and promesit to delyuer to him angell nobles tharfoir, quharof the said George is fund to bear na ventur and the saidis [gildbrethir *? text obscured*] acceptit the said decreit and oblished thame to abyd tharat and fulfill the samyn in all poynttis.

[*in margin*: [H?]arie [M?]udie enterit] That day Harie Mudie was enterit gildbrothir as ane that hes mareit ane frimannis dochter be reassoun of Margaret Reid his spous beand ane frimannis dochter peyand tharfoir conforme to the last actis and was sworne tharto. [*addition*: peyit spyce and vyne and all.]

[*Fo. 88*]

> [*entry incomplete : folio torn*] - - - - - - - tharof be Jam - - - - - - - - - Pratus baillie and gild brethir the thrid [day *?*] of the yeir of God j^m v^c foure scoir and fourtene yei[ris?].

The quhilk day anent the appoyntment maid betuix the

gildbrethir [and *? folio torn*] craftismene of this toun tuiching the intertainment of mvtuall love and amitie amang the inhabitantis of this toune thairfoir that na occasioun of contra veyntioun thairof result of ony of the saidis breth[rine *? folio torn*] in tyme cuming it is statut and ordanit be the dane of gild baillie and haill brethrine convenit that gif ony of the [said *? folio torn*]gild brithir hereftir happinis to mak ony manier of pro- vocatioune to ony of the saidis craftismene in woord deid or countenance contrar the tenor of the said appoyntitment, that he salbe ansuerable for his awin deid and falt and sall refound [*? folio torn*] the remanent brethrin of gild all and quhatsumeuir damnage [*? folio torn*] and expense thay happin to sustein thair throw and salbe simpliciter dischargit of his fridome of the said gildrie in tymis cuming exceptit be notourlie knavin that he be first provokit invadit or persewit of his lyff be ony of the saidis craftis contrair the persounis invadit and persewit may defend thame selffis provyding alwayis that it salbe lesum to ony of the saidis brethrine havand civile actiounis aganis the said craftismene to persew the samin conforme to the lawis of the realm. In witness of the quhilk thingis the saidis dane of gild baillie and gild brithir hes sub- scryvit this act witht thair handis as[seillit *? text obscur- ed*] day yeir and place forsaidis.
James Reid den of gild
Robert Pattoune witht my hand   Williame Pratus [baillie *?*
Dauid Stewart vitht my hand   *folio torn*]
Wilyeom Fillane with my hand   Tomas Cowper witht my hand
Robert Wylsoune witht my hand Laurence   Hutoun   witht
George Peirsoune witht my hand   my hand
                                Jhone Andersone litster
                                         witht my [hand
                                         ? folio torn]
                                Johne Walkare witht my
                                         hand
                                Gilbert Kennedy   witht
                                         my hand
Be Robert Turnbull Edward Thamsoune Henrie Turnbull John Law Robert Nicholl Waltir Crystie William Mowtray William Waluod Harie Mudie William Wryght with [our hand *? folio torn*] at the pene led be nottar vndirwrittin at our command becaus we can[nocht *? folio torn*]

Ita est Dauid Broune notarius publicus demandatis dictarum personarum vt asserunt nescientium scribere requisitus manu propria.

Ita est Jacobus Kingorne notarius publicus de mandatis dictarum personarum scribere nescientium (vt asserunt) cum conotario suprascribente requisitus testando manu mea propria signoque.

[Fo. 88v]

> [entry incomplete : folio torn]
> - - - gildbredir of - - - - - - - -the- - - -
> - - - -bruch thairof the xxix of Julij 1595.

The quhilk day the dane of gild and gildbrithir convenit convictit Alexander Stevin and Jonet Sibbald his spous comperand personalie in contraventioune of the last act maid anent the sell[ing of ? folio torn] thair wyne in selling the samin for tene schillingis the [? folio torn] being ordanit to sell the samin in Maij last for [? folio torn] sex pennies the pynt. Thairfoir convictis thame [? folio torn] vnlaw of foure pundis money for the said contra[ventioune ? folio torn] and ordanis thame to sell the rest of thair wyne [? folio torn] have in this toun for nyne schillingis the pynt [? folio torn] derar fra this hour furth.

> The gild court holden be James Reid dean [of ? folio torn] gild and gild brethir off the burcht of Dunf[ermline ? folio torn] in the tolbuth tharoff the vij day of October.

The quhilk day Patryk Macartan merchand was ad[mitit ? folio torn] gildbrthir be the consent of the den off gild and gildbethir [sic] and to pay tharfoir xx lib mony f[or ? folio torn] entres conform to the ordinance and wes sw[orne ? folio torn] and the spyce and wyn and gaiff his fyth as efferis.

> The gild court of the brucht of Dunfermlyne haldyn [be ? folio torn] Reid dane of gild and gild brethir in the tolbuitht the nynt of Februarij 1595.

That day James Reid lait dane of gild dimittit his [? folio torn] thaireftir Robert Pattoun Thomas Cuper and James Cudbert [? folio torn] lyttis for electing the new dane of gild.

That day Thomas Cuper be voitting of the brethir was [electit ? folio torn] and chosin dane of gild for ane yeir to come quha [? folio torn] and maid fayth thairto.

[in margin: [La ? folio torn]urence [Wi ? folio torn]lsone enterrit.] The quhilk day Laurence Wilsoun eldest sone and air to [? folio torn] Wilsoun burges and gild broder of this brucht was [? *folio torn*] gildbrother to his vmquhill fatheris fridome and maid f[ayth ? *folio torn*].

[*Fo.* 89]

[*entry incomplete* ; *folio torn*]
The gild court of – – – – – – – – – – – dane of gild and gildbrethir the xij day of October 15 – – .
The quhilk day James Reid lait dane of gild maid his compt of his intromissioun of the gild syluir vnlavis and contributioune sen he making of his last compt quhilk was vpoun the aucht day of Nouember 1594 vntill his dimissioun of his office quhilk was vpoun the nynt of Februar 1595. His haill charge extendis to xxxix lib ij^S his discharge thairof to xxvij lib xvij^S. Sua restis awin be him of his intromissioune elevin pundis fyve schillingis to be payit to Thomas Cuper in pl of peyment of the xij lib x^S awin to him.
I Thomas Cowpar grantis me to have ressauit fra James Reid this forsaid sovm according to the act abonewrittin.
Thomas Cowper witht my hand.
The gild court of the brucht of Dunfermlyne haldin be Thomas Cowper dane of gild and gildbrethir the first of December 1596.
[*in margin*: Johne Watson entirrit] The quhilk day Johne Watsoun merchand was be consent and vcitting of the brethir convenit was enterit gildbroder withtin this brucht and maid fayth tharto peyand thairfoir tuentie pundis money with the spyce and wyne quharof the brethir for sindry guid caus[is ? *text obscured*] and consideratiounis moving thame dischargis him of tene markis.
xxix Decembris 1597.
The quhilk day in presens of the dane of gild and gildbrethir convenit Thomas Cowper last dane of gild maid compt of his intromissioun with the gild syluer during his office all his compt haid and auwit to him the brethir dischargis him of his intromissioun preceiding the dait heirof for evir except of xx^S to be peyt be him to Johne Fraser wyff.

[*Fo.* 89 v to 94v *inclusive blank*]

[*Fo.* 95]

– – – – [*folio torn and worn*] – – – –
Item that na burges suit onie procutour duelling withtowt our libertie to plaid againis his nichtbours for gif he do it he shall pay a puncion of wyne vnlaw.

Item that na woman haiving a 1 husband by woll in the villadg na burges haif ofter acces to by woll or hyddis nor danis. And gif onie by darrar [deleted: than] the forsaidis than our statutis maikis pryce the gear bought shalbe taicking and the byar condempnit in viij ^{s}.

Off conspiratouris.

Item that nain maik conspiracie againis the commontie of our gild to dispers or separat the sam vnder a puncion vyn vnlaw.

Off handmillis.

Item that na man haw ma handmillis nor twa and gif onie haif ma thay shalbe taiking frome him for the spaice of yeir and day nevertheles the graice and pardone of the gild to be exceptid for dispensation and relenting the rigour of the act.

Item that na man presum to grind onie kynd of corne witht handmillis except compellit be tempest of wedder or penurie and scairstie of other millis. And gif onie in sick caice grind witht hand millis let him gyf xiij lumfull for multure for gif onie mane braick this our act he salbe depryvit of handmillis for ever and sal for grinding his bear in the millis gif of multure xxiiij lumfull.

We ordean that nan shall by hydis wooll or skinis to sell again nather cutt claith except he be a brother of our gild. As for the extramean and other townismen or merchantis for sustening of thair lawfull custum quhilk is to pas to mercattis we will permit bot yit to haif na lott nor cavil witht our [? folio worn]

[Fo. 95v]

We ordain that na cordynar [?- - - - - folio torn and worn] of the hornes and the earis are of equall lenth [---- ? folio torn and worn] na barkar sault hydis.

We ordain gif onie of our brether taik silver to cuire his bissines frome onie owtlandish merchand and of the sam advantadg onie thing at merkat to him self eather in sack of wooll in hydis skinis or onie other merchandreis let him be condempnit first in xl ^{s}. Secundlie and thridlie gif of sick thingis he be convictit he sal tyn his gildschip.

We ordain that nane by hearing salmund or onie sort of fish quhilk vsis be carriit oursee in schip, and bring to the towne befoire the schip taik schoore and grund [hir ? folio worn] saillis and oirris sett. This be also done of peis beinis all cornis and salt, gif onie be convictit of the mis let him pay a puntion of vyn to the gild for vnlaw or ellis be the spaice of the yeir and day be eiectid from the villadg.

Item gif onie man by hearing salt, quhyt, beinis or peis or onie sick other thing at the schip or of onie soirt of fish he sall nocht deny a pairt to his nichtbour for his awin meat and famileis of the sam pryce he bought his self, quhilk gif he do nocht let him gif a puntion of vyne for his vnlaw.

Lyikwayis quha byis mair nor servis his awin meat and sellis it vnder pretence of his meat onlie let him be punishit.

Off skinners.

Item that na skinner nor onie other man maik woll of the skinnis from Witsunday vnto Michaelmes bot let the skinnis be sauld as thei ar, for gif a skinner or other be convictit of thir he salbe depryvit of his office for yeir and day gif onie burges be convictit of sicklyik he shall pay a puntion of vyn vnto the gild.

The impairting of gearing.

Item quha evir by hearing quhatsoevir nichbouris salbe present at the bying of tham shall also have gif thei neid efter a [pairt *? folio worn*] of tham of the sam pryce thay war bought [withtowt fraud *? folio worn*]

[*Fo.* 96]

fraud. Bot gif onie nocht being present at the bying of the saming shall seik a pairt of thame let thame be gevin for xii^d vantadg to the secund sellar according to the quantitie. And gif onie satisffie nocht the sellar of the said hearing in tyme and plaice convenientlie bot convictit in the contrar he sall gif to the gild a puntion of vyn for vnlaw. And this apperteinis to the brether of gild and to na other.

Off the Regiment and Rowll of the commontie.

Item we statut be the haill communitie of our towne of Bervik that the said communitie be governit be xxiiij of the best discreitest and faithwordiest of the said brough witht the mair, minor and provestis. And quhasever quhat plaice soever thir xxiiij convenis and assemblis to hauld thair common consill cumis nocht warning maid lawfullie in the night preceding shall pay twa s.

Off the election of the mair and provestis.

Item that the mair and provestis be chosin be the communitie. And gif thair sall onie contraversie in the election let it be maid then to the sacramentis and symbollis of thay xxiiij that war chosin be the deane to rowll the communitie.

Twiching bying of beastis.
Item we statut be our haill communitie assemblid on Weddinsday the xxviij of October callit Simon and Judis day in the yeir of God 1293 that frome the xv eftir Michaelmes vnto Yuill na flesher pas withtowt the villadg in purpos to meit bestiall cuming to the merkat and towne to be sauld nor yit in the merkat by onie quhill efter none in cais he be fund and sein fraudfull and convictid tyn his office for yeir and day.

[Fo. 96v]

Off Barkat ledder.
Item that na extramean haifing barkat to be sauld sell onie withtin the hous bot in the merkat plaice and that onlie on sett merkat day for gif he transgres this our act quhither he sell thame cuttit or heall he shall pay ane vnlaw.

Off gathering the gildbrethir.
Item it was ordanit on Saturnday nixt efter the Feast of Trinitie the yeir of God, 1284, that quhen alderman and ferthingman willis the brether of gild to be congregat for to cuire thair bissinis be common consill, a little bell in a row of the towne shalbe rung thryis for warning, and severallie to witt first shortlie or a little spaice, and so secundlie and thridlie quhilk being rung and hard to the last ting, onie brother of the gild nocht present shalbe vnlawit in xij^d.

Off lott and cavill.
Item that na brother of gild haif lott or cavill witht ane other vnder les nor half quarter skinnis and half dakar hydis and twa packis woll.

Off portadge or careing of the gear bought.
The first cuirt haldin on Weddinsday befoir Witsonday the yeir of God, 1294, at quhilk tym it was constitut and ordanit be vnanimitie and common consent of all the gild brether that na man by onie kynd of corne, salt, collis or onie uther venallis cuming be see to our towne of Bervick except it befoir schipbuird that is to say owt of the

[*Fo. 97*]

Off the way. And that he bring nocht the guidis bought frome the schip befoire the sun rysing but frome the rysing to the going to lett the portadge be done for gif onie do vtherwayis he shall gif to the gildbrother a pvntion of vyne.

Off premonishing the gildbrether.

We statut the quhatsumever gildbrother lawfullie premonishit in the day befoire to cum to halding of our gild befoire ten howris of the day cumis noch shall pay iiij^d forowt remission. Also quha gois owt of the gild for owt licence of the deane he shall pay iiij^d. And gif onie of the constablis premonish nocht his nightbour he shall pay xij^d forowt remission.

Off speacking in the cuirt.

Item that na gildbrother speack witht a lowd voice to perturb the cuirt vnder the pain of iiij^d bot keip silence at the commandment of the deane.

Off bearing weapinnis in the cuirt.

Item that na brother of the gild bring withtin the bar of the cuirt onie twa handit weapin or suird vnder the pain of iiij^d.

Off bying be wemen

Item it is ordainit that na women eather cled witht a husband or vidu by woll, skinis or hydis except black woll and black skinis vnder pain of escheating the woll skinis or hydis bought efter this maner saving in tym of proclamit merkat.

[*Fos. 97v, 98 and 98v blank.*]

[*Fo. 99*]

Anno Domini millesimo cccc xxxv^{to} penvltimo die mensis Octobris Thom Cristyson ga[u ? *folio torn*] of the deynscyp of the gyld of the twa yeris gayn befor and his ch[arge ? *folio torn*] be the fwt of Lawrens Boys entrie remanand in the buk xxxvj lib xj^s iiij^d.

Item be Jhon Mychalsoun of owr male of ij yeris gan befor iij^s.

Item be Thom Grangiar of ii yeiris male ij^s.

Item be Jhon of Loktoun of ij yeris male vj^s viij^d.

Item be Jhon of Cupir of his entre xl^s.

Item be Alan Lytstar for his craffte of the twa yeris gan befor xij^s.

Item be Jhon Wilson cordwnar of the yer by gan vj^s viij^d.

Sum of the chargis xl lib xx^s.

This is the sum ressawyt be the said Thom Cristysoun in his tym. In primis fra Will of Bar x^s
Item fra Wyl the Ramsay iiij^s
Item fra Huchun Mason v^s
Item fra Dawy Store v^s
Item fra Jhon Mychalsoun vj^s
Item fra Thom Grangiar xij^d
Item fra Jhon Yong v^s
Item fra Wyl Logan v^s
Item fra Jhon of Lokton vj^s viij^d
Item fra Jhon of Cupir ij^s
Item fra Jhon of Cupir viij^s
Item fra Jhon of Cupir in papir ij^s to the gyld buk
Item fra Alan Lytstar vj^s
    Sum of his ressate iij lib v^s viij^d.
This is the sum of the disspens. In primis to Schir Mathew x^s
Item spendyt at Stirlyng v^s
Item in colationis xiij^d
Item spendyt in colationis ij^s viij^d
Item for hallyn owt of a payr of walswris iiij^d
Item drunkyn in wyn xij^d
Item for the borw mayl of ij yeris xiiij^d
Item for the makyn of owr gyld buk ij^s iiij^d
Item for papir ij^s
Item to Jhon Wrych the aldirman xxj^s vj^d
    Summa expensarum xlvij^s j^d

    Sic remanet in suis manibus xviij^s vij^d.
    Sic remanet in bursa de summa prescripta xxxvij lib xiiij^s vij^d.

[Fo. 99v]

[? folio torn] be the [co ?] of the gyld to the kyngis gol[d on ? text obscured] the said day.
In primis of Wyl Logan x^s.
Item of Jhon Yowng x^s.
Item of Jhon of Cupir xx^s.
Item of Jhon Wilsoun cordinar of this yer v^s. Item of the yer by gan vj^s [? text obscured].
Item of Ramsay vj^s.

Anno Domini j^{mo} cccc xxxvij the xviij day of October Huchon Mason gef his cont of the denschip of the gyld of the yer befor and hys charg was in primis be the fut of Thom Cristisonis act remanand in the buk xxxvij lib xiiij^s vij^d.
Item fra Alan Littystar vj^s. Item fra John of Loktoun

iij^s iiij^d.
Item fra John Mechel xviij^d.
Item fra Thom Grangiar xij^d.
Item fra John William [*deleted*: vj^s viij^d] vs.
[*deleted*: Item fra Jo] Sum of the hall charge is xxxviij lib xj^s v^d.
Resauit þe the said den. In primis fra John of Loktoun iij^s iiij^d.
Item fra Alan Littistar vj^s.
   Summa recepcionis ix^s iiij^d.
Expens. In primis for vax and wyndouclath to John of Seras wyf v^s iiij^d.
Item to collationis dronkyn xvj^d.
   Summa expensarum vj^s viij^d.
Sic remanet in suis manibus ij^s viij^d.
Sic remanet in bursa de summa oneracionis xxxviij lib iiij^s ix^d.

[*Fo. 100*]

Anno Domini j^m cccc xxxviij^o the xij day of [*deleted*: Nove November] October Dawy [Haket ? *folio torn*] gef his count of twa yeiris gan befor and hys charge was liij lib ix^s.
Item our malis. In primis fra John of Lokton of the twa yeris vj^s viij^d.
Item fra John Mechelsoun of the twa yeirs iij^s.
Item John Wrych of the twa yeris of the land besid the cors ij^s.
   Soum total witht the malis liiij lib v^s v^d
Receptis. In primis be the said deyn of the soum aboun wrytyn.
Item in primis fra Jhon Mechalsoun of the sovm lent to the kyngis gold xlv^s.
Item fra Jhon [*deleted*: Mechalsoun] of Loktonis of mayl vj^s viij^d.
Item fra Loktoun xx^d.
Item fra Jhon Mechalsoun iij^s.
Item fra Nychol Jhonsoun vj^s viij^d.
Item fra Wyl of Anand v^s.
Item fra Jhon of Cupir and Robyn Hacat ij^s viij^d.
Item fra the mene of Mastirtoun xx^s.
Item fra Fawsyd xviij^d.
Item fra Alane Lystar v^s.
Item fra Wyl Jacson x^s ix^d.
Item fra Thom Bra x^s.
   Summa recepcionis v lib xvij^s xj^d.
Expensis. In primis of the gyld land xix^s ij^d.

Item to the herdyng of Henry Lytstar ix^s viij^d.
Item for the borw mayl of iij yeris of the gild land xxi ^{d}.
Item for the hidis fechit fra Leth ij^s iiij^d.
Item for the costis of a dyner [deleted: qwen we war at Mastirtoun] xix^s viij^d in Jhon Wrycht [handis ? folio worn]
Item in dyner qwen the hidis war takyn at Mastirtoun x^s.
Item xij^d gyffyn the men of Mastirtoun of thar xx^s.
Item xxviij^s spendyt in dyneris colationis be the dene and the brethir.
    Summa expensarum iiij lib xj^s vij^d.
Sic remanet secum in suis manibus xxvj^s iiij^d the quhilk sum the nichbouris [? folio torn] John Wricht.

[Fo. 100v]

[Ann ? text obscured]o Domini j^m cccc xl^o the xxviij day of Januar John of Coupir gef hys count of the y[er ? text obscured] the deneship of the gild and his charg vas xlix lib xiij^s x^d that remanys aw[in ? text obscured] Dawy Hacattis count nest befor. Item of entrais in hys tym iiij lib x^s.
[Item ? text obscured] our malis. In primis fra John of Loktoun iij^s iiij^d.
[Item ? text obscured] fra John Mechelsoun xliij^d. Item fra John Wrych xij^d.
 Summa totalis oneracionis witht the malis is liiij lib ix^s viij^d.

[Rec ? text obscured]eptis. Inprimis be the said den of the soum abone wrytyn fra Will Jakson x^s.
fra John Mechelsoun   v^s
fra Robyn Hacat   v^s
fra Will Jakson   v^s
fra Balmanouch   ix^s
fra Alan Littistar   v^s
fra Andrew Hoge   x^s
fra Will of Gelland   x^s viij^d
  Summa recepcionis lix^s and viij^d.

[Exp ? text obscured]ensis in primis dronkkyn be the nychbowris the den and the brethir x^s and viij^d [? text obscured] day that the nychbouris sat to consedyr and put in wryt al that vas to be [? text obscured] of the gild guddis. [? text obscured] day that the vij personis sat that chosyn be the nychbouris to motefey the [guddis ? text obscured] rasynyn dronkyn iiij^s j^d.

[The *? text obscured*] makyn of the sclope of the gild land and the thornyn of it ij^s iiij^d.
[*? text obscured*] Jacsonis vnlaw vas dronkyn of the skynis byen fra the sallerer iiij^d mar than it com to.
[D *? text obscured*] ronkyn be the nychbowris in John Wrychtis for all and wyn [*? text obscured*]^s iiij^d.
Item lent the balyeis to the toun kepyng John Chepman and Alan [Lyt *? text obscured*] star of the comonis behaulf borouyt xxxiiij^s and viij^d.
[L *? text obscured*]ent to the said balyeis v^s iiij^d the quhilk the nychbouris drank quhen t[hai red *? text obscured*] the marchis of the comon mur.

Summa expensarum iij lib ix^s viij^d. Sua is the expensis mar than I hafe resauit x^s the quhilk hafe laid doun.

[*? text obscured*]net in bursa de summa oneracionis lj lib. Item xxxiiij^s and viij^d awand the qu[hilk *? text obscured*] borowtt Alan Littistar and John Chepman.

[*Fo. 101*]

Anno Domini j^m cccc^c xlj^o the xviij day of the moneth of Nouember Alane Litstar gaue his count of the yher befor of the denschip of the gilde and his charge was lj lib that remanys in John of Couperis count next be for.
Item owr malis. In the first fra John of Loktoun iij^s iiij^d. Item John Michalsoun xviij^d. Item fra John Wricht xij^d. Item xxviij^s for hidis. Item fra Will Ramsay xxx^d. Item fra Schir Alexander xxx^d.

Summa totalis oneracionis and siluir lij lib xviij^s x^d.

Receptis. In primis be the sayde Alane dene of the sowme abwne wrytyn ffra John of Loktoun iij^s iiij^d.
Item fra Will Jacsoun iiij^s ij^d.
Item fra Patoun Valange for John Duncansoun xij^s.
Item fra Will of Balmanoch x^s.
Item fra Will of Gellalde v^s.
Item fra Will Logane v^s.
Item fra Will the Ramsay xxx^d.
Item for hidis xxviij^s.
Item fra Schir Alexander xxx^d.

Summa recepcionis iij lib xij^s vj^d.

Expense. In primis drunkyn be the gildebrethir and the den in John Wricht hous xiij^s vj^d.
Item to Andro Hoggis qwhen the gildbrethir and the den com fra Kinglassy at a super xxiij^s ix^d.
Item at a colacioun in John Wrichtis xij^d.
Item be the brethir and the den in John Bothuelis tavern

iij ^{s}.
Item the den and Thom Cristysoun at Lithkew the gild brethir is avande iiij ^{s}.
Item for a hors to Thom Cristysone to Kinglassy xij ^{d}.
Item be for the chawmerlane ayr xvj ^{d} in to John Bothuelis hous.
Item at the selling of the hydis xvj ^{d}. Drunkyn be the balyheis.
Item ij ^{s} vij ^{d} be the modefyaris of the gilde gudis.
Item in the tolbuth drunkyn be the gilde brethir and the den iiij ^{s} ij ^{d}.
Item that ilk day viij ^{d} in John Bothuelis tavern.
Item for a common kist to the gild brethir xij ^{s}.
Item drunkyn at Michalmes last bypast xj ^{s} in John Bothuelis.
Item for a lok to the forsaid kist xviij ^{d}.
Item to John of Coupir x ^{s}.
Item to Will of Anande xl ^{d}.
  Summa expensarum iiij lib xiiij ^{s} ij ^{d}. Swa is the expensis mar than I haue rasauit xxij ^{s} vj ^{d} that I haue laide doin.
Sic remanet in bursa de summa oneracionis xlix lib vij ^{s}.

[*Fo. 101v*]

Anno etc. xlij the first day of December Wilyham of Kircaldy gaue his count of the yher be[for ? *text obscured*] of the denschip of the gilde. And his charge was xlix lib vij ^{s} that ramanyt in the fwt of Alan Litstaris count next befor. Item owr malis. In primis fra John of Loktoun iij ^{s} iiij ^{d}. Item fra John Michalsoun xviij ^{d}. Item John Wricht xij ^{d}. Item fra Alan Litstar for ane vnlaw vj ^{s} viij ^{d}. Item ab eodem xviij ^{d}. Item ab eodem iiij ^{d}. Item fra Malis Lech for ane vnlaw xviij ^{d}.
  Summa totalis oneracionis cum firmiset amerciamentis l. lib ij ^{s} x ^{d}.

Receptis. In primis be the said den rasauit of the soum abone writin. In primis fra John of Loktoun iij ^{s} iiij ^{d}.
Item fra John Wricht xij ^{d}.
Item fra John Michalsoun xviij ^{d}.
Item fra Alan Litstar pro amerciamento vj ^{s} viij ^{d}. Item ab eodem xviij ^{d}.
Item ab eodem iiij ^{d}.
Item fra Malis Lech xviij ^{d}.
Item fra Alan Litstar xxij ^{s} of his entre.
Item fra John Wricht for Will of Walwode v ^{s}.
Item fra Thom of Bra for John Ywngis entrie v ^{s}.
Item fra Alan Litstar of his entre v ^{s}.

DUNFERMLINE GILD

Summa recepcionis lij^s x^d.

Expense. In primis in vino drunkyn in John Bothuelis diuersis tymis xij^s viij^d.
Item in expensis Johannis Bothuel and Johannis de Cupar apud Lithkew v^s.
Item in vino drunkyn in the tolbuth qwhen Alexander of Irland payit his entre ij^s viij^d.
Item Alano Litster pro suis superexpensis sui ultimi computi xxij^s.
Item in vino drunkyn in John Chepmanis hous ij^s.
Item pro firma burgi terrae nostrae de gilde vij^d.

Summa expensarum xliiij^{s}xj^d. Que summa deducta de summa recepcionis. Sic remanet in manibus vij^s xj^d. Sic remanet in bursa xlvij lib xvij^s xj^d.

[Fo. 102]

Anno etc. cccc xliijj the vij day of Januar Wilyham of Kircaldy gaue his count of the yhere gane befor of the denschip of the gyld. And his charge was xlix lib xix^s ix^d.
Debitoris of the sayd soum. In primis.
In his awn handis of the last count vij^s xj^d.
Item oure malis John of Lokton iij^s iiij^d.
Item John Michalsone xviij^d.
Item John Wricht xij^d.
Item the soume that was anyss in bursa.
In primis. John Wricht xxij^s x^d for dwris and window.
Item John Wricht for Wyll of Walwode xx^s.
Item John Wricht that Dauid Hacat lent him of oure syluir xxj^s iiij^d.
Item Schir Alexander of Kinglassy vj^s ix^d.
Item Dauid Story xv^s of lent syluir.
Item Patoun Turnbulle xij^s iiij^d.
Item Lowrans Boyis xxx^{s}ix^d.
Item Thom Cristysone xviij^s vij^d.
Item Huchun Mason ij^s viij^d.
Item Thom Granger ij^s of oure malis.
Item John Wricht ij^s of malis.
Item the balyeis and the commonis vj^s viij^d.
Item John Chepman and Alan Litstar balyheis xl^s of lent syluir.
Item Thom Cristysone and John Wincister for John Goslyn xx^s.
Item Wyll of Bar for barkyt lethyr ij lib xvj^s xj^d.
Item Wyll of Bar xij^s for barkit lethir in Dauid Hacatis tym.

COURT BOOK, 1433-1597   161

Item awand of entreis. In primis
Schir John Wilyhamsone xix ^{s}
Item Nichole Jonsone iiij ^{s}
Item Wyll Cristysone xxiij ^{s}
Item John Chepman xxv ^{s}
Item Thom Cordynar xxxij ^{s} iiij ^{d}
Item Thom Cristysone xxvj ^{s}
Item Law of Bra xxv ^{s}
Item Thom of Bra xl ^{s}
Item Wyll of Cowris xl ^{s}
Item Malis Leche x ^{s}
Item Philp of Lochgwhor xxviij ^{s} xj ^{d}
Item Thom of Dalgles vj ^{s} viij ^{d}
Item Huchun Masone xx ^{s}
Item John Scoby xl ^{s}
Item Schir Alexander of Kinglassy xxij ^{s}

Item Wyll Ramsay xxx ^{s}
Item Thom of Bra for John Ywng ix ^{s}
Item Wyll Logane xv ^{s}
Item John of Coupir vj ^{s} viij ^{d}
Item Thom of Bra for John Wylsoune xx ^{s}
Item Nichole Jonsonis ayr and his land xiij ^{s}
Item Wyll of Anande v ^{s}
Item Alan Litstar vij ^{s} vj ^{d}
Item Law Fox xx ^{s}
Item Robyn Hacat xxiij ^{d} iiij ^{d}
Item Wyll Jacsone xx ^{s} j ^{d}
Item Nichole Brwne xl ^{s}
Item Wyll of Balmanoch xxj ^{s}
Item Wyll of Gellalde xiiij ^{s} iiij ^{d}
Item Andro Hog xxx ^{s}
Item John of Spens harrald xx ^{s}
Item John Boyis xxx ^{s}
Item Malis Dawsone ix ^{s}

Summa totalis oneracionis ut supra xlix lib xix ^{s} ix ^{d}.

[*Fo. 102v*]

Receptis. In primis be the sayd dene abone writyn fra John of Loktone for malis iij ^{s} iiij ^{d}.
Item fra John Michalsone xviij ^{d}. Item fra John Wricht xij ^{d}. Item fra Thom Cristysone iij ^{s} [v ^{d} *? text obscured*] Item Huchun Masone ij ^{s} ix ^{d}. Item fra Schir Alexander vj ^{s}. Item Thom Cristysone for John Goslyn xx ^{s}. Item vij ^{s} xj ^{d} of the yhere befor in his handis.
        Summa recepcionis xlvj ^{s}.
Expensis. In primis in vino drunkyn in the tolbuth and in John Chepmanis tavern at diueris tymes ix ^{s}.
Item for borw malle of the gyldland vij ^{d}.
        Summa expensarum ix ^{s} vij ^{d} que summa dicta de summa recepcionis sic remanet in suis manibus xxxvj ^{s} v ^{d}. Sic remanet in bursa and per debitores vt supra xlix lib x ^{s} ij ^{d}.
Of the soum the quhilk is callit in bursa and per debitores saivyn of be the gyld brethir that the sayd dettouris

swor thai had payit befor. In primis
To Thom Cristysone xiij^s iiij^d the quhilk he swor he payit to Nichole Jonsone.
Item to the sayd Thom Cristyson forgevin xviij^d.
Item forgevin to the sayd Thom Cristysone of his entres xix^s iiij^d
Item alowit to Schir Alexander ix^d.
Item John Wricht xviij^s the quhilk he swor he had payit of befor in hewin work.
Item to Thom Granger xij^d.
Item forgevin to Schir Dauid Stewart anent John Scoby xiij^s iiij^d the quhilk he swor he payit to Schir Dauid Stewart.
   Summa sworne and forgevin iij lib vij^s iij^d.
Item forgevin to the brint men of thar entrie of thaim that begouth to byg thar land withtin a yher thareftir. In primis Schir John Wilyhamsone xix^s.

Item Wyll Cristysone	xxiij^s
Item Thom of Bra	xl^s
Item Wyll Logane	xv^s
Item Wyll of Anande	v^s
Item Alan Litstar	vij^s vj^d
Item John Chepman	xxv^s
Item Wyll Jacson	xx^s j^d
Item Wyll of Balmanoch	xxj^s

   Summa forgevin to the brint men viij lib xv^s vij^d.

[*Fo. 103*]

Thir ar the namys of thaim vndirwritin awand the sowmis in to the charge abone writin in Wylyham of Kircaldis count the qwhilkis sowmys ar out sittin as than the qwhilk mycht nocht gudly be rasit for knawin mysterie quhill thai or thar ayris micht racover to pay the sayd sowmis. In primis Dauid Story of lent syluir xv^s.
Item Patone Turnbule xij^s iiij^d syn he was den of the gild in his handis.
Item Wyll of Bar ij lib xvj^s xj^d for barkit lethir the quhilk syluir was in bursa.
Item Wyll of Bar xij^s for barkit lethir.
Item Nichole Jonsone iiij^s away [*deleted*: Item xlij^s iiij^d ane othir way]
Item Thom Cordynar xxxij^s iiij^d.
Item Law of Bra xxv^s.
Item Wyll of Cowris [*deleted*: x] xl^s.
Item John Boyis xxx^s.
Item Malis Dawsone ix^s.
Item Nichole Brwne xl^s.

Item John of Spens harrald xx^s.
Summa of the respit xiiij lib xvj ^s vij^d.
Thir ar the sowmis forgevin be the gild brethir of the charge in Wylyham of Kircaldie count. In primis to Lowrans Boyis xxx^s ix^d.
Item of lent syluir to the balyheis and the commonis in the tym of the pestinens for dikyn of the toun xlvj ^s viij^d.
Item to Robyn Hacat at the instans of James of Levingstone captane of Strevelyn xxiij ^s iiij^d. Item Andro Hog x ^s. Item to John Wricht ij ^s.
Summa forgevin v lib xii ^s ix^d
Summa total forgevin to brint men and all otheris abone writtin and resp[itit *? folio torn*] xxxij lib xij ^s ij^d Sic remanet in bursa xvj lib xvij ^s [d *? folio torn*] in Wilyham of Kircaldie handis and be the dettouris.

[*Fo. 103v*]

Anno etc. cccc xliiij the viij day of Januar John of Coupir gaue his count of the yher gane befor of the denschip of the gylde. And his charge was in primis be the fwt of Wylyham of Kircaldis count xvj lib xvij^s x^d be the dettouris vndirwritin. In primis levyt in bursa be Wylyham of Kircaldy and delyuerit to John of Coupir den xxxvj^s v^d .
Item Thom Cristysone vj ^s viij^d.
Item Schir Alexander of Kinglassy xxij^s for the quhilk Anny of Spyr com dettour to be payit the next Michalmes.
Item Malis Leche x^s
Item Philp of Lochqwhor xxviij^s xj^d
Item Thom of Dalgles vj ^s viij^d
Item Huchun Masone xx ^s
Item John Scoby xxvj ^s viij^d
Item Wyll Ramsay xxx ^s
Item Thom of Bra xxix^s
Item Wyll of Gellalde xiiij ^s iiij^d
Item John of Coupir vj ^s viij^d
Item Andro Hog xx ^s soluit
Item Nichole Jonsonnys ayris xiij^s iiij^d of the quilk some the nychtburis forgaf John [*? text obscured*] vj[s *? - - text obscured*].
Item Law Fox xx ^s.
Item John Wricht xlvij ^s ij ^d of the qwhilk some rasauit be John of Bothuel dene xxxviij[s. *? text obscured*].
Summa vt supra xvj lib xvij^s x^d.
Item in John of Coupiris tym den of malis. In primis fra John of Loktone iij ^s iiij^d.
Item John Michalsone xviij^d. Item John Wricht xij^d. Item of enteris. In primis John Sym vj ^s viij^d and his wyn

syluir drunken.
Item Wyll of Dwnlop x^s. Item xxxij^d of wyn syluir.
Item Law of Furmoris x^s. Item xxxij^d of wyn syluir.
Item John Bakstar x^s his wyn syluir drunkyn.
Item Richard of Walwode x^s. Item xxxij^d of wyn syluir.
Item de amerciamentis Wyll of Balmanoch xij^d.
Item John Wylsone xij^d.
    Summa of malis enteris and amerciamentis iij lib ij^{s}vj^d.
    Summa totalis oneracionis xx lib iiij^d.

Receptis. In primis fra Wylyham of Kircaldy of the fwt of his count xxxvj^s v^d.
Item [*deleted*: fra] in malis iij^s iiij^d fra John of Loktone. Item fra John Mechalsoune xviij^d. Item [fra ? *text obscured*] John Wricht xij^d. Item fra John Sym vj^s viij^d. Item fra Wyll of Dunlop xij^s viii^d. Item Law of Furmornis xij^s viij^d. Item John Bakstar x^s. Item Richarde of Walwode xij^{s}viij^d. Item ij^s viij^d fra John Bakstar of his wyn syluir.
    Summa recepcionis iiij lib xix^s vij^d.

[*Fo. 104*]

Expense. In primis in vino drunkyn in John Chepmanis ij^s. Item drunkyn in John of Coupiris tavern at diueris tymis ij^s viij^d. Item drunkyn in John of Bothuelis v^s. Item drunkyn in John Chepmanis at Wyll of Kircaldie count makyn and expendyt xj^s [-^{d}? *folio torn*]. Item at John of Coupiris count geving expendyt vj^s vj^d. Item for borwmale of the gyld vij^d. Item in papir and to the writar xij^d.
    Summa expensarum xxix^s vj^d. Quae summa deducta de summa [recepcionum ? *folio torn*] remanet in suis manibus iij lib x^s j^d. Sic remanet in bursa et per debitores. [? *folio torn*]
    xviij lib x^s x^d. Of the qwhilk some tretyt be Joh[? *folio torn*] xv^s and forgevin be the brethir and othir xv^s of the said some the said John [? *folio torn*] is cummyn dettour to be payit be Witsonday, Wilyhame of Kircaldy borch.

Anno etc. cccc xlvj^o the vij day of Januar John of Bothuel gave his compt of the twa yher [gane befor ? *folio torn*] of the denschip of the gyld. And his charge was in primis be the fwt of John of Coupir [is compt ? *folio torn*] xviij lib x^s x^d. Item the malis in his tym xj^s viij^d. Item enteris in his tym l^s [? *folio torn*] tym v^s vj^d.
    Summa totalis oneracionis xxj lib xviij^s.

Expense. In primis forgevyn to John Wincister of Nichole
Jonsonys det vj^s viij[^{d} ? *folio torn*].
Item to John Valange forgevyn of Ramsayis det xv^s.
Item to Schir Thomas Steylle xvij^s vj^d.
Item gevyn to Law Segy v^s.
Item for a cowell to the gyld crosse iiij^s.
Item drunkyn in wyne xviij^s x^d.
Item in wyne gevyn to the larde at his ham cuming
ix^s iiij^d.
Item expendyt at a dynar xxviij^s vij^d.
Item drunkyn that day the compt was gevyn ij^s iiij^d.
    Summa expensarum v lib vij^s iij^d.
    Summa totalis oneracionis vt supra xxj
    lib xviij^s quae summa deducta de summa
    exp[? *folio torn*].
    Sic remanet in bursa xvj lib x^s ix^d the
    qwhilk some restis [? *folio torn*] handis vn-
    dirwritin.
In primis Malisse Leche x^s. Soluit.
Item Thom Cristysone vj^s viij^d.
Item John Michalsone for Philp of Lochqwhor xxviij^s xj^d.
Item Thom of Dalgles vj^s viij^d.
Item Huchon Masone xx^s. Conceidyt witht hym for iiij^c of
lym for x^s and to owr syt the remanis qwhyt [? *folio torn*]
for the lym [? *folio torn*].
Item Johne Scoby xxvj^s viij^d.
Item Thom of Bra for John Ywng and John Wylsone xxix^s.
Item Wyll of Gellald xiiij^s iiij^d.
Item Law Fox xx^s. Item he and Law Segy iiij^s for the
qwaril mell.
Item John Wricht ix^s ii^d.
Item Johne of Coupir vj^s viij^d. Summa in the dettouris
handis viij lib xviij^s j [^{d} and ? *folio torn*] restis in the
denys handis vij lib [*deleted*: vii^s viii^d] viij^s viij^d.

[*Fo. 104v*]

   Anno etc xlviij.
Anno Domini etc. cccc xlviij the xxii day of March John
of Bothuell gef his compt of the [twa ? *folio torn*] last gan
befor of the denschip of the gild. And hys charg was in
the fut of hys [last ? *folio torn*] compt xvj lib x^s ix^d.
Item the malis of the said twa yeris xj^s viij^d. Item fra
[? *folio torn*] Logan for fauour to occupy gild fredom v^s.
   Summa totalis oneracionis xvij^s lib vij^s v^d.
Expense. In primis in win giffin to the abbot at the
deliuerans of the decret of our [fredom ? *folio torn*] of Gaytmylk betuyx ws and Kyrcaldy xj^s. Item dronkin be the

nichbouris of the said [twa *? folio torn*] yer in win vij ^{s} x ^{d}. Item gyffin for stanis to the tolbuth xiij^s iiij^d . Item gyffin [for skla *? folio torn*] to Robin Sklattaris to the tolbuth iij lib xij ^{s}. Item forgewin to Malice Lech x ^{s} [Item geffin to *? folio torn*] Snawdon harrald x ^{s}. Summa expensarum vj lib iiij ^{s} ij^d.

   Summa totalis oneracionis vt supra xvij lib vij ^{s} v ^{d}.

   Summa expensarum vt supra vj lib iiij^s ij^d.

Quae summa deducta de summa oneracionis sic remanet in bursa xj lib iij ^{s} iij ^{d}.

In the mennis handis vndirwritin. In primis Thom Cristisoun vj ^{s} viij ^{d}. James Mechelsou[n *? folio torn*] Philp of Louchor xviij ^{s} xj^d. Thom of Dalgles iij^s v^d. [*deleted*: Huchon Mason x]. Johne Scobe xiij ^{s} iiij ^{d}. Item Thom of Bra xvj ^{s} . Item Will of Gelland vij^s ij^d. [Item *? folio torn*] Law Fox xx ^{s}. Johne Wrich ix ^{s} ij ^{d}. Johne of Coupir iij ^{s} iiij^d. Item Law Fox [and *? folio torn*] Law Segy viiij ^{s} coniunctly for a quarell mell. Item Huchun Masone xx ^{s} the qwhilk is forgevin for xij ^{s} vj ^{d}. Soluit. Summa in the mennis handis abonwritin vj lib ij^s.

   Sua remanis in the said Johne of Bothuell handis v lib xv^d.

   And tharof deliverit to the mastyr of the skull than den be Mor[is *? folio torn*] Blayk sergeand xxxiiij ^{s} xj ^{d} of the soum befor writtin that restis [in *? folio torn*] Johne of Boihuell handis. Sa remanis in Johne of Bothuell ha[ndis *? folio torn*] iij lib vj ^{s} iiij^d the qwilk soum he deliuerit to the said dey[n *? folio torn*] Johne Wylyamsoune the xiij day of the moneth of May anno etc. xlix°.

[*Fo. 105*]

Anno etc. cccc xlix the xxv day of the moneth of October Schir John Wylyhamsone den of gylde gaue his compt of the yher gane befor of the denschip. And his charge was in primis be the fute of John of Bothuelis compt xj lib iij ^{s} iij ^{d}.

Entreis of this yhere vij lib vii^s iiij^d.

Item resauit fra James Strang of formalle for viij yher xx ^{s} of a land lyand in the Newraw the qwhilk gane befor xviij ^{d} and now set him in fee for xxx ^{d} yherly and his [*addition in margin ? folio worn and torn*] is at the Witsonday next eftir this date. Item

Item the malis of that yher v ^{s} x^d.

   Summa totalis oneracionis xix lib xvi ^{s} v^d.

Expense. In primis delyuerit to John Chepman balye to the

biging of the tolbuth xvij lib j^d.
Item expendyt in drink and colacionis viij^s viij^d. Item to
John Wricht for the malle of his both ix^s ij^d. Item defaukit
to Philp of Lochqwhor of the som that he aucht iij^s j^d.
Item defaukit to Huchun Mason vij^s vj^d.

    Summa totalis expensarum xviij lib viij^s vj^d. Quae
    summa deducta de summa oneracionis remanet in
    bursa xxvij^s xj^d in thir mennys handis vndir
    writyn.
In primis Law Fox xv^s. Item Thom Cristysone vj^s viij^d.
Item in the masteris handis of the malis vj^s iij^d.

    Summa that John Chepman is chargit witht to the
    tolbuth of the common purs iiij lib. Item of the
    gyld purss xvij lib j^d. Summa totalis xxi lib
    iiij^s xj^d.
Expense made vpon the tolbuth be John Chepman master of
the werk xxj lib xvij^s ij^d.

    Summa expensarum xxj lib xvij^s ij^d. Sic supra-
    expendentur xij^s iij[^{d}? *folio torn*]. Summa totalis
    of the costis made on the tolbuth the yher befor
    and this yher of the common purss and the gylde
    purss xxvj lib iij^s iiij^d of the qwhilk som laide
    don be the gyldebrethir xxj lib xviij^s vj^d and
    be common purss iiij lib iiij^s x^d.
Memorandum that on Sant Thomas evyn John of Coupir
aldirman and John of Bothuell den witht consent of the
brethir thai forgaffe Law Fox for the luff of God the
xv^s the qwhilk he was awand to the den and the brethir
for his entrie.

[*in margin* : nota] Anno etc. cccc quinquagesimo the xx
day of Januar John of Bothuell den of the gy[ld ? *folio torn*]
gaue his compt of the yher gane befor of the denschip and
his charge was in [primis ? *folio torn*] be the fute of Schir
John Wyllyhamsounis count xxvij^s xj^d. Item of malis
iiij^s iiij^d [of ? *folio torn*] that yher. Item the amercements
of that yher iij^s vj^d.

    Summa totalis oneracionis xxxv^s ix^d.
Expense. In primis forgevin to Law Fox xv^s. Item drunkin
in wyne vij^s iiij^d.
Item forgevin to Thom Cristysone vj^s viij^d.

    Summa totalis expensarum xxix^s. Quae summa
    deducta de summa oneracionis remanet in bursa
    vj^s ix^d[*deleted*: that is] the qwhilk is iij^s [? *folio
    torn*] Wylylhamsone handis den.
Item Philp Stoylis wyn syluir vnpayit.

[*Fo. 105v*]

Anno etc. cccc quinquagesimo primo the xvj day of December Schir John Wylyhamso[ne *? text obscured*] den of the gilde gaue his count of the [*deleted* : twa] yher gane befor of the denschip. And his charge was in primis be the fute of John of Bothuel count vj^s ix^d. Item of malis iiij ^{s} iiij^d of that yher.
    Summa totalis oneracionis xj^s j^d.
Expense. In primis in his count of befor v^s iiij^d the qwhilk was drunk[in *? text obscured*] in till his tothir count and nocht put in his expense. Item in wyne drunkin in Andro Hog [*? text obscured*] xij^d.
   Summa expensarum vj^s iiij^d. Quae summa deducta de summa oneracionis reman[*? text obscured*] in bursa iiij^s ix^d the qwhilk Rob Patonsone has.
[*in margin*: nota] Anno etc. cccc quinquagesimo secundo the xvij day of December Dauid Wrych dene of the gild gave his compt of the yhere befor of the denschip. And his charge was in primis be the fute of Schir John Wilyhamsounis cumpt iiij^s ix^d. Item of mal iiij^s iiij^d of that yher.
    Summa totalis oneracionis ix^s j^d.
[*in margin*: nota] Expense. In primis gevin to Jonate of Guthrie iij^s iiij^d. Item drunkin in Wyll of Kircaldis houss in Sanct Stephins day xij^d.
   Summa expensarum iiij^s iiij^d. Quae summa deducta de summa oneracionis remanet in bursa iiij^s ix^d the qwhilk is in Rob Patonsone handis.

Anno etc. quinquagesimo tercio xxiiij die mensis Nouembris John of Cokburn den of the gilde gave his count of the yher gane befor of the denschip. And his charge was in primis be the fute of Dauid Weris count iiij^s ix^d. Item of mal iiij^s iiij^d of that yher.
   Nota. Summa totalis oneracionis ix^s j^d. Quae supra remanet in bursa.

Anno etc. cccc quinquagesimo quarto xv^o die mensis Decembris John Chepman den of the gilde gaue his count of the yer gan befor of the denschip. And his charge was in primis be the fute of John of Cokburnys count ix^s j^d. Item of mal iiij^s iiij^d.
    Summa totalis oneracionis xiij^s v^d.
Expense inde. In primis gevin to the bying of a collacioun vj^s viij^d. Item drunkyn in the tolbuth into wyne xij^d. Item gevin to Jonat of Guthrie xij^d.
   Summa totalis expensarum viij^s viij^d. Quae summa deducta de summa oneracionis remanet in bursa

iiij ˢ ixᵈ.

[Fo. 106]

[in margin: nota] Anno etc. cccc quinquagesimo quinto decimo tercio die mensis Decembris Thom [? folio torn] dene of the gild gaue his count of the yer gane of befor of the denschip [and ? folio torn] his charge was in primis be the fute of John Chepmanis count iiij ˢ ixᵈ. Item of mal iiij ˢ iiijᵈ. Item fra Andro Litstar for the fredom to occupy his craf[t ? folio torn] vj ˢ viij ᵈ. Amerciamenta for berking of Henry Fowlar ij ˢ. Item of the said Henry for h[ym ? folio torn] to berk hors hydis and huddrownis iij ˢ iiijᵈ.
    Summa totalis oneracionis xxj ˢ jᵈ.
Expense inde. In primis drunkyn be the dene and the brethir in Thom of B[ra ? folio torn] hous in Yuille ijˢ.

    Summa totalis expensarum ij ˢ. Sic remanet in bursa xix ˢ j ᵈ.

[in margin: nota] Anno etc. lviijᵒ xv ᵒ die mensis Maij Alane Litstar den of gilde gaue his compt yere gane of befor of the denschip. And his charg was in primis be the fute of Thom of Brais compt xix ˢ jᵈ. Item of malis iiij ˢ iiijᵈ that is to say iij ˢ iiijᵈ of J[? folio torn] Loktownis houss and xijᵈ of John Wrycht houss at the corss.
    Summa totalis oneracionis xxiijˢ vᵈ.
Expense inde. In primis gevin to Andro Litstar for stanis leding and sand leding to causa vjˢ viijᵈ. Item drynkyn xijᵈ.

    Summa expensarum patet sic remanet in bursa xv ˢ v [? folio torn] quhilk is delyuerit to Lowry Foular sergiand. Item in [? folio torn] handis iiijˢ iiijᵈ delyuerit him be Andro Logane.
    Summa xxˢ jᵈ.

Anno etc. lviijᵒ xvj die mensis Augusti John Fleming dene of the gilde gaue his compt of the yere gane of befor of the office of denschip, and his charge was in primis of the fute Alane Litstaris compt xxˢ jᵈ. Item of malis vj ˢ x ᵈ. Item entreis that yer xxvjˢ viijᵈ.
    Summa totalis oneracionis [deleted: xxviˢ xlᵈ] liij ˢ vij ᵈ.
Expense inde. In primis gevin to Schir Henry Logane vˢ.
Item Andre Butlar for wyne drunkyn be the dene and the gild brethir iiij ˢ [? folio torn].
Item gevin to the causamakar at diuers tymis xviij ˢ xᵈ.
Item for sand and stanis and serment to the causamakar viij ˢ vijᵈ.

Item gevin to the causamakar for erllis xij^d.
>Summa expensarum xxxvij^s v^d [*deleted*: summa] summa de [ducta *? folio torn*] de summa oneracionis remanet in bursa xvj^s ij^d.

[*Fo. 106v*]

Anno etc. lix^o primo die mensis Decembris Thomas of Coupir dene of the gilde gave compt of the denschip of the yeir gane of befor. And his charge was in primis xvj^s ij^d of the fute of John Flemyngis compt. Item of malis vj^{s}x^d. Amercements ij^s. Summa totalis oneracionis xxv^s.

Expense inde. In primis forgevin to Wyll Jacson ij^s. Sic remanet in bursa xxiij^s quhilk was richt than delyuerit to Alan Litstar dene.

Anno etc. lx^o vltimo die mensis Octobris Alan Litstar dene of the gilde gave compt of the denschip of the yer gane of befor. And his charge was in primis xxiij^s of the fute of Thom of Coupiris compt next of befor. Item of mal vj^s x^d. Item of entreis of that yer. In primis of Andro Butlar xl^s. Item of Dauid Brais entre xiij^s iiij^d.

>Summa totalis oneracionis iiij lib iij^s ij^d quhilk restis in his handis.

Item in Lowry Foularis handis of wyne siluir of Schir Robert Graunt ij^s vj^d. Item Andro Butlar ij^s viij^d. Item Dauid Bra ij^s viij^d. Item of the said Lowry ij^s viij^d. Item John of Hill ij^s viij^d. Summa of that yer wyne siluir xiij^s.

Anno etc. lxij^o septimo die mensis Augusti Thom of Coupir gaue compt of the office of the denschip and of the yer of lxj. And his charge was [in *? folio torn*] primis of the fute of Alan Litstaris compt iiij lib iij^s ij^d. Item of xiij^s [q *? folio torn*]uhilk was in Lowry Foularis handis the quhilk halle some was expendit vpon [the *? folio torn*] causa the day of the making of this compt excep v^s viij^d as the commone buke beris witnes in Alan Litstaris compt and Wyll Jacsonis. Item of the gilde malis [o *? folio torn*]f that yer of John Wrycht xij^d. Item of Loktownis houss iij^s iiij^d. Item of James [Str*? folio torn*]angis houss ij^s vj^d. Summa [*deleted* : totalis] vj^s x^d. Summa totalis xxxix^s ij^d. And thairof [de *? folio torn*] lyuerit to Wyll Jacsone to the causa xxvj^s viij^d. Swa remane in the said den [is *? folio torn*] handis xij^s vj^d the quhilk he delyuerit the said day to Dauid Wer dene of gil[de *? folio torn*]. Item the said Dauid has to tak in of Dic of Orok xxxij^d of wyne siluir. Item fra Andro Gervas xxxij^d.

[Fo. 107]

[deleted: Anno etc. cccc lix septimo die mensis Decembris Thomas of Coupir den of the gilde gaue compt of the denschip of the yere gane of [befor ? folio torn]. And his charge was in primis xvj^s ij^d of the fute of John Flemingis [compt ? folio torn]. Item of malis vj^s x^d. Amercements ij^s.

                Summa totalis oneracionis xxv^s.

Expense inde. In primis forgevin to Wyll Jacsone ij^s. Sic remanet in bursa xx [? folio torn] quhilk was richt than richt than delyuerit to Alan Litstar den.]

Memorandum the yeir of God j^m cccc lxx ande fywe apone Sanct Thomas ewyn Andro Litstar ande Andro Geruas war put in frenchip and the saide Andro Geruas wes conuickit in xl^d for his amercement and to ask the said Andro forgyfnes. And the saide Andro Gerues sall nothir heir nor se his schaith bot he sall warn hym be caus he gaif a bill of complant to the to lorde of [deleted: the] Andro Litstar, the qwhilk complant wes fund of na waill be ane offis.

                Summa xix lib xij^s ij^d.

Memorandum quod anno Domini j^{mo} cccc lxxvj [sic] xij^o die Septembris the quhilk day the aldirman John of Kircaldy, Andro Litstar dene, Dauid Bra and William of Spitell balyeis and a part of the consalle of the toune herd the comptis of viij yeris of the quhilk of this instant yer was a yer. And the hale charge of the forsaid yeris extendis to xvij lib ix^s ij^d. And the expens of the forsaid yeris x lib xiiij^s. Restis vj lib xv^s iiij^d the quhilkis is in thir mennys handis vndir writtyn. In primis Laurence Foular xlv^s iiij^d. Item Thomas Covpir xv^s x^d, William of Spetell vj^s x^d, Andro Litstar iij lib vj^d. Item John Fleming vj^s x^d.

[Fo. 107v]

[? folio torn]- - - etc. lxvj^{to} xxvij day of Aprille Dauid Weir gaffe compt of [the ? folio torn] denschip of the gilde. And his charge was iij lib iiij^s viij^d, the quhilk [? folio torn] haly expendit on the cawsa.

Anno etc. lxvij, ix day of Maij Thomas of Coupir gaff compt of the yer of lxij and of the yer of lxiij of the office of the denschip of the gyld. And his charge of the sayde twa yeris xj lib x^s vj^d as the buke of the countis of the sayde ij yeris [ber ? folio torn]is witness, the quhilk halle some is spendit vpone the causais excep xiiij^d.

Anno etc. lxvij ix day of Maij Alan Litstar gaff compt of the yer of lxiiij of the denschip of the gild. And his charge was in primis of the fute of Thomas of Coupiris [com ? *folio torn*]pt xiiij^d. Item of Andro Litstaris entre xv^s and ij^s viij^d of wyne siluir. Item of malyis vj^s x^d.
       Summa totalis oneracionis xxv^s viij^d.
Expense inde. In primis ij^s gevin to Ffynlay Broustaris wyff till a purr barn. Item xiij^s gevin to the causamackar Summa expensarum xv^s. Sic remanet x^s viij^d quhilk was gevin to Thomas of Coupir dene.

Anno etc lxvij, ix day of Maij Thomas of Coupir geff compt of the yer of lxv of the office of the denschip of the gilde. And his charge was in primis of the fute of Alane Litstaris compt x^s viij^d. Item Jok Flemingis wyne siluir ij^s viij^d. Item of the malis vj^s x^d.
       Summa totalis oneracionis xx^s ij^d.
Expense inde. In primis to Michale causamackar in the Colyeraw v^s.
       Summa expensarum v^s. Sic remanet xv^s ij^d quhilk was deliuerit to William Jacsone dene. And incontinent the said dene delyuerit the said xv^s ij^d to Michale in the Colyeraw.

[*Fo. 108*]

[Anno etc. cccc ? *folio worn*] lxxix, viij die Novembris quinquagesimo Willelmus Spetell decanus de gi[? *folio torn*]. In primis of the gild male vj^s x^d.
Item of the entreis of Rob Blakwode xl^s.
Item Johne Broune xl^s.
       Summa totalis oneracionis iiij lib vj^s x^d.
The quhilk soum was delyuerit to Laurens Foular bursour. Expense inde. In primis superexpendit in the bursaris last compt of the causa vj^s viij^d.
Item delyuerit to the common clerk for his fe x^s, the quhilk was nocht in [the common purs ? *folio torn*]
       Summa expensarum xvj^s viij^d. Remanet in [? *folio torn*] iij lib x^s ij^d.

Anno Domini j^{mo} lxxx, ix die mensis Octobris Llowrens Fowlar dene of the gyld [? *folio torn*] haill cownt of twa yerris by gayn and of all mall and ressate of gild [maill ? *folio torn*] siluyr deliuerit till hym of befor the said Lowrens haffand a fre disch[arg ? *folio torn*] of all entreis gayn of befor.

[*in margin*: memorandum] Memorandum etc. anno Domini j^m cccc lxxxv vltimo die mensis Decembris the quhilk day

the alderman balyeis the dene the common clerk witht the
part of the [? *folio torn*] and eftir the deliuerans of the
communite has set westmist hauf of the [? *folio torn*] to Wilyam Pattonsoune for all the dais of his lyff payand
[? *folio torn*] at Witsunday and Mertimes be ewyn portiones
and the said [? *folio torn*] sal bettir the haus and mendit
withtin a yer xxx ˢ at the syte [of ? *folio torn*] discret nychtburris and uphaldit as efferis falyeand thairof h[? *folio
torn*] waik.

[*Fo. 108v*]

Anno etc. cccc lxxvij xj die Octobris.
[The ? *folio torn*] quhilk day Laurence Foular bursar
resauit fra Thom of Coupir vjˢ xᵈ of [the gi ? *folio torn*]ld
siluir and of the soum of xv ˢ.
Item in the said bursaris handis xlvˢ iiijᵈ.
Item fra Johne Fleming vj ˢ xᵈ.
Item payit be Andro Litstar iij lib vjᵈ.
Item pait be Wilyame of Spittall vjˢ xᵈ.

Anno etc. cccc lxxviij penultimo die Nouembris Laurens
Foular dene gaff compt of the gilde siluyr. And his
chargis was of the fute of the compt gane of befor vj
lib [? *folio torn*] iiijᵈ. Item of gild male vjˢ xᵈ.
Summa vii lib ijˢ ijᵈ.
[*deleted*: Expense inde Roberto Thomsone xijˢ iiijᵈ for
stanis and sand to the causa.
Item delyuerit to Purrokis xvˢ for stanis and sand to the
causa. Item eidem xvˢ.
Item Alexander Budge for stanis and sand xvˢ. Item eidem
Alexandro xv ˢ.
[Item ? *text concealed*] Johne Coudone and Ochtre for stanis
and sand xvˢ. Item xˢ.
[memorandum ? *folio torn*] that Andro Butlar is awand of
the soum that the said Laurens is chargit witht ix ˢ .
Qu[hilk sou ? *folio torn*]m is hale payit to the said
Laurens be the said Andro.
Item delyuerit be the said Laurens to Michale causamakar
xl ˢ.
Item John Wilsone for gwter stanis leding xxxᵈ.
Item delyuerit be the said Laurence to the aldyrman
xlijᵈ, the quhilk he delyuerit to [M ? *folio torn*]ichael cawsa makar for erlys to the calsa makyng vjᵈ in primis.
Item to the said Michaelis costis quhen he com our the
wattir to commoun with ws anens the [sai ? *folio torn*]d caw-
say ij ˢ. Item for drynk siluyr at the bigynyng off the
cawsa vjᵈ.
Item for the copying off the kingis lettoris vndir an

instrument vj^d.
Item delyuerit to the causemakaris childer xx^s. Item v^s.
Item delyuerit to Purrokis for sand and stanis till a rude of causa v^s.
Item for squill ij^d.]

[? *folio torn*] anno etc. lxxix, vltimo die mensis Octobris, Laurens Foular bursour gaff compt [of ? *folio torn*] the common siluyr and of the gild silyur quhilk he was chargit with. In primis of the [common siluyr ? *folio torn*] iiij lib ij^s vij^d.
Item of the gild sylyur vij lib ij^s ij^d. Summa totalis oneracionis xj lib iiij^s [ix^d ? *folio torn*]
   Expense inde gevin to the causamaking x lib iiij^s. Item for copying of the king[is lettoris ? *folio torn*] vndir ane instrument vj^d. Item for lym and sand to the tolbuth iij^s. Item Thom Blaik iiij^s. [Item ? *folio torn*] for ane instrument to Sant Saluatouris altar vj^d. Item for squill ij^d.
Item forgevin to [? *folio torn*] of Spetell at the request of the abbot xviij^s.
Summa expensarum xj lib x^s iij^d.
[Item xlj ? *folio torn*]^d attour gevin for meking of the causa. Swa restis superexpendit v^s.

INDEX

In indexing, where possible, both surnames and forenames have been modernised and variants given. Surnames have been modernised according to G.F. Black, *The Surnames of Scotland* (New York, 1974, 1979). Place-names have been given both original and modern spellings, and cross-referenced where necessary.

To differentiate between individuals of the same name, information has been used from other primary source materials, as well as from the Dunfermline Gild Court Book.

abbey, of Dunfermline, xvi, xvii, xxi, xxviii, 50.
abbot, of Culross, 1.
   of Dunfermline, xvii, xviii, xx, xxii, xxiv, xxviii, 5, 6, 8, 9, 12, 15, 16, 17, 18, 25, 29, 165, 174.
   John (of Strathmiglo ?), abbot of Dunfermline, xvii.
   Richard, abbot of Dunfermline, 18.
Aberdeen, xiv; gild merchant of, xv; gild records of, xii, xiii, xxvi.
accounts of gild, xix, xxii, 41, 42, 43, 47, 49, 51, 52, 57, 61, 88, 89, 92, 94, 101, 102, 118, 119, 123, 125, 131, 137, 141, 150, 154 to 174.
Addison (Adesone, Adison), John, 138.
   Lawrence, 127.
   Robert, 132.
Adnbro, see Edinburgh.
Aiken (Aaking, Aitkine, Aitkyne , etc.), Sir Alexander, gild priest, 83.
   David, 90, 94, 95, 97, 99, 100, 102, 103, 104; as dean of gild, 97, 98, 99, 101.
   Richard, 48.
   Sir Robert, 37.
ais (as, ass, ays), see potash.
Alan (Allane, Allanne), James, 143.
albs, 102.
alderman of burgh, xviii, xxviii, *passim* to p. 73, 154 to 174 *passim*. See *also* provost.
ale, xxii, 3, 28, 30, 35, 42, 46, 158.
alehouses, see taverns.
Allanson (Alanson, Alansone, Alansoun), Alexander, 21, 28.
   Sir James, 50.
   Sir John, 39.
   Sir William, 6.
almery, see cupboard.
almoner, of Dunfermline abbey, 7, 10, 11, 13, 47, 50, 51; land of, see eli-mosinar's land.
altars, xxi, xxii; chalice of, 52; cloths of, 102; frontal of, 102; towels of, 102.
   of the Holy Blood, in Dundee, xxx.
   of the Holy Blood, in

INDEX

Dunfermline, xxi, 34, 35, 37, 41, 47, 49, 50, 51, 54, 55, 56, 57, 58, 63, 65, 66, 68, 69, 71, 93, 94, 97, 99, 135, 138; annuals, offerings, silver of, 34, 41, 54, 55, 56, 57, 58, 59, 63, 66, 68, 70, 97; chaplains of, 41, 58; kist of Holy Blood silver, 59; lands of, Holy Blood acres, 41, 47, 55, 58, 59, 63, 65, 66, 70; patrons of, 135; tutours to, 70.
of the Holy Blood in Edinburgh, xxx.
of the Holy Blood in Perth, xxx.
of the Holy Blood in St. Andrews, xxx.
of the Holy Rood and Our Lady, 31; priest of, 69.
of St. John, 35.
of St. Margaret, 34, 37, 50, 65, 66; chaplains of, 69, 88; offerings of, 34.
of St. Michael, 51; lands of, 51.
of St. Rynyein (Ninian), xxi, 35.
of St. Salvator, xxi, 34, 35, 36, 51, 52, 57, 174; tutours to, 34.
Anderson (Andersone, Andersoun, Anderston, Andirson, Andirsoune, Androson, etc.), Adam, father of John, 142.
Andrew, father of John, 15.
Andrew, 106.
George, 127.
John, son of Andrew, father of John, 15, 19, 20, 21, 23.
John, son of John, 27, 29.
John, 85, 87, 95.
John, flesher, 94.
John, 'at the cross' (*another ?*), father of John, 131.
John, son of John 'at the cross', 131, 132, 133, 134.
John, son of Adam, husband of Bessie Christie, 142.
John (*another ?*), litster, 148.
Robert, 48.
Robert, 117.
Thomas, 6.
William, 42, 44, 46, 64, 65.
William, 75, 80.
William, 136.
Angus, William, 93.
Annan (Anand, Anande, Annand), William, grandson of Lawrence Boyce, 3, 8, 11, 156, 159, 161, 162.
annuals of gild, *see* accounts of gild.
archbishop, of St. Andrews, Andrew, 57.
Arnot (Arnoit), Alexander, husband of Janet Jackson, father of John, 52, 64.
John, son of Alexander, 64.
Antwerp, 82.
Asloan (Aisoim, Aisoune, Aslone), John, 86.
William, 128.
assault, 2, 4, 19, 21, 148.
assizes, of burgh, xxix.
auditors of gild accounts, xxx, 45.
Ayr, gild records of, xiii, xxvi; gild merchant of, xxvii.

Baad (Bad), Henry, 64, 65.
Nichol, 80.

INDEX

bailies, xviii, *passim*; choosing of, 122.
Baldridge (Baldrig), by Dunfermline, 146.
Balfour, James, 85; as collector of light silver, 74.
Ballunie (Ballone, Balloune, Ballune, Balluny, Balwny), John of, son of William of, 40.
William of, father of John of, 25, 29, 30, 40.
Balmanno (Balmanoch, Balmanouch), William of, 5, 8, 9, 11, 157, 158, 161, 162, 164.
Baltic Sea, xix, xxx. See also easter seas.
banishment from town, 1, 152.
Bar, Will of, 5, 155, 160, 162.
Barber (Barbor, Barbour, Barbur), Henry, 40, 43, 44, 45, 49; as dean of gild, 40, 41, 42, 44, 47.
Barclay (Barklay), Marian, 102.
Bardner (Bardnar), Master David, 28, 35.
Barker (Berkar), James, 78.
barkers, see tanners.
barking, bark pots, see tanning, tanning pits.
barley, 151.
Barnet (Barnat), George, 114.
barns, xxiii.
Baxter (Bakstar, Baxstar, Baxster, Baxtar, Baxtir), Dotho, 11.
John, 10, 164.
John, 29, 30, 32, 34, 35, 39, 40, 42; as dean of gild, 40, 41, 50; father-in-law of John Wellwood, 42.
Walter, 72.
Walter, 77, 80, 81, 83, 87, 88, 89, 92, 94, 95, 96, 97, 99, 100, 105; as bailie, 77, 78, 79, 80; as deputy for dean of gild, 109, 111.
Walter (*another?*), 136.
William, 108.
beans, 152.
bear, see barley.
Beath, 48.
beer, xxiii, 46.
Beitht, see Beath.
bell, 52, 53, 54, 55, 153; bellhouse (steeple), 53, 55.
Bennie (Benyn, Benyng, Benynge), Sir Thomas, 31, 37.
William, husband of Janet, 1, 4.
Berwick, xv, xvi, 152, 153; gild of, xv; gild laws of, see *Statuta gilde*.
bishop, of St. Andrews, 13.
Roger, xv.
Black (Blaik, Blak, Blayk), Alexander, 138.
David, 66, 67.
David, 138; father of Isobel, 144.
Isobel, daughter of David, wife of Simon Hair, 144.
Dean John, almoner, 7, 13.
John, 50.
John, burgess of Dunfermline and citizen of Swiecen, Prussia, xxx.
Maurice, 10, 13; as serjeand of gild, 11, 166.
Thomas, 174.
William, 59.
Blackwood (Blacat, Blackat, Blacot, Blakwod, Blakwold, etc.), Adam, weaver, 45, 46, 47, 52, 53, 57, 65, 66; as bailie, 54; as dean of

INDEX

gild, 55, 56, 58, 59.
Adam, 73, 74, 78.
Adam, 135.
David, 71.
John, 25, 26, 27, 35.
Robert, 23, 24, 25, 26, 27, 33, 35, 172.
Robert, 51.
William, 20, 22; father of William, 45.
William, son of William, 45, 57, 63.
William, 66; as dean of gild, 68, 69, 70, 71; as tutour to Holy Blood altar, 70; 'elder', 72; as collector of light silver, 72; as kirkmaster, 73; father of William, 89.
William, son of William, 89.
Blake, see Black.
Blaw (Blawe), James, husband of Christian Shorthouse, 135.
Blyth, James, 64.
books; burgh court book, xiii, xiv, xix, xx, xxiii, xxix; book of accounts, 171; common book, 170; gild court book, xi, xiii, xiv, xviii, xix, xx, xxii, xxiii, xxxii, 155, and repairs to, xii; regality court book, xiii.
booths, xxv, 19, 38, 93, 96, 106, 115, 118, 138, 167.
Bothwell (Boissuell, Boiswell, Bosuale, Boswald, Bothuele, Bothuell, etc.), David, 24, 32; as dean of gild, 26.
George, 130; as bailie, 140.
Henry, 47; as alderman, 47, 49, 50.
John, 2, 4, 7, 8, 14, 158, 159, 160, 164; as dean of gild, 10, 11, 12, 13, 14, 25, 163, 164, 165, 166, 167, 168.
John, 79.
John (another? two others?) 86, 87, 89, 94, 95, 96, 97, 98, 99, 100, 103, 104, 105, 107, 108, 110, 113, 114, 127, 135; as bailie, 94, 98, 128, 131, 132; as dean of gild, 87, 88, 89, 90, 91, 92, 94, 124.
Dean John, sacristan of Dunfermline abbey, 83.
Richard, sacristan of Dunfermline abbey, 6.
William, 100, 105, 106, 110, 113, 114.
Bourne, Thomas, 115.
Boyce (Boyis, Boys), Alexander, 5, 8.
John, 18, 161, 162.
Lawrence, 2, 154, 160, 163; grandfather of William Annan, 4.
Dean William, sacristan of Dunfermline abbey, 12.
braid yard, the, 138.
Brand, Adam, 62; as collector of light silver, 74.
David, 83, 94, 95; wife of, 83.
Robert, 59.
Bray (Bra), David, 4, 16, 17, 30, 35, 170; as bailie, 20, 171; as dean of gild, 23.
David, common clerk of burgh, xi.
John, son of Thomas, 13, 14; grandfather of John Welwood, 46.
Lawrence, 161, 162.
Thomas, 3, 5, 7, 8, 11, 12, 13, 14, 15, 156, 159, 161, 162, 163, 165, 166, 169; as bailie, 13; as dean of gild, 15, 169;

INDEX

father of John, 13; wife of, 14.
breach of the peace, 2, 3, 4, 6, 9, 11, 12, 15, 16, 23, 25, 31, 38, 114, 146. See also assault.
bread, xxiii, 42, 46.
Brewster (Broustar), Findlay, 19, 172; wife of, 172.
brewsters (brostirs), 28, 35.
Brown (Bron, Broun, Broune, Browne, Brovnne, Brwne), David, 48.
  David, common clerk of the burgh, notary public, xii, 142, 148; husband of Gelis Reid, 142.
  George, 48.
  Henry, 34.
  John, 23, 24, 27, 28, 172.
  John 'in the Netherton', 135.
  Lawrence, 51.
  Nichol, 4, 5, 8, 161, 162.
  Robert, 45, 46.
Bruce, Robert, of Baldridge, 146.
Bruges, xvii.
Bryson (Brison), John, 21.
Budge, Alexander, 173.
building control, see lining decisions.
Bull (Bulle), John, 48. Master Nichol, 69.
Buncle (Boncle), Robin of, dean of gild, 21.
burgage plots, see tofts.
burgesses, xiv, xvi, 150, 151; of Dunfermline, xvii, xviii, xxiv, 99, 114.
burgess freedom, 35; entry to, 14, 64.
burgh clerks, see clerks.
burgh officers, xvii, xviii, xix, 114. See also alderman, bailies, farthingmen, mayor, minor, provosts.
burghs, holding of crown, xiv, xvi, xviii.
burghs, of regality, xvii, xx, xxix, xxx, 137.
Burn (Bowrn, Burne, Bwrn), Andrew, 78.
  Edward, 138.
  James, 89, 90, 92, 94, 95, 99, 100, 104, 116, 119, 120, 121, 124, 127, 130.
  John of, 12, 13.
  John, grandson of John Welwood of the Wynd, 50.
  John, younger (another ?) 54.
  John, (another ?) 54, 56, 65; as collector of light silver, 72.
  Lawrence, 124.
  Thomas of, 50.
  William, 127.
bursar, of gild, xxx, 24, 27, 172, 173, 174. See also treasurer.
Butler (Butlar), Andrew, brother of John of Cupar, 17, 18, 25, 26, 169, 170, 173; as bailie, 26; as dean of gild, 25.
Byres (Byris), John of, 14.

Cady, Thomas, 8, 18, 20, 21, 22.
Cairns (Carnis, Carnys, Cranis, Karnis, Karnys), John, cordiner, 41, 43, 44, 46, 59, 65, 67.
  John, plumber, son of John, 52, 67.
  Sir Thomas, chaplain, 46.
Callan (Calland), Thomas, 39.
Calsagate, 47, 50, 138.
Campbell (Cambell), George, husband of Isobel Hutton, 140.
Campheir, see Veere.
candles, xxi, 68, 70, 93.
Cant, Alan, 29, 35.

canvas (canwes), 87.
Carmuir (Carmour, Carmur), James, 104, 105, 108; wife of, 105.
carnifex, see fleshers.
Carver (Carvor, Carvour), Simon, 58, 62, 63.
causa, repairs to, see roads.
causamackar (causamaker), 169, 170, 172, 174.
Michael, 19, 172, 173.
Cavil, see Keavil.
cellarer, of monastery, 6, 158.
Ceres (Seras), John of, wife of, 156.
chamberlain ayre, xv, 159.
chandeliers, 103.
chaplains, xxi, 41, 46, 50, 53, 58, 69, 88, 90, 134.
Chapman (Chepman), John, 2, 8, 10, 12, 14, 158, 160, 161, 162, 164, 167; as merchant, 12; as master of works to tolbooth repairs, 167; as bailie, 7, 13, 160, 166; as dean of gild, 15, 16, 168, 169; wife of, 14.
chapmen, 48.
charity, xxii, 19, 42, 93, 102, 125, 126, 127, 172. See also orphans, support of; women and widows, support of.
Charles V, Holy Roman Emperor, 82.
chasubles (chaissaippis), 102.
Cheyne (Chayn), John, 8.
Christie; Christison (Carste, Crestye, Cristie, Crystie, Cryste, etc; Cristiason, Cristison, Cristisoun, Cristysone, Cristysune, etc.), Andrew, 35.
Andrew, 120, 124, 125, 130.
Bessie, daughter of Patrick, wife of John Anderson, 142.
Cristell, 22, 34, 36.
Master John, 27, 59; as dean of gild, 53.
Sir John, 67.
John, 77, 82, 86, 87, 96; as collector of light silver, 74; husband of Janet Martin, 75.
John (another ?), 135.
Patrick, son of Walter, 133; father of Bessie, 142.
Thomas, 2, 4, 8, 11, 15, 20, 159, 160, 161, 162, 163, 165, 166, 167; as dean of gild, 2, 154, 155.
Walter, 48, 51, 52, 61.
Walter, 99, 101, 103, 104, 105, 107, 108, 112, 115, 130, 135, 148; father of Patrick, 133.
William, 1, 161, 162.
William, 46, 50, 58.
William, 121, 124; husband of Isobel Templeman, 133.
claret wine, 105.
Cleish (Cleische), vicar of, 47.
clerks, 58; common clerk, xi, xx, xxiv, 142, 172, 173; and fee of, 172; of gild book, xi, xx, xxv; of the parish, 69; of the regality, 144. See also writers.
Clermont-Ferrand, xi.
cloth, xviii, 11, 21, 87, 151; window cloth, 156.
coal, 42, 46, 153.
Cochrane, William, litster, 69.
Cockburn (Cokburn, Cokburne), Sir John of, 14, 35; knight, 25, 26; as dean of gild, 168; as alderman, 16, 20, 22, 25,

INDEX

26, 27, 28, 29, 30, 32. William of, 30, 36.
cocket seal, see regality of Dunfermline cocket seal.
Codane Beitht, see Cowdenbeath.
coinage, coins, 38, 57, 62, 67, 70, 71, 84, 98, 99, 110, 129, 147.
colations, 3, 10, 14, 75, 155, 156, 157, 158, 165, 167, 168. See also feasts.
collectors of gild money, 123, 124, 125, 126.
Collier Row, 34, 172.
Colyaraw, see Collier Row.
common book, see books.
common gate, the, 138.
common goods, 7. See also common silver.
common muir, 158.
common purse, xix, 32, 85, 167, 172.
common silver, 174. See also common goods.
Congregation, Lords of the, xxi, 99.
constables, 154.
Convention of Royal Burghs, Records of, xxv.
cooking utensils, xxiii.
Cooper (Coupar, Coupyr, Covpir, Cowpar, Cowpere, Cupir, Cwppyr, etc.), Alan, 55, 60, 65, 66; as dean of gild, 60.
David, 26, 32, 35; as alderman, 32, 33, 34, 37, 38, 39, 40, 42, 43, 44, 45, 46; father-in-law of James Preston, 50; uncle of William, 70.
John of, 1, 2, 3, 4, 5, 6, 10, 11, 18, 154, 155, 156, 159, 160, 161, 163, 164, 165, 166; of gild, xxii, 6, 7, 9, 157, 158, 163, 164; as alderman, 14, 18, 167; brother of Andrew Butler, 17.
Sir John, chaplain, 90, 134, 135, 137, 138; father of John, 117.
John, son of Sir John, 117, 120, 122.
Katherine, 34, 36.
Thomas, 13, 14, 15, 21, 171, 173; as bailie, 16, 18, 19; as alderman, 21; as dean of gild, 17, 19, 20, 170, 171, 172.
Thomas, 122, 124, 126, 128, 139, 141, 145, 148, 149; as bailie, 131, 134; as dean of gild, 141, 142, 143, 144, 145, 146, 147, 149, 150; brother of William, 139.
William, 82, 84, 88, 95, 99, 100, 108, 110; as collector of light silver, 72, 74; as head deacon, 77; nephew of David, 70; father of William, 122.
William, son of William, 122, 135; brother of Thomas, 139.
copper, 119.
Cordiner (Cordynar), Thomas, 161, 162.
cordiners, xxiv, 2, 3, 5, 9, 40, 41, 43, 44, 46, 80, 81, 143, 151, 154, 155.
corn, 48, 151, 152, 153.
council of the burgh, xviii, xxix, 14, 19, 171.
Coutts (Coutiss), Alan, 136.
Cowan (Cauane, Cawone, Couane, Cowene, Covane), John, 85, 88, 93, 94, 95, 100, 105, 110, 115, 119, 120, 127.
Patrick, 124, 130; husband of Gillie Wilson, 126.

INDEX

Cowden (Coudone), John, 173.
Cowdenbeath, 48.
Cowpir, see Cupar.
crafts, 1; incorporations, xxv, and deacons of, 33, and head deacon of, 77; craftsmen, xvi, xxv, 109, 148; and disputes with gild, xxv, 147, 148.
Craigduckie (Cragdukye), by Dunfermline, 48.
Crichton (Crechton, Crechtone), Dean James, sacristan of Dunfermline abbey, 64, 69.
cross, market, xxiii, 61, 72, 73, 131, 133, 138, 156, 169.
Culross (Culros), 135; abbot of, see abbot.
Culross (Cowris), Will of, 161, 162.
Cunningham (Cwnynghame), John, notary public, xi, 120.
Cupar, 34; gild merchant of, xxvii.
cupboard, of gild, 62, 63.
customs, of town, 144; great customs, xvii, 125.
Cuthbert (Cudbert, Culbart, Culbert), James, 126, 144, 145, 146, 149; husband of Bessie Nichol, 145.

Dalgleish (Dalglas, Dalglasche, Dallgles, Daugles, Dawgleische, Dowglas, etc.), Janet, 136.
Lawrence, 71, 75, 77, 78, 79, 81, 87, 92, 95, 96, 97, 99, 100, 104; husband of Katherine Syme, 107.
Lawrence, 'younger' (another ?), son of Thomas, 98.
Lawrence, (another ?), 135.
Robert, 92, 98, 99, 101, 108, 110, 112, 113; as dean of gild, 102, 103, 104, 105, 106, 107.
Thomas, 161, 163, 165, 166.
Thomas, 62, 63, 67, 77, 79, 80, 82, 85, 88, 89, 92, 94, 95, 97, 98, 111, 136; as collector of light silver, 72; as dean of gild, 67, 68, 69, 71, 74, 93, 94, 95, 96, 97; father of Lawrence, 98.
Daniel (Danyel), William, 53.
Danzig (Danskin, Danskyne), 67, 70, 71, 75. 84, 86, 96, 110, 124, 145.
David I, king of Scotland, xv, xvi, xxviii.
David II, king of Scotland, xvii.
Dawson (Dawsone), Malis, 161, 162.
dean of gild, as head of gild court, xx and *passim*; appointment of xx, 32, 73, 79, 95, 104, 107; choosing of, 58, 75, 97, 113; deputy to, 104, 107, 111, 124; election of, 67, 87, 92, 101, 105, 111, 114, 116, 117, 119, 121, 122, 123, 126, 128, 131, 132, 133, 137, 141, 143, 145, 146, 149.
death, of gildbrothers, xxi, xxii, 16, 42, 64.
debt, 5, 8, 11, 13, 18, 21, 29, 30, 36, 37, 43, 64, 79, 80, 88, 90, 102, 113, 147, 163, 165.
destitute gild brothers, support of, xxii, 107.
Dewar (Dawar, Deware, Dewer, Devar), David, 68, 77, 82, 89; as collector of light silver, 72; as dean of gild, 75; wife of, 104.

INDEX

David, 135, 136, 138.
John, husband of Bessie Welwood, 140.
diking, of town, 163.
dinners, see colations.
Disart, see Dysart.
Donaldson (Donaldsone), William, 65.
Dougal (Dowgall), James, 129.
Dow, Paton, 2.
Drumcapye, see Drumchapel.
Drumchapel, 48.
dry closets, xxiii.
Duguid (Dewgait, Dewgart), Robert, husband of Katherine Porteous, 137, 138.
Duly (Daly, Dwly), James, 83, 93; as collector of light silver, 72, 74.
James (another ?), 135.
Dumbarton, gild merchant of, xxvii.
Duncan (Duncane), John, 59, 92; as collector of light silver, 72, 74.
Duncanson (Duncansoun), John, 158.
Dundee, xiii, xiv, xxx; gild merchant of, xv.
Dunlop (Dwnlop), William, 10, 164; grandfather of John Johnson, 41.
(no forename), 5.
Durie (Dury, Durye), Patrick, 123, 125.
dyeing, xviii, 15.
Dysart, 67, 140.

easter seas (esteir seyeis), 82. See also Baltic Sea.
Edbrocht, see Edinburgh.
Edinburgh, xxviii, xxx, 113, 115, 123, 130, 132; gild court of, xiii; gild merchant of xxvii.
Edisoune, Robert see Addison.
Edmonston, Archibald, 50.

Elder (Eldar), David, 142.
Elgin, gild merchant of, xv.
elimosinar's land, 50.
Elsinore (Elsonevre), 98.
emperor, see Charles V.
England, xvii, xix, xxviii, 98. 144.
extramen, 151. See also unfreemen, outmen.

factor, 87; factor fee, 144.
fairs, xviii, xxix.
farthingmen, 153.
Fawsyde (Falsid), John of, 5, 156.
feasts, xxii, xxiii, 43, 44, 46, 51, 55, 57, 64, 91, 102, 111, 114, 117, 120, 125. See also colations.
Ferguson (Fargesone, Fargisone, Fargusowne, Ferguisoune, Fergujsone, etc.), Elizabeth, wife of Gavin Lawson, 61.
James, 61, 62, 64, 67; father of William, 71.
John, 39, 44, 46, 49, 52, 53, 56, 58; as bailie, 58; as dean of gild, 57.
John, 'younger', 60.
Lawrence, 49, 51, 52, 65, 66, 67, 76, 77, 79, 80, 83, 87; as dean of gild, 62, 64, 65; as kirkmaster, 68, 71; as collector of light silver, 72.
Lawrence (another ?), 136.
Robert, merchant, 68, 77, 82, 83, 86; father of Robert, 127; as collector of light silver, 72; as bailie, 76; wife of, 83.
Robert, son of Robert, 127.
William, son of James, 71, 87.
William (another ?), 135.

(Ferge, 42.)
Fillan (Fallane, Fallene, Fellane, Fillane, Filleine, Fyllane, Phillane), John, 94.
   Robert, 91, 94, 95, 98, 99, 100, 101, 105, 110, 114, 116, 118, 121, 125, 127; father of William, 143.
   William, 148; son of Robert, 143.
Fin (Fyne), Thomas, 53, 57, 61.
   Thomas (*another ?*), 136.
fire in town, xxiv, 10, 14, 162, 163; reduction in gild entrance fee as result, 10, 162.
fish, 151, 152. See also herring, salmon.
Flanders (Flanderis), xxx, 22, 82. See also Low Countries, Netherlands.
flax, 76, 84, 127, 140, 145.
Fleming (Flemyn, Flemyng), John, 15, 171, 172, 173; as dean of gild, 15, 169, 170, 171.
   John, 19, 20.
   Patrick, 15, 20, 28, 30.
   Peter, 42.
   Thomas, 12.
   William, 12.
fleshers, 4, 81, 83, 94, 112, 130, 153.
flessour, see fleshers.
Flockhart (Flokart), John, 45.
foodstuffs, control of quality and quantity, xix, 35, 104, 105, 130, 131, 132, 149, 151, 152, 153.
forestalling, see trading privileges, malpractice in.
Forfar, gild merchant of, xxvii.
Forthrik, dean of, 52, 58.
Fowler (Foular, Fowlar), Henry, 15, 169.
   Lawrence, 16, 20, 21, 22, 27, 31, 170, 171; as bursar of gild, 24, 172, 173, 174; as dean of gild, 22, 25, 26, 172, 173; as serjeant of gild, 17, 169.
   Thomas, 14.
Fox, Lawrence, 2, 4, 13, 161, 163, 165, 166, 167,
France, xi; men of, xxi, 99.
Fraser (Frasar, Frasor, Fresor, Fressall, Fresser, Friser, etc.), John, wife of, 150.
   Robert, 91, 94, 97, 103; as bailie, 94, 95, 101.
   Robert, 129.
freedom of gild, *passim*; loss of, xxii, 3, 8, 11, 31, 41, 65, 66, 68, 74, 75, 76, 77, 80, 81, 85, 93, 96, 103, 108, 109, 112, 114, 119, 124, 125, 127, 130, 131, 134, 139, 148, 151.
Frenchmen, see France.
Frog, Master John, 23.
fuel, see coal.
furs, xviii.
Furmoris (Furmornis, Furmornys), Lawrence of, 10, 11, 20, 21, 164.

gates of town, see ports.
Gay (Gaij), William, 118.
Gaytmylk, see Goatmilk.
Gellet (Gellat), xvii, 48.
Gellet (Gelland, Gellald, Gellalde), William of, 6, 8, 9, 157, 158, 161, 163, 165, 166.
Geneva, xi.
Germany, xi.
Gervase (Geruas, Gerues, Gervas, Gerwes), Anddrew, 17, 19, 20, 27, 29, 30, 31, 170, 171;

INDEX

grandfather of Alexander Stevenson, 75.
John, 31.
gild altars, xxi, xxii. *See also* altar of Holy Rood, of St. Salvator.
gild box, 103. *See also* gild purse.
gild cross, xxi, 38, 44, 61, 62, 63, 67, 68; cowl of, xxi, 165.
gild cross silver, 42, 45, 48, 52, 61, 63, 90; account of, 44, 49, 52.
gild goods, 157, 159. *See* kist of gild, contents of.
gild land, 8, 156, 157, 158, 160, 161.
gild priest, 83.
gild purse, 2, 3, 178. *See also* gild box.
gild silver, see accounts of gild.
gilds, early, xiv, xxi.
Glasgow, xiii, xiv.
Glass (Glas), Henry, 88.
Glen, Sir Alan, 54.
Goatmilk, xxix, 165.
gold, 31, 32.
Goodswain (Gudeswane, Gudsuan, Gudsuane, Gudswan, Gudswane), Andrew, 13, 17, 21.
  Sir James, 25, 31, 33, 34, 35, 36, 37, 39, 41; as dean of gild, 27, 28, 29, 30, 31, 32.
Goslyn, John, 5, 8, 9, 160, 161.
Gourlay, Thomas, collector of light silver, 72.
Granger (Grangiar), Thomas, 1, 8, 9, 154, 155, 156, 160, 162.
Grant (Graunt), David, 28.
  Sir Robert, 16, 28, 170.
  William, 34, 61; as bailie, 54.
  Sir William, 63.

Grantisthorne, 50.
Gray, Robert, 57, 65, 66, 68, 69; as collector of light silver, 72.
  (*another ?*) 103, 107, 108, 136.
Greig (Greg), Henry, 51, 57.
Guthrie (Guthre), Janet of, 168.

Hair, Simon, xxx, 138; husband of Isobel Black, 144.
Halkett (Hacat, Hachet, Hackat, Haicheid, Haikheid, Hakett, Hockat, etc.), Andrew, 48.
  Andrew, 55.
  David, 1, 8, 160; as dean of gild, 3, 4, 5, 6, 156, 157.
  David, 60.
  Master George, 85; as Robin Hood, 85.
  George, of Pitfirrane, son of Patrick, 134.
  Henry, of Pitfirrane, 44; as dean of gild, 46, as alderman, 51.
  James, 15.
  John, of Pitfirrane, 55, 56, 57, 58, 59, 60, 68, 73; as alderman, 52, 78; father of Patrick, 76.
  Patrick, as dean of gild, 65.
  Patrick, of Pitfirrane, 76, 95; as alderman, 77, 81, 82, 90, 95, 97, 98; father of George, 134.
  Patrick (*another ?*), 136.
  Peter, 65; as dean of gild, 65, 66; as tutour to Holy Blood altar, 70.
  Robin, 4, 156, 157, 161, 163.
handmills, 151.
Handwart, Handwerp, *see* Antwerp.

handwriting, xi, xxiii, 34, 56, 69, 100, 120, 148, 149.
Hart (Hert), William, 38, 42, 44; as bailie, 45.
Hawick (Hawyk), Dean William of, 4.
heirship, queried, 29, 41, 46, 131, 132, 133.
hemp, 127.
Henderson (Hendresone), Nicol, 80, 82.
herald, 7, 161, 163; Snowdon herald, 166.
herring, 151, 152.
hides, xviii, 2, 3, 5, 7, 9, 11, 15, 22, 26, 51, 59, 71, 73, 80, 82, 84, 90, 97, 99, 107, 112, 130, 134, 151, 153, 154, 157, 158, 159; of horse, 15, 169; of young heifers, 169; rough, 81.
Hiegate, see Calsagate.
Hill (Hil), John, 17, 28, 32, 170.
Sir John, chaplain, 53, 56, 63.
William, 61.
Hogg (Hog, Hoge, Hogg), Andrew, 6, 8, 12, 157, 158, 161, 163, 168.
Sir Andrew, 18.
Hoile, the, 133.
Horne, Andrew, 85.
Thomas, 54.
William, merchant, burgess of Edinburgh, 132.
Hume (Hwywme), James, 78.
Sir Thomas, of Langschaw, knight, 39.
William, 78.
William (another ?), 135.
Hutton (Hautone, Hovtoune, Howtene, Howtoune, Huttoun, Hwtone, etc.), Elizabeth, daughter of John, 69, 70; wife of William Wilson, 69, 70.

Isobel, wife of George Campbell, 140.
James, 68, 86.
John, elder, 34.
John, younger, 34, 57, 63, 67; father of Elizabeth, 69, 70.
John, merchant, 91, 94, 95, 102, 103, 104, 105, 108, 110.
Lawrence, 138, 144, 148.
Thomas, 71.
Inverkeithing (Innerkething, Inuirkethtyn), 34, 56; gild merchant of, xxvii.
Inverness, gild merchant of, xxvii.
Ireland (Iraulyn, Irland, Yrland), Alexander, 11, 160; son of John Wilson, 9.
iron (jrne), 15, 96, 124, 127.
Irvine, gild merchant of, xxvii.
Irvine (Irwane), Patrick, 122.

Jackson (Jacson, Jacsoun, Jakson, Jaksone, etc.), Janet, wife of Alexander Arnot, 52.
James, 42.
John, 3, 11, 12, 13, 14.
William, 4, 6, 8, 11, 12, 13, 14, 15, 20, 156, 157, 158, 161, 162, 170, 171; as bailie, 16; as dean of gild, 19, 172.
William, 'younger', 23, 25, 27, 28, 30, 37, 38, 39, 41, 42, 43; as dean of gild, 35, 36, 37.
jail, see tolbooth.
Johnson (Jhonsoun, Jhonsoune Jonson, etc.), John, 41, 43; grandson of William Dunlop, 41.

INDEX

Nicol, 3, 5, 156, 161, 162, 163, 165.
Robert, 113.

Keavil, 48.
Keir (Keyr, Keyre), John, 74, 80, 89, 94, 107, 108, 110; as collector of light silver, 72; as kirkmaster, 74, 77, 78, 87, 90, 92, 93, 95, 96, 99.
John, 118, 135.
Kellock (Kellik, Kellok), Alexander, 85, 95, 103, 108, 130.
James, 138.
Kennedy (Kanetye, Kelnedye, Kennidy, Kennydy), Gilbert, 114, 120, 148; as bailie, 128, 130.
kilns, xxiii.
king and burgh, xx, xxiv, 4, 137, 138, 155, 156, 173, 174.
Kinghorn, 34.
Kinghorn (Kingorne, Kyngowrn), David, 39.
James, clerk of the regality of Dunfermline, 144; notary public, xii, 149.
Kinglassie (Kinglassy, Kynglassy), xxix, 8, 158, 159.
Kinglassie (Kinglassy, Kynglassy), Sir Alexander of, 7, 8, 160, 161, 162, 163.
Thomas of, 50.
William of, 7.
Kingseat Hill (Kyngis sid hil), 32.
kirk light, see light silver.
Kirkcaldy, xvii, xviii, xxix, xxx, 165.
Kirkcaldy (Kircaldie, Kircaldis, Kircaldy, Kyrcaudy), Master Henry of, 22; as dean of gild, 25.
John of, 22, 23; as alderman, 22, 23, 24, 25, 171.
Nicol of, 20; as alderman, 21, 22.
William of, 7, 10, 12, 13, 20, 168, as alderman, 17, 18, 20; as dean of gild, 8, 159, 160, 162, 163, 164.
kirkmaster, 66, 67, 68, 71, 73, 74, 77, 87, 90, 92, 95, 99.
kist of gild, 102, 103, 104, 106, 108, 159; contents of, 102–103.
Kyngorne, see Kinghorn.
Kyrcaldy, see Kirkcaldy.

Lad (Lade) Wynd, 36.
Lamb (Lam), Robert, 32.
William, 34.
Lambert, Margaret, wife of William, 41, 42.
William, 38, 39, 42, 54, 55, 58; husband of Margaret, 41; husband of Christian Reid, 58, 59.
Langschaw, 39.
Lathrisk, 39.
Law (Lawe), John, 147, 148; husband of Barbara Stewart, 140.
Lawson (Lauson, Lavsone, Lawsoun, Lawsoune), Gavin, 61, 68, 70, 71; husband of Elizabeth Ferguson, 61.
Leach (Lech, Leche, Leich), John, 30.
Malise, 8, 13, 30, 159, 161, 163, 165, 166.
leather (ledder, leddir, lethyr), xvii, 143, 153, 160, 162.
Leges Burgorum, xv, xxvii.
Leishman (Leichman, Leis-

INDEX

man), Mark, 71, 73.
Leith (Leth, Leytht), 67, 113, 130, 157.
light silver (kirk light), xxi, 31, 32, 49, 53, 54, 55, 59, 61, 62, 63, 66, 74, 87, 92, 99; box of, 55, 59, 72, 78; collectors of, 32, 57, 72, 74; conservators of, 32; treasurer of, 61.
lime, 1, 165.
Limekilns, 6.
liners, 40, 54.
lining decisions, xxi, 39, 40, 54, 63, 173.
Linlithgow, 34, 159, 160.
lint (lynt), see flax.
literacy, xxiv. See also handwriting.
Lithkew, see Linlithgow.
litsters, 69, 148.
Litster (Litstar, Littistar, Littystar, Lytstar), Alan, 1, 3, 4, 6, 8, 10, 12, 13, 14, 19, 154, 155, 156, 157, 158, 159, 161, 162, merchant, 12; as bailie, 6, 7, 160; as dean of gild, 7, 8, 16, 17, 18, 158, 159, 169, 170, 171, 172; wife of, 6.
Andrew, 15, 18, 20, 30, 34, 169, 171, 172, 173; as dean of gild, 22, 23, 171; as serjeant of gild, 19.
David, 22, 23, 27, 29, 32, 35; as bailie, 31.
Henry, 157.
John, 21.
Thomas, 1.
Livingston (Levingstone), James, captain of Stirling, 163.
Llythtgwhow, see Linlithgow.
Loch (Loich), James, 78.
Patrick, 78.
Lochore (Lochgwhor, Lochqwhor, Louchor), Philip of, 161, 163, 165, 166, 167.
Logan (Logane), Andrew, 16, 169.
Sir Henry, brother of William, 13, 169.
William (two of the same name), 8, 11, 12, 13, 34, 155, 158, 161, 162; brother of Sir Henry, 13.
(no forename), 165.
Lords of the Congregation, see Congregation.
Lothian (Lawdian, Loudeene, Louthiane, Lowdeene, Lowdiene, Lowthyane), John, 100, 106, 107, 110, 120, 130.
Low Countries, xvii. See also Flanders, Netherlands. Gilds of, xv.
Lowrie (Lowry), James, 135.
Lude, parson of, 47.
Lugton (Logtoune, Lokton, Loktone, Loktoun, Loktown), John of, 154, 155, 156, 157, 158, 159, 160, 161, 163, 164.
Richard, 62.
(no forename), 169, 170.
Lumsden (Lumisdene), Dean William, 97.
Lym Kill, see Limekilns.
Lyon, xi.
lyttyn, see dyeing.

Macartain (Macartan), Patrick, merchant, 149.
Malaris croft, 31.
Malcolm (Makum, Malcom, Malcome, Malcum), John, 20, 28, 29, 33; father of William, 68.
Sir Thomas, 64, 68; as collector of light silver, 74; as tutour to Holy Blood altar, 70.
William, son of John, 68.

INDEX

William, cordiner, 80.
mallet, for quarrying (qwaril mell), 165, 166.
malmsey, 12.
malt, 28, 35, 58, 68, 69, 110.
maltmakers, maltmen, 28, 35, 110.
markets, xviii. xix, xxix, 19, 81, 151, 153, 154; market cross, see cross; market day, 19, 75, 153.
Martin,(Martyne, Martynne), Gilbert, 73, 75, father of Janet, 75. Janet, daughter of Gilbert, 75; wife of John Christie, 75.
Martinson (Martynsone, Martyson), Alan, 8, 13.
Mason (Masone, Masoun), Huchon, 1, 155, 160, 161, 163, 165, 166, 167; as dean of gild, 3, 155.
Sir William, 74.
masons, xxiv, 36.
masters of works, see parish church, tolbooth.
Masterton (Mastirton, Mastirtoun), by Dunfermline, 5, 156, 157.
Mathew, (no surname), Sir, 155.
mayor, xvi, 152.
meal (meil), 28.
meat, 152.
Meiklejohn (Meikiljhone, Mekkyjohn, Mekiljohn, Meklejhone, Mvkklihone, Mvkyihone, etc.). William, 105, 106, 114, 115, 116, 118, 120, 121, 123, 141; as bailie, 129, 130, 146; as dean of gild, 116, 117, 123, 124, 125, 126.
Melville (Malwyn, Malwyne), John, 27, 32, 37, 38.

merchants, xiv, xvii, xxiv, xxv, xxx, 6, 12, 26, 59, 70, 81, 82, 84, 91, 98, 105, 107, 108, 116, 120, 124, 128, 129, 131, 132, 133, 149, 150, 151; merchant bill, 70, 71, 84; merchant fee, 144; merchant mark, 70, 82, 100.
Millar (Myllar), Alexander, 98.
mills, xxiii.
minor, 152.
Mitchell; Mitchelson (Mechall Mechel; Mechalson, Mechelsoun, Michalsone, Mychalsoun, etc.), James, 166.
John, 2, 3, 4, 7, 8, 13, 154, 155, 156, 157, 158, 159, 160, 161, 163, 164, 165, wife of, 2.
William, 99.
Mochrie (Muchrie), James, 140.
money-lending, 18, 20, 21, 24, 44, 49.
Monimail (Monimeile), Dean Thomas, sacristan of Dunfermline abbey, 33.
monks, xxii.
Monteith (Menteht, Mentetht), John of, 30, 35, 37, 45; as alderman, 36.
Montrose, gild merchant of, xxvii.
Mony Roddis (Monyrodis), 92.
morning priest, 69.
Moubray (Movbray, Movbry, Mowbra, Mowbray), James, 102, 103, 106, 108; as bailie (?), 104; as dean of gild, 105, 108, 109, 110.
John, 101, 121, 123.
Peter, 73, 75.
Moutray (Multray, Moltrar, Movtrar, Mowtray, Mult-

urar, Mwtray, (etc.), David, 46.
Helen, wife of Henry Turnbull, 136.
John, 64, 65, 73; as collector of light silver, 72, 74.
John 'in the New Row', collector of light silver, 74.
John, 93, 108, 110, 120, 136; as collector of gild money, 123, 124; father of William, 131.
John, merchant and burgers of Edinburgh, 132.
William, son of John, 131, 148.
Mudie (Mudy), Harry, 145, 147, 148; husband of Margaret Reid, 147.
William, 47, 50.
Murray (Muray, Murra, Murrai, Mvray, Mwrray), Harry, son of James, 91.
James, 61, 67; as collector of light silver, 72; father of Harry, 91.
James (another ?), 136.
Patrick, 101, as bailie, 128.
Robert, 34, 36.
Robert, 61, 86, 93, 98, husband of Bessie Spittal, 111; as bailie, 82, 83.
Robert (another ?), 135.
Musselburgh, xvii, xviii.

Nairn (Narn), William of, 7, 8.
Netherlands, xi. See also, Flanders, Low Countries.
Netherton (Neddirtoune, Nethertoun), 50, 51, 54, 132, 135, 138.
Newcastle, customs of, xxviii.
Newman (Nevman), James, 73, 75; wife of, 83.

New Row (Nevraw), 74, 137, 138, 166.
Nichol (Nechol, Neikeill, Nichell, Nichole, Nockhal, Nycholl, etc.), Alexander, 80, 100, 101, 111, 115, 119, 120, 125, 126, 127; as bailie, 133, 134; as dean of gild, 129, 130, 131; as treasurer, 118.
Bessie, wife of James Cuthbert, 145.
Robert, 116, 118, 121, 122, 127, 144, 148; as collector of gild funds, 126.
William, 86, 87, 95, 101, 103, 105, 106, 108, 111, 136.
Ninian (Niniane, Ringane), Sir David, parson of Lude, 47.
Northampton, customs of, xxviii.
north croft, the, 35.
notary public, xi, xii, 120, 148, 149.
Nottingham, customs of, xxviii.

oath de calumpnia, 144.
Ochiltree (Ochtre), (no forename), 173.
Ochterlonie (Ochterlowny), Elspeth of, 11.
odman, 60.
Ogilvie (Ogelvy), lord of, 11.
oil, 52, 60.
orchards, xxiii.
orphans, support of, 137, 139.
Orrok (Orok), David of, 17.
Dick of, 170.
John of, 27, 28.
outmen, 22. See also extramen, unfreemen.
oxen, 60.

INDEX

paper, xi, xii, xviii, xxii, 155, 164; watermarks of, xi.
parish church, xxi, xxii, 59, 92, 93, 106; aisle of and master of works of aisle, 36; choir of, 69, 74; clerks of, see clerks; congregation of, 69, 74; Protestant minister in, xxii; seat in, 106. See also altars, chaplains.
Paton (Paittoune, Paltoun, Pantoun, Patting, Pavtoune, Pawittan, Pawtoune, etc.), John, 68, 71, 79, 82, 87, 92, 94, 95, 97; as collector of light silver, 72; as dean of gild, 71, 72, 75, 76, 77, 78, 92, 93.
John (another ?), 136.
Patrick, as dean of gild, 78.
Robert, 103, 105, 110, 114, 121, 122, 123, 124, 125, 127, 145, 148, 149, as dean of gild, 111, 113, 117, 119, 120, 121, 122, 127, 128, 131, 132, 133, 134, 135, 136, 137, 138, 139, 140, 141, 142.
William, as dean of gild, 131.
Patonson (Patirsone, Patounsoun, Pattonson, etc.), Master John, 29.
John, 55, 60, 63; as dean of gild, 61; uncle of John, 65.
John, nephew of John, 65.
Robert, 14, 168.
Richard, 34, 38, 45; as serjeant of gild, 39.
William, 173.
Peacock (Pacok, Pakcok), Sir Andrew, xxi, 50, 51, 54, 55, 65.

Andrew, 116, 119.
Morris, 80.
peas, 152.
Peebles, xxxi.
Penny, Thomas, 47, 50.
pepper, 42.
Pert, see Perth.
Perth, xxviii, xxx, 34; gild of, xv; gild records of, xiii, xxvi.
pest, pestilence, see plague.
peter, see saltpetre.
Petfuran (Pitfirren, Pitfurane), see Pitfirrane.
Phillane, Robert, William, see Fillan.
Pierson (Pairsoune, Peirson, Person, Peyrsone, etc.), Sir Andrew, chaplain, 35, 50.
George, 128, 129, 145, 147, 148.
John, 36, 45.
John, 95, 105, 106, 108, 110, 120; brother of Lawrence, 119.
Lawrence, 106, 120; brother of John, 119.
Pitfirrane, 44, 48, 55, 56, 90, 95, 97, 134; lord of, 51, 54, 60.
Pittencrieff (Pettincrif, Pittincreff, Pittyncreff), 60, 102, 105, 130; lord of, 60.
plague, xxiii, xxiv, xxxi, 22, 138, 163.
plays and pageants, xiv, xxi, xxiv. See also Robin Hood.
plumbers, xxiv, 52, 67.
Poland, towns in, xxx.
poor, the, xxii, 42, 93, 102, 125, 126, 172.
population of burgh, xviii, xxix.
Porteous, Katherine, wife of

Robert Duguid, 137.
ports, xxiii, 40.
potash, 81, 89, 92, 96.
Potter (Pottar), John, 85; as collector of light silver, 72, 74.
Pratus (Prateris), John, 85. William, 141, 146; as bailie, 147, 148.
prepositus, see alderman and provost.
Preston (Prestone), James, son-in-law of David Cooper, 50; as dean of gild, 52.
Primrose, by Dunfermline, 48.
prior, 28.
Privy Council, xxii.
Proud (Prowd), Robert, 59.
provost, xxix, and 81 onwards, *passim*. See also alderman.
Prumros, see Primrose.
Prussia, xxx.
Purrock (Purrok), John, 151, 173, 174.

Queensferry, xvii, xviii.

Ramsay, William, 7, 155, 158, 161, 163, 165; wife of, 7.
Randill Craggis, by Dunfermline, 48.
Ray, William, 117.
Reformation, xxi, xxii, 99.
regality of Dunfermline, xviii, xxix; burghs of, xvii, xviii, xxix; clerks of, see clerks; cocket seal of, xvii; court of, xiii; court book of, see book, serjeant of, see serjeant.
Reid (Raid, Rayd, Red, Reyd), Alan, 48.
Andrew, 66, 67, 70, 71; father of Gelis, 142.
Christian, wife of William Lambert, 58, 59.
David, brother of James, 145.
Gelis, daughter of Andrew, 142; wife of David Brown, 142.
Henry, 109, 110, 121, 123, 141; father of James, 143.
James, 146; son of Henry, 143; brother of David, 145; as dean of gild, 148, 149, 150.
John, 112, 113, 126.
Margaret, wife of Harry Mudie, 147.
William, 48.
rentals, on gild property and land, 27, 37, 47, 51, 132, 154, 156, 157; diverted to support of church, 34, 36, 37, 49, 50, 54, 134, 135, 138. See also accounts of gild.
Richmond (Rechmont), (*no forename*), 80.
rigs, cultivated, xxiii.
Ringane, David, see Ninian.
roads, condition of, xxiii; road-making, repairing, 6, 169, 170, 171, 172, 173, 174. See also causamackar.
Robert I, king of Scotland, xvii.
Robertson (Robertsoune, Robsoune), Sir Andrew, 56.
George, 48.
John, 5, 13.
John, 109, 120.
Robin Hood (Robene, Robyne Hud), xxiv, xxxi, xxxii, 85.
Rodger (Rogar, Roger, Rogger), Henry, 140.
John, 48.
Thomas, 28, 32, 35, 37.
William, 90.
rope, 87.

Rosyth (Rossicht), xvii, xxiv, 43, 52.
Rouen, xi.
Rowan (Rovand), Robert, 48.
Roxburgh, gild merchant of, xv.

sacristan of Dunfermline abbey, xxii, 6, 7, 8, 12, 33, 34, 64, 68, 69, 83.
St. Andrews, xxx, 57; archbishop of, see archbishop; bishop of, see bishop; gild merchant of, xv.
sallerer, see cellarer.
salmon, 151.
salt, 152, 153.
saltpetre, 41.
Sanctandrois, see St. Andrews.
Sanders (Sandis), Andrew, 78.
school, master of, xxiv, 166.
Sclater (Sklattaris), Robin, 166.
Scobie (Scobe, Scoby), John, 55, 56, 161, 162, 163, 165, 166.
 Lawrence, 61, 62.
 Thomas, 62.
Scone, xxviii.
scot and lot, 70.
scribes, see clerks.
seal, common, of burgh, 69.
Seggie (Segy), Lawrence of, 13, 165, 166.
Seras, see Ceres.
serjeant, of gild, xx, 11, 16, 17, 19, 33, 38, 39, 86, 166, 169.
serjeant, of regality of Dunfermline, 40, 43.
Sharp (Scharap, Scharep, Scharp), John, 108,
 Robert, 25, 26, 27, 31, 42, 43, 49.
Shearer (Schara, Scharay, Scheraris), John, 105, 109, 110.
ships, shipping, 5, 67, 82, 98, 104, 107, 111, 119, 125, 129, 145, 151, 152, 153, 154.
Shorthouse (Schortes, Schorthous, Schorthus, Schortoris, Schurtus, Scurtuus, etc.), Andrew, 48.
 Christian, daughter of James, 135; wife of James Blaw, 135.
 James, 75, 79, 88, 92, 94, 95, 98, 99, 100, 101, 104, 105, 106, 110, 112, 114, 116, 120, 121, 122, 123, 130, 135, 136; as dean of gild, 114, 115, 116; father of Christian, 135.
 William, 48.
 William, 'the younger', 90.
Sibbald, Janet, wife of Alexander Steven, 149.
silver, 25, 31, 32, 99, 103, 104, 119, 145, 151.
Skaithmuir (Skaithmur), Dean Edward, almoner of Dunfermline abbey, 47.
Skinner (Skynner), James, 71.
skinners, xxiv, 41, 43, 44, 46, 152.
skins, xvii, xviii, 2, 3, 5, 6, 7, 26, 39, 41, 69, 73, 81, 84, 85, 90, 97, 99, 101, 107, 112, 130, 134, 151, 152, 153, 154, 158; black, 154; of cattle, 85; of sheep, 71, 73, 85.
Smart (Smert), Alexander, grandfather of Thomas, 24.
 Thomas, grandson of Alexander, 24.
Smith (Smyth, Smythis, Smytht), Andrew, 50.
 John, 85; as collector of light silver, 72.
 John, 'younger', 'junior',

INDEX

103, 105, 108.
John, 'elder', 138.
Lawrence, 138.
William, 70.
(*no forename*), as collector of light silver, 72.
smithies, xxiii.
Snowdon herald, *see* herald.
soap (seip), 118, 132.
Somerville (Somerwell), John, 84.
souters (suttaris), see cordiners.
Speir (Spyr), Annie of, 163.
Spens, John of, herald, 7, 161, 163.
　Master John, 72, 76, 82, 83, 126; as bailie, 77, 78, 83.
　Robert, 85; as collector of light silver, 72, 74.
　Thomas of, 31.
spices, xviii; and wine, xxiv, xxxii and *passim*. *See also* pepper.
Spittal (Spetell, Spetyll, Spitell, Spittaell, Spittailll, etc.), Bessie, widow of Robert Murray, 111.
　William, 17, 20, 21, 171, 173; as bailie, 19, 20, 171; as dean of gild, 21, 22, 24, 33, 34, 172.
　William, 27, 34, 35, 42, 45, 51, 52, 53, 55, 59. 60, 61, 63; as bailie, 45, 58, 59; as dean of gild, 37, 51, 52, 60.
　(*no forename*), 174.
stables, xxiii.
staple goods, xviii, 73, 89, 116, 140.
Statuta gilde, xii, xv, xvi, xxvii, 150–154.
steeple, *see* bell; bellhouse.
Steill (Steylle), Sir Thomas, 165.
Steven (Stevin, Stewin),
　Alexander, 133, 149; husband of Janet Sibbald, 149.
Stevenson (Steinsone, Stevinsoune, Stewinsone, Stewynsovne, etc.), Alexander, grandson of Andrew Gervase, 75.
　Thomas, 32, 61.
　Thomas (*two of same name ?*) 79, 89, 92, 95, 96, 99, 103, 108, 110, 135, 138; merchant, 81, 91.
　William, 119.
Stewart (Steuart, Stevart), Alexander, 70, 71.
　Master Andrew, 60, 61; father of Sir David, 117; as dean of gild, 61, 62, 73, 74.
　Master Andrew (*another ?*), 136.
　Archibald, 33, 45, 57.
　Barbara, wife of John Law, 140.
　Sir David, 4, 5, 7, 8, 162
　Sir David, 30, 33.
　David, laird of Rosyth, 52.
　Sir David, son of Master Andrew, 117; bailie, 117.
　David, 120, 134, 135, 136, 139, 148.
　Henry, 8; as alderman, 3, 7, 9.
　Henry, 120, 122.
　James, 48.
　James, 56.
　M.D., 67.
　Robert, 10.
　Robert, 60, 67.
　Thomas, 76, 77, 82; as bailie, 87, 88; as dean of gild, 79, 80, 81, 82, 86.
　Thomas (*another ?*), 136.
　William, 15; as alderman, 23, 33.
　William, 23, 32, 35.

INDEX

William, of Rosyth (another ?), 43.
Stewarts of Rosyth, xxiv. See also Stewart.
Stirling, xiv, xxviii, 34, 155, 163; gild merchant of, xv; gild records of, xii, xiii, xxvi.
Stirlyne, see Stirling.
stole, 103.
Storie (Store, Story), David, 1, 2, 155, 160, 162.
Stoyll (Stoylle), Philip, 14, 167.
Strang, James, 13, 166, 170.
John, 26, 27.
Strevelyn, see Stirling.
strublance, see breach of the peace.
suppers, see colations.
Swiecin, Prussia, xxx.
Swinton (Swynton), Dean Robert, 40.
Sword (Swerd), (no forename), 48.
Sym (Syme, Symm), Dean David, 37.
John, 10, 11, 15, 20, 163, 164.
John, 22, 29.
Katherine, widow of Lawrence Dalgleish, 107.
Symson (Symsone), William, of Lathrisk, 39; as alderman, 40, 41, 42, 43.

tanners, 81, 151.
tanning, xviii, 5, 9, 13, 15, 81, 169; tanning pits, xxiii, 81.
tapsters, dry, of ale, 35.
Tarvit (Tarwat), Lord, 11.
tavern, xxii, xxiii, 105, 158, 159, 161, 164; tavern keeper, xxiv.
taxation, royal, 54.
Templeman, Isobel, widow of William Christie, 133.
terar (terrar), of abbey, 42, 58.

Thain (Than), Alexander, father of John, 6.
John, son of Alexander, 6.
Thomson (Thamsoun, Thamsoune, Thomeson, Thomsone), Sir Andrew, 28.
Edward, 142, 148.
Morris, 34.
Robert, 173.
Tod, David, 118, 120.
tofts, xxiii.
tolbooth, xxiii; as jail, 31, 57, 65, 80, 91, 94, 109; as meeting place of gild court, xx, xxii and passim; master of works to, 167; repairs to, xix, 14, 79, 166, 167, 174.
toll, xvii, xix, 98.
tow, see rope.
town hillock, 36.
trade, xv, xix and passim; overseas, xix, xxv, xxx, 7, 67, 76, 82, 84, 86, 87, 96, 98, 110, 124, 132, 145.
traders, xvi, xix, xx. See also merchants.
trading privileges, of Dunfermline abbey, xvii.
of early burghs, xv, xvi, xvii.
of gild of Dunfermline, xviii; encroachment into, xviii, xx, xxiv, 5, 11, 24, 48, 69, 71, 73, 75, 78, 80, 107, 109, 119, 121, 127, 140, 145; malpractice in, xix, 3, 5, 6, 8, 9, 11, 22, 44, 48, 70, 74, 75, 78, 84, 101, 105, 107, 108, 110, 111, 115, 116, 125, 151, 152, 153.
treasurer, 61, 118. See also bursar.
tron (trone), xxiii, 120, 134, 139.
Trotter (Troter), John, 59.

Tulloch (Tulch), Andrew, 24.
John of, 13.
Turnbull (Trowmbill, Trumbill, Trumble, Trumbul, Turnbul), George, 138.
Henry, 146, 148; husband of Helen Moutray, 136.
Master John, 52, 53, 55; vicar of Cleish, 47.
Lawrence, 120, 134, 135.
Paton, 1, 2, 4, 160; as dean of gild, 162.
Robert, 122, 125, 148.
William, 122.

unfreemen, 5, 8, 35, 44, 70, 74, 75, 78, 89, 91, 104, 105, 107, 108, 109, 111, 115, 117, 118, 125, 126, 129, 132, 140, 143, 145. See also extramen, outmen.

Vallance (Valange), John, 165.
Paton, 158.
Veere, 132.

Wales, xvii.
Walker (Valcar, Valker, Walcar, Walkar, Walkare), Andrew, 78, 98, 101, 105, 136; son of William, 78.
David, as collector of light silver, 72.
John, 100, 114, 118, 148; son of Richard, 141.
Richard, 130; father of John, 141.
William, 48, 55.
William, (*two of same name* ?), 56, 94, 101; father of Andrew, 78.
Waswat, William, 118.
Watson (Watsoun), John, merchant, 150.
Wawane, (*no forename*), 138.
wax, xxi, xxxii, 32, 45, 53, 54, 55, 57, 58, 68, 71, 73, 86, 87, 88, 89, 93, 156.
weapons, 2; in court, 154.
weaver, xxiv, 45.
webstar, see weaver.
weights of town, 109.
Weir (Wer), David, 9, 10; as dean of **gild**, **17**, **22**, **168**, 170.
David, 36.
Wellwood (Vallud, Wallat, Wallo, Waluod, Walwode, Walvod, etc.), Abraham, 98, 105, 108, 110.
Alan, 26, 27, 35, 36, 42; as dean of gild, 32, 33, 36.
Bessie, wife of John Dewar, 140.
John, of the Wynd, 18, 33; as serjeant of the gild, 33; grandfather of John Burn, 50.
John, 23.
John, son of Richard, 24; as bailie, 26; as dean of gild, 26, 27, 33, 38, 39, 40.
John, 29, 32, 33, 37, 42, 45.
John, serjeant of regality of Dunfermline, 40, 43.
John, 40, 42.
John, cordiner, 40, 43, 44, 46.
John, skinner, 40, 41, 43, 44, 46.
John, grandson of John Bray, 46.
John, son-in-law of John Baxter, 42.
Marjorie, xxiii.
Richard of, 10, 164; father of John, 24.
Robin, 18, 20, 21, 23, 27.
Thomas, 81.
William, 2, 4, 159, 160.

William, 58, 62, 65, 67; as dean of gild, 66, 67; as tutour to Holy Blood altar, 70; as collector of light silver, 72.
William (*another ?*) as bailie, 88.
William, 110, 111, 112, 114, 115, 116, 121, 123, 130, 136, 138, 148; as bailie, 120; as dean of gild, 113, 114, 126, 127.
Wemyss (Wemis, Wems, Wemys), John, of Pittencrieff, 102, 130; as provost, 105, 131; son of Patrick, 102.
Patrick, of Pittencrieff, 60, 64, 65; as dean of gild, 62, 63, 64; as kirkmaster, 67; father of John, 102.
Westluscar (Westir Luscour), 48.
wheat, 17, 28, 152.
White (Quhit, Quyth), Sir Andrew, 64, 65, 66, 67; chaplain of St. Margaret's altar, 88.
Whitson (Quhitsone), Richard, collector of light silver, 72.
widows, see women.
Williamson (Wilyamson, Wilyhamsoun, Wylyamsoune, Wylyhamsone, etc.), Sir John, 7, 8, 156, 161, 162; as dean of gild, 13, 14, 166, 167, 168.
William the Lion, king of Scotland, xv.
Wilson (Vilson, Welsone, Willsoun, Wyllson, Wylsoune, etc.), Alexander, 33.
David, 84, 136.
Gillie, wife of Patrick Cowan, 126.
John, cordiner, 2, 3, 5, 9, 154, 155, 161, 164, 165, 173.
John, father of Alexander Ireland, 9.
John, 38, 42, 52, 53, 57; as bailie, 55; as dean of gild, xi, xxiii, 42, 43, 44, 45, 46, 47, 48, 49, 50, 51, 58; husband of Marjorie Welwood, xxiii.
John, son of Robert, 77, 84.
John (*another ?*), 136.
Lawrence, 149, 150.
Robert, 62; as collector of light silver, 72; father of John, 77.
Robert, 94, 101, 111, 114, 116, 126, 129, 148, as dean of gild, 128, 129.
William, 70; as collector of light silver, 72; husband of Elizabeth Hutton, 69; 'elder', 76.
William, 75, 76; 'younger' (*the same ?*), 76, 80, 82, 84, 91, 94, 95, 100, 110, 112.
William (*another ?*), 135.
Winchester, customs of, xxviii.
Winchester (Wincister), John, 160, 165.
wine, xxii, 13, 15, 32, 42, 46, 83, 89, 104, 105, 108, 125, 130, 131, 132, 149, 151, 152, 154, 155, 158, 160, 161, 164, 165, 166, 167, 168, 169; spice and, *passim. See also* claret wine, malmsey.
woad (wad, wald, wud), 20, 79, 80.
women, widows, and entrance to gild through, 23, 32, 39, 43, 50, 52, 61, 70, 75, 90, 91, 126, 135,

136, 140, 142, 143, 144,
147; holding land, 58,
59; in court, 1, 2, 12,
14, 105; and permission
to marry, xxiv, 43, 107,
111, 126, 133, 139, 147;
support of, xxii, xxiii,
19, 172; and trade, 11,
42, 83, 104, 108, 133,
139, 140, 145, 149, 151,
154, 156, 168.
wool, xvii, xviii, 5, 7,
26, 41, 73, 130, 151, 152,
153, 154; black, 154.
woolfells, xviii.
Workman (Warkmen, Werk-
    man, Werkmane), George,
    80.
    James, 59, 63.
Wright (Wrecht, Wreicht,
    Wricht, Wrych, Wrycht,
    Wryght, etc.), Christian,
    43.
    David, 168.
    John, 2, 4, 6, 8, 11, 12,
    13, 156, 157, 158, 159,
    160, 161, 162, 163, 164,
    165, 166, 167, 169, 170;
    as alderman, 3, 13, 14,
    155; wife of, 12.
    John, 14; as dean of
    gild, 20.
    John, 21, 24, 35, 49, 53,
    54, 59; as dean of
    gild, 37, 38, 53, 55, 57,
    60, 61; father of John,
    43.
    John, son of John, 43.
    John (*another ?*), 134, 138.
    Wa(*lter ?*), 100.
    William, 103, 105, 109,
    111, 112, 115, 116, 148.
writers, xxii, 163. *See also*
clerks.

Young (Yong, Yowng, Yung,
    Ywng), John, 3, 155,
    159, 161, 165.
    John, flesher, 4.

Yrland, Alexander, see Ireland, Alexander.